RECONSTRUCTION FICTION

RECONSTRUCTION FICTION

HOUSING AND REALIST LITERATURE IN POSTWAR BRITAIN

PAULA DERDIGER

THE OHIO STATE UNIVERSITY PRESS
COLUMBUS

Copyright © 2020 by The Ohio State University.
All rights reserved.

Library of Congress Cataloging-in-Publication Data
Names: Derdiger, Paula, author.
Title: Reconstruction fiction : housing and realist literature in postwar Britain / Paula Derdiger.
Description: Columbus : The Ohio State University Press, [2020] | Includes bibliographical references and index. | Summary: "Assesses the impact of World War II and the welfare state on literary fiction by focusing on how housing reconstruction created a sheltered space for the mediation between individual subjects and the social and geographical environments that they encountered. Argues writers spanning various social positions and aesthetic tendencies—Elizabeth Bowen, Graham Greene, Patrick Hamilton, Doris Lessing, Colin MacInnes, and Elizabeth Taylor—engaged with literary realism as a way to shape postwar life"—Provided by publisher.
Identifiers: LCCN 2020022224 | ISBN 9780814214527 (cloth) | ISBN 0814214525 (cloth) | ISBN 9780814280768 (ebook) | ISBN 0814280765 (ebook)
Subjects: LCSH: English fiction—20th century—History and criticism. | Buildings—Repair and reconstruction—Great Britain. | Dwellings—Great Britain—History—20th century. | Postwar reconstruction—Great Britain—History—20th century. | World War, 1939–1945—Literature and the war. | Architecture, Domestic, in literature.
Classification: LCC PR881 .D47 2020 | DDC 823/.914093564—dc23
LC record available at https://lccn.loc.gov/2020022224
Other identifiers: ISBN 9780814257708 (paper)

Cover design by Derek Thornton
Text design by Juliet Williams
Type set in Adobe Minion Pro

CONTENTS

List of Illustrations — vii

Acknowledgments — ix

INTRODUCTION	"We Shall Look Out Through Glass"	1
CHAPTER 1	An Urgent Invitation: Theorizing Postwar Realist Writing	25
CHAPTER 2	Billets and Boardinghouses: Shared Space and the Reconstruction Novel	43
CHAPTER 3	Mobile Housing: Realizing Movement in 1950s City Fiction	85
CHAPTER 4	Country Houses: Nostalgia and the Realist Challenge	119
CHAPTER 5	Safe Houses: Seeking Shelter and Connection Post-Consensus	157
CONCLUSION	Reconstruction as Departure and Return	195

Bibliography — 201

Index — 211

ILLUSTRATIONS

FIGURE 1	Golden Lane Network	94
FIGURE 2	Golden Lane Sketch	95
FIGURE 3	Collage view of Golden Lane drawing superimposed on photograph of site	95
FIGURE 4	Robin Hood Gardens	96
FIGURE 5	Park Hill Estates, Sheffield, aerial view	96
FIGURE 6	Corridor, or a "street in the sky," Park Hill Estates, Sheffield	97

ACKNOWLEDGMENTS

I wish to acknowledge and thank the editors and readers who have helped to shape this book. At The Ohio State University Press, Ana Jimenez-Moreno has been a wonderfully supportive editor, and anonymous readers offered generous yet attentively critical suggestions that helped make the final version of this manuscript as polished as it could be. A section of chapter 2 focusing on Elizabeth Taylor's *At Mrs. Lippincote's* appeared in an earlier form in Petra Rau's edited volume, *Long Shadows: The Second World War in British Fiction and Film* from Northwestern University Press; likewise, a previous analysis of Colin MacInnes's *Absolute Beginners* was published in an article in *Modern Fiction Studies*, which here is found in a revised form in chapter 3. These previous iterations of my thinking were crucial to developing the bigger project undertaken here. I also wish to acknowledge and thank staff from the following archives who have granted permission for documents and images that appear in this book: The National Maritime Museum Archive and Record Centre, The Smithson Family Collection, and the RIBA Library Photograph Collection. To Rob Newman: I owe a special thanks for his help with the permissions process.

This book has benefited enormously from the wisdom of my mentors, conversations with colleagues and students, and the support of family and friends. Allan Hepburn encouraged me at every step as the project evolved, offering indispensable insight and editing suggestions. Phyllis Lassner likewise offered continuous support, asking the questions that helped my critical voice flourish. To Allan and Phyllis, both, I owe a debt of gratitude for nurturing my scholarly life and for inspiring me, especially with their work on Elizabeth Bowen. I am also thankful to Ned Schantz for his advice on the book and his efforts to foster intellectual risk-taking. Many conversations with peers at McGill University sharpened my thinking about the literature and culture of World War II and the midcentury and modernist periods. I am particularly grateful to Ariel Buckley, Caroline Krzakowski, Robin Feenstra, Justin Pfefferle, and Ian Whittington for the countless discussions of books and films that we shared. Colleagues at the Space Between Society's annual conferences offered generous feedback on my research over the years and reinvigorated my commitment to work on comparatively neglected writers and texts. I am grateful to the University of Minnesota Duluth, and the College of Liberal Arts, in particular, for providing funds to support various aspects of my research as I completed the manuscript. I would like to thank my colleagues in the English program, especially Evan Brier, Paul Cannan, Hilary Kowino, Burke Scarborough, John Schwetman, Krista Twu, Katie Van Wert, and Rochelle Zuck. Michele Larson also provided indispensable personal and professional support. Students at McGill and UMD indulged my interest in space and architecture, and regularly inspired me as we discussed twentieth-century British literature.

Many friends offered invaluable intellectual and emotional support that I could not have done without. A heartfelt thank you to Ben Barootes, Natalie Belsky, Becky Boyle, Amanda Clarke, Amanda Cockburn, Amy Danzer, Joel Deshaye, Tom Evans, Sarah Kmosena, Michelle LeDonne, Greg Phipps, Eve Rabinoff, and Bob and Jeanine Schroer. I am endlessly grateful for the love and support of my family. Many thanks to my parents, Jan and Terry Derdiger; my brother and sister-in-law, David and Sara Derdiger; and the MacPhail and Doggett families. Finally, Kelly MacPhail, thank you for your wit, intellect, and tireless support; you and our son, Owen, have made this project worth doing.

INTRODUCTION

"We Shall Look Out Through Glass"

> All my life I have said, "Whatever happens there will always be tables and chairs"—and what a mistake.
>
> —Elizabeth Bowen, in a letter to Virginia Woolf after the 1940 bombing of Woolf's London home[1]

ELIZABETH BOWEN'S admission to Virginia Woolf at first appears trivial, a passing observation that, at most, reveals Bowen's keen interest in interiors and furniture. In the context of the blitz and directed toward Woolf, however, the comment can be read as nothing less than a declaration of historical and literary sea change. It echoes but notably shifts the implications of Woolf's own infamous, sweeping pronouncement sixteen years earlier that "in or about December 1910 human character changed."[2] Woolf's oft-quoted line from "Mr. Bennett and Mrs. Brown" responded to changes "in religion, conduct, politics, and literature" that have come to be understood as commonplace facets of modernism. Woolf herself had articulated one of the more resilient characterizations of how literature had changed—or needed to change, from her perspective—several years earlier in her 1919 essay "Modern Fiction":

> Look within and life, it seems, is very far from being "like this." Examine for a moment an ordinary mind on an ordinary day. The mind receives a myriad impressions—trivial, fantastic, evanescent, or engraved with eh sharpness of steel. From all sides they come, an incessant shower of innumerable atoms;

---

1. Bowen, "Letter to Virginia Woolf, 5 Jan. 1940," 216.
2. Woolf, "Mr. Bennett and Mrs. Brown," 396.

and as they fall, as they shape themselves in the life of Monday or Tuesday, the accent falls directly from of old; the moment of importance came not here but there; so that, if a writer were a free man and not a slave, if he could write what he chose, not what he must, if he could base his work upon his own feeling and not upon convention, there would be no plot, no comedy, no tragedy, no love interest or catastrophe in the accepted style, and perhaps not a single button sewn on as the Bond Street tailors world have it. Life is not a series of gig lamps symmetrically arranged; life is a luminous halo, a semi-transparent envelope surrounding us from the beginning of consciousness to the end. Is it not the task of the novelist to convey this varying, this unknown and uncircumscribed spirit, whatever aberration or complexity it may display, with as little mixture of the alien and external as possible?[3]

This directive to novelists, to "look within" and chart the "luminous halo" of consciousness, to eschew plot and the details of material life and instead to invest in character perception and interiority, dominated interwar high modernist writing and continues to be the dominant critical story of what defines most modernist fiction.[4]

Bowen's wartime letter to Woolf coupled with her 1953 essay "English Fiction at Mid-Century" demonstrate how, instead of consciousness and character, material conditions and housing specifically, along with realist representation, would be the pivotal forces shaping postwar, midcentury fiction. In that essay, Bowen explains that the experience of the war led writers to shift their interests and change their techniques. The physically destructive historical realities of the war could not be ignored:

> The salutary value of the exterior, the comfortable sanity of the concrete came to be realised only when the approach of the Second World War forced one to envisage whole-sale destruction. The obliteration of man's surroundings, streets and houses, tables and chairs sent up, for him, their psychological worth. Up to now, consciousness had been a sheltered product: its

---

3. Woolf, "Modern Fiction," 397.

4. This is not to suggest that all interwar modernist writing blindly and uniformly follows Woolf's prescription for literary transformation. There are, of course, countless examples of interwar fiction that demonstrate their representational commitments to something other than consciousness. Kristin Bluemel's edited volume, *Intermodernism: Literary Culture in Mid-Twentieth-Century Britain*, is an indispensable introduction to a range of writers whose work might be characterized in this way. As Bluemel notes in her introduction, "Writers like George Orwell, Storm Jameson, William Empson, Harold Heslop, and Stella Gibbons . . . saw their responsibilities, as writers, primarily to 'the people,'" challenging T. S. Eliot's insistence, aligning with Woolf, that the writer should be first and foremost responsible to language (1).

interest as consciousness diminished now that, at any moment, the physical shelter could be gone.[5]

Bowen's observation helps to account for the realist mode that dominated midcentury literary fiction. The realities of wartime and postwar life turned realist fiction-making into a revelatory and important task rather than, as Woolf had characterized Edwardian realism, "a series of gig lamps symmetrically arranged."[6] Midcentury realism was anything but a conservative retreat to safety and tradition, as has often been argued, especially in relation to claims about modernism.[7]

The wartime decimation of buildings and streets called for reconstruction, and reconstruction called not just for bricks and mortar, architectural drawings, town plans, and new policies, but for fiction that invited particular ways of inhabiting an environment that had been irrevocably changed. Fiction, like actual buildings, creates a sheltered space for the mediation between individual subjects and the social and geographical environments that they encounter. Realist fiction, specifically, insists that such mediation is possible and that it is socially valuable. This book argues that literary realism was a necessary, generative response to the war and Welfare State conditions.

HOUSING: THE DEFINING POSTWAR ISSUE

Housing is, arguably, the defining issue of the postwar period. Over 2.5 million homes were destroyed in Britain during the war. Writing for the *New Yorker* in October 1944, London correspondent and novelist Mollie Panter-Downes noted, "Building reconstruction is the biggest domestic issue for this government, and possibly for many a government to come."[8] New construction was at once a pragmatic antidote to homelessness caused by the war and an opportunity to express the broad Welfare State mandate to provide for its

---

5. Bowen, "English Fiction at Mid-Century," 322.
6. Woolf, "Modern Fiction," 397.
7. In *British Fiction after Modernism: The Novel at Mid-Century*, Marina MacKay and Lyndsey Stonebridge also work against this critical commonplace. They argue that the period between the late 1930s and the 1960s has been neglected and "too often characterized as a conservative literature of retreat" (Introduction, 2). As a rejoinder, they emphasize the relentless warfare of the midcentury years and observe that "for those writing at mid-century, after two wars and in the middle of an undeclared chilly third, the historical resonances of what had come before loomed as large as (and as part of) the task of imagining the present and the future" (2).
8. Panter-Downes, *London War Notes*, 422.

citizenry. The 1942 "Report of the Inter-Departmental Committee on Social Insurance and Allied Services" (the Beveridge Report)—one of the foundational documents of the Welfare State—designated housing as a basic right for British citizens alongside health, education, and employment.[9] The landscape was transformed between 1945 and 1951 as the Labour government laid the foundation for the Welfare State by building approximately one million new homes across the nation. A substantial number of suburban dwellings were built as part of "New Towns," such as Harlow, Milton Keynes, and Stevenage, which conceived of housing in terms of planned, multiuse neighborhoods and employed the most up-do-date construction and design technologies. In the early 1950s, the Welfare State housing mandate was further realized through slum clearance programs, especially in northern urban centers such as Manchester and Liverpool, which demolished neglected working-class residences in inner-city areas and relocated inhabitants to single-family, "two-up, two-down" houses built on town peripheries. By 1960, the seeming success of postwar recovery efforts was evident in Britain's largest urban center: London's skyline became increasingly dominated by architectural verticality as over 500,000 new flats in council estates and tower blocks were added to the city.

Changes to major British cities were impossible to miss, but the built environment of rural Britain was also transformed, if less obviously, as a result of the war. Many country houses had been requisitioned for evacuation and military purposes and were later demolished, liquidated, or sold, and then repurposed as public facilities or heritage industry museums in the 1950s and 1960s. For country houses that survived, the disappearance of an already minute servant class transformed how those spaces, literally, would work. After Margaret Thatcher's rise to leadership of the Conservative party in 1975 and their subsequent majority Government in 1979, the Welfare State mandate to provide housing for all was decisively reversed as the construction and maintenance of public housing were largely privatized alongside other major public services and industries. British citizens thus once again found themselves facing ruins—not of a bombed landscape, but of a dismantled postwar consensus—that would require yet a new reconstructive vision.

"Reconstruction fiction," as I call it, accounts for the legacy of the war, and it mediates and critiques Welfare State interventions through its realist engagement with housing, which is represented throughout the period as unstable and in the midst of transformation. In the first postwar decade, reconstruction fiction aims to take stock of destruction and confront the ruined landscape in no uncertain terms. This means that it often works as a

---

9. Calder, "UK: Domestic Life, War Effort, and Economy," 885.

revealing and critical counterpart to the overtly politicized, utopian rhetoric of the nonfictional reconstruction discourse that emerges from the Beveridge Report and building and planning documents such as the *County of London Plan*. This discourse was marked by the reinforcement of a resilient mentality that defined official government propaganda. A different, often more painfully realistic picture of wartime Britain emerges through much of this decade's fiction. In Elizabeth Taylor's *At Mrs. Lippincote's* (1945), for instance, the protagonist feels "burdened" by someone else's possessions in the wartime billet: "We shall never make a home of this," she complains.[10] Five years later, in Rose Macaulay's *The World My Wilderness* (1950), London ruins dominate the story of a young girl trying to find moral and political direction in the midst of "shells of flats," which "soared skyward on twisting stairs, staring empty-eyed at desolation."[11] As late as the mid-1960s, the legacy of war damage remained potent. In 1963, Muriel Spark's *The Girls of Slender Means* returns to the war as the setting for a story in which a women's boardinghouse falls victim to an unexploded bomb, and Iris Murdoch set her 1966 novel, *The Time of the Angels*, amidst the ruins of an East End London church that is still classified as a "building site" more than twenty-five years after the blitz.[12]

ACCOUNTING FOR THE WAR THROUGH REALISM: "RECONSTRUCTION FICTION" AS CRITICAL INTERVENTION

Domestic space and domestic issues are by no means innovative subjects for British fiction or for literary scholarship. Wartime and postwar writers, however, were in a position to capture the unique significance of the domestic in this specific historical moment. As the literature, historical documents, and events examined in this book indicate, living space in this period was subject to dramatic transformation and repurposing, disturbing any kind of secure relation between individuals, their communities, and their homes. While many people were rehoused in new properties, the literature of the period often represents the many others who were left behind in housing that needed full reconstruction but that instead was repurposed and modified, as in the many Victorian terraced houses that were divided up into flats and bedsits. "Reconstruction," then, as the central term of this book, acknowledges both the sociopolitical primacy of reconstruction efforts as well as the problems inherent in executing idealistic reconstruction plans, including, in

---

10. Taylor, *At Mrs. Lippincote's*, 13.
11. Macaulay, *World My Wilderness*, 110.
12. Murdoch, *Time of the Angels*, 8.

some cases, the failure to do so at all. Works of "reconstruction fiction" clarify and mediate the complex challenges of postwar reconstruction in its various permutations.[13]

This book posits "reconstruction fiction" as both a critical term and a set of texts that emphasize the impact of the war and crucial moments of historical change within the Welfare State. As a critical term, it theorizes the cultural and social relationship between works of realistic literature and environmental transformation. As a set of texts, it responds to altered urban, suburban, and rural landscapes alongside new sociopolitical attitudes and policies regarding housing by persistently demonstrating renewed artistic attention to the exterior world. Crucially, it is invested in social and material conditions just as much or more than characters' interior lives; in other words, it is committed to realist representation.

As a historically specific term, "reconstruction fiction" reflects the fact that, in the midst and aftermath of World War II, writers often thought about the craft of literature, daily life, and national culture in terms of an architectural and planning discourse that was directly responding to an unstable physical landscape. Most notably, writers expressed a desire for transparency—in life and in literature. Elizabeth Bowen offers one of the more suggestive commentaries linking the desire for transparency with the challenges of architectural reconstruction as well as the broad task of representation. In a 1944 essay on the effects of continual bombing, she asserts the need for new plans and building materials after the total destruction of wartime: "The old plan for living has been erased, and you do not miss it. . . . When the war is over, there will be no more of this nonsense; we shall look out through glass."[14] As with so many of Bowen's wartime writings, this comment refers to the physically altered surroundings she confronted, but it also has a metaphorical resonance

---

13. Although Matthew Taunton's *Fictions of the City: Class, Culture, and Mass Housing in London and Paris* addresses a slightly earlier time period and takes a comparative approach with a focus on London and Paris, I share with his work the basic assumption that fictional narratives "form a continuum" with nonfictional documents and artifacts of all sorts, and that "the home should be placed at the centre" of this discourse during key moments of environmental transformation (1). For Taunton, whose interest lies specifically in explaining the emergence of the modern city, these key moments are Haussmann's rebuilding of Paris in the 1850s, '60s, and '70s, and the two waves of growth producing the modern London suburbs in the late nineteenth century and the 1930s (1–2). Just as I understand reconstruction fiction as playing a mediating role within the transitional environment and discourse in which it is embedded, Taunton asserts that urban fiction often will "involve a critical engagement with the structures, institutions and mechanisms that shape the city's social life. Fictions of the city thus frequently contain projections about the ways in which that city could be improved or perfected, or go to wrack" (1).

14. Bowen, "Calico Windows," 184, 186.

with her ideas about writing. The desire to look out through glass is literal: during the war, bombed-out windows were replaced with "Calico windows," glass that had been coated in blackout material, obscuring the outside world. But the desire is also symbolic of a widespread longing for renewed clarity and order in an environment that had neither, a desire that expressed itself stylistically in a revisionist realism that characterized much of the literature of the wartime and postwar period.[15] Not long after the war ended, George Orwell echoed Bowen's materially attuned plea for transparency when he defined literary excellence in terms of glass: "Good prose is like a window pane," he wrote in his 1947 essay, "Why I Write."[16]

Such ideas about representation responded directly to the material conditions of wartime life: air raids, blackouts, bomb shelters, evacuations, financial strain, and rationing. Throughout her regular wartime reporting for the *New Yorker*, Mollie Panter-Downes documented the widespread preoccupation with light, darkness, and vision as a result of these conditions. In February 1941, reporting on the population's response to blitzed London, she wrote, "These days, people find themselves looking at England with a new eye, almost as though they were seeing it for the first time."[17] As the war continued and blackout conditions took their toll, she noted that "the command 'Let there be light' sounds like just about the most beautiful sentence in the language."[18] In the final months of the war in Europe, the feeling only intensified: "People feel that everything can wait until after that almost unbelievable hour when the lights go on again."[19] Indeed, her American *New Yorker* colleague, S. N. Behrman, visited London in January 1945 and described the blackout as "profound, terrifying, impenetrable," and he noted that "in a poll taken to discover what people considered the greatest hardship of the war, the blackout won hands down. I didn't wonder. This blackout was inhuman; it was too literal, it couldn't take a joke."[20] Like Bowen, Orwell, and Panter-Downes, Behrman thus became more attuned to the promises of renewed vision granted by light and transparency; he reflects on one benefit of the blackout: "For once a full moon overcame it and London lay bathed in silver.... I realized that this was

---

15. In *Literature of the 1940s: War, Postwar and 'Peace,'* Gill Plain similarly notes that the literature of the 1940s aimed "for transparency, assuming the duty of bearing witness to momentous historical events, but in the process inevitably revealing the limits of both articulation and imagination in the face of war's violence" (10).

16. Orwell, "Why I Write," 320.

17. Panter-Downes, *London War Notes*, 165.

18. Panter-Downes, 325.

19. Panter-Downes, 446.

20. Behrman, "Suspended Drawing Room," 28.

the first time I had really ever seen London by moonlight."[21] The wish to see clearly, to have the material world illuminated, was widespread among writers and civilians alike by the end of the war.

After immediate postwar recovery, reconstruction questions and architectural rhetoric persisted in literary criticism to both aesthetic and ethical ends. The writer was often likened to an architect and identified, thus, as a powerful cultural figure. V. S. Pritchett, for instance, wrote in his introduction to a new edition of *Wuthering Heights* (1956) that the logic of Emily Bronte's "construction is masterly," and he went on to say of the novel, "There is nothing careless or amateur about its architecture."[22] In "A Small Personal Voice" (1957), Doris Lessing's meditation on the state of contemporary British literature and her impassioned call for a renewed commitment to realism, she aligns architecture not only with realist writing but with a morally responsible, humanistic civic vision:

> The act of getting a story or a novel published is an act of communication, an attempt to impose one's personality and beliefs on other people. If a writer accepts this responsibility, he must see himself, to use the socialist phrase, as an architect of the soul. . . . But if one is going to be an architect, one must have a vision to build toward, and that vision must spring from the nature of the world we live in.[23]

For Lessing, the writer/architect has the ability to affect social change through the literary communicative act, but such an act depends on transparency, on materially engaged "vision." Indeed, she further remarks in this essay that the most important justification for reading novels is "illumination, in order to enlarge one's perception of life" (5), and she specifies realism as the narrative mode most able to provide such illumination. "Reconstruction fiction," with its historical relation to transparency, planning, and architecture, is thus a term that is useful for addressing questions of form and representational

---

21. Behrman, 61.

22. V. S. Pritchett, introduction to *Wuthering Heights*, x. This book does not provide a history of literary criticism and theory, but the continued development of structuralism and the emergence of poststructuralism in Europe could be productively read in terms of the significance of architectural reconstruction in this period. Similarly, and as the new edition of *Wuthering Heights* with Pritchett's introduction suggests, the postwar reconstruction of the English literary canon could also be a subject for a related project. Marina Mackay's recent work on the impact of the war on Ian Watt and his emerging theories of the English novel moves productively in this direction (See "Wartime Rise of the Rise of the Novel").

23. Lessing, "Small Personal Voice," 7.

technique as well as questions of meaning and social implication. How are postwar texts, alongside transformed and transforming postwar homes, communities, and landscapes, built—and to what end?

In identifying reconstruction fiction as a necessary postwar realism, this book aims to complicate conventional literary periodization schemes as well as critical theories of realism that have not yet persuasively accounted for postwar realist writing as such. It is not my intention to make claims about realism as a universal, homogeneous concept, nor as a mode that should be understood in stark opposition to experimentalism or genre fiction. Instead, I use "realist" to describe postwar fiction that takes up techniques and ideas about the purpose of literature that have been associated with the realist tradition in historically various ways since the eighteenth century. Namely, postwar realist reconstruction fiction represents and interrogates a human-scale world that is recognizable through the specificity and accessibility of its social and material content. These representations are generally supported, rather than complicated, by language and syntax—although some of the examples in the book, such as Elizabeth Bowen's more experimental *The Little Girls* (1963), notably stretch the limits of conventionally recognized realist fiction. Similarly, while postwar realist texts may take up the same content or themes of genre fiction, like romance in the case of Taylor's *At Mrs. Lippincote's* or espionage in that of Graham Greene's *The Human Factor* (1978), they resist formulaic plots and archetypal characters that tend to characterize more purely defined genre fiction, as in the example of Ian Fleming's James Bond novels. Certainly, overtly experimental writing and genre fiction may contain realist representations of housing that respond to the same conditions as more thoroughly realist work, and these are moments that demonstrate how the boundaries between various genres and modes are more mutable than our reliance on literary terminology often conveys. In J. G. Ballard's 1975 dystopian novel *High-Rise*, for example, the expectedly paranoid plot centered around dehumanization, social inequality, and greed run amok unfolds in a setting that, more or less, realistically represents mass housing constructed between the late 1950s and 1970s:

> Together they [the five high-rises] stood on the eastern perimeter of the project, looking out across an ornamental lake—at present an empty concrete basin surrounded by parking-lots and construction equipment. On the opposite shore stood the recently completed concert-hall, with Laing's medical school and the new television studios on either side. The massive scale of the glass and concrete architecture, and its striking situation on a bend of the

river, sharply separated the development project from the run-down areas around it, decaying nineteenth-century terraced houses and empty factories already zoned for reclamation.[24]

Despite such realistically represented moments, however, there is a key distinction for my argument: overtly experimental writing and genre fiction typically do not display what Pam Morris identifies as "the artistic impulse behind realism: a complex, ambivalent responsiveness towards, rather than repulsion from, the tangible stuff of reality. Realism is committed to the material actuality we share as embodied creatures."[25] I argue that postwar realist writing demands formal attention when considering twentieth-century literary history because it responds to material and social conditions that are essentially distinct from those conditions that preceded the war, and that realist technique was central to that response.[26]

Chapter 1 fully elaborates the category of reconstruction fiction in light of critical and theoretical engagements with realism, but I want to emphasize a few salient points here about the historical specificity of reconstruction fiction as realist narrative. Reconstruction fiction is a generative mode. At the height of the first postwar decade, Georg Lukács observed in *Studies in European Realism* (1948) that the method of realism is a method of discovery, not of representation of preestablished realities.[27] George Levine later echoed Lukács in *The Realistic Imagination*, describing realism as a "highly self-conscious

---

24. Ballard, *High-Rise*, 15.
25. Morris, *Realism*, 23.
26. My argument is indebted to Andrzej Gąsiorek's ground-laying literary historical work in *Post-War British Fiction: Realism and After* (1995). Gąsiorek is concerned with dismantling the entrenched critical binary of realism/experimentalism that he identifies as limiting analysis of postwar literature. He argues, "The realism/experimentalism dichotomy is formalist. It construes realism as a set of narrative techniques and experimentalism as their subversion. This is inadequate. Realism, I argue, needs to be seen as a heterogeneous phenomenon. Only then can the post-war writing practices that engage with it be seen in their full diversity and complexity (*Post-War Fiction*, v). Gąsiorek's observation that the critical insistence on opposing realism and experimentalism is formalist points to the tendency in twentieth-century literary scholarship to prioritize aesthetic innovation over social content by privileging terms such as "modernism" and "postmodernism" as organizing categories. He challenges this tendency by recuperating "realism" and grounding it in the fiction as well as discussions among postwar novelists about the function and significance of British literature at the time. He concludes persuasively, "The novels of these [postwar] writers suggest that distinctions between 'realist' and 'experimental' or between 'traditional' and 'innovative,' which were of such significance to the modernists and the avant-garde in the earlier part of the century, are so irrelevant to the post-war period that they should be dropped altogether" (*Post-War Fiction*, v).
27. Quoted in George Levine, *Realistic Imagination*, 11.

attempt to explore or create a new reality."[28] Although Lukács and Levine were describing nineteenth-century realism, which continues to dominate critical discourse, there are formal and epistemological connections with postwar realism. Like earlier instances of realist writing, the postwar mode should not be understood as being synonymous with uncritical documentary, mimesis, or comprehensiveness. Rather, realism in the postwar context characterizes a mode of expression and representation, following Bowen, Orwell, and Lessing, that emphasizes the effort to bring new material to light, to see the familiar anew, and therefore to imagine what might or ought to be.

The emphasis on generative discovery in theories of nineteenth-century realism holds true for reconstruction fiction, but there are two crucial historically specific characteristics that distinguish the two modes. First, writers in the postwar period faced wholesale destruction of the material environment, which meant that there was not merely an "attempt" but a *need* to "create a new reality," to use Levine's phrase.[29] Responding to this need with a mode of fiction that realistically imagined what might or ought to be emphasized the demand for human scale and humanist sensibility in the wake of unprecedented, global wartime dehumanization and alienation. These writers were concerned with human beings' relation to their environment, not primarily for the sake of increasing empirical knowledge of the self or of the human world, as we might characterize the project of earlier forms of realism, but more urgently as a crucial sign of human welfare and connection.

The second important distinction between nineteenth-century realism and the realism of postwar reconstruction is that postwar writers were aware of—and sometimes participated in—the aesthetic and philosophical struggles that defined interwar modernism, even if the problem of representation as such is not foregrounded in reconstruction fiction as it so often is in avant-garde modernist fiction. As Bowen's reflection on midcentury fiction suggests, postwar writers came to see the modernist problem of representing consciousness in particular as a privileged one, and therefore less urgent or relevant, in the aftermath of wartime destruction. With that said, the experiments and existential queries of modernism were often present in reconstruction fiction in an adapted form that allowed postwar writers to foreground a commitment to representing an accessible social reality in all its complexity. Colin MacInnes's reinvention of the city novel in *Absolute Beginners* (1959), for example, echoes the modernist interest in representing cities and time through the form of the one-day novel, but the style and content of his novel remain sociologically

---

28. Levine, 20.
29. Levine, 20.

realist, emphasizing the detailed, often interracial and interclass relationships among characters and between characters and their environment.

Although stylistic approaches vary among the works I discuss, reconstruction fiction is characterized by a number of recurring preoccupations and tropes that help to define postwar realism as distinct. First, it is interested in the visible, exterior world. I trace this investment in what can be seen to the wartime experience that made clear or well-lit vision difficult.[30] Elizabeth Bowen's prognosis, "When the war is over, there will be no more of this nonsense; we shall look out through glass," perfectly expresses the postwar link between realist representation of the exterior and reconstruction.[31] Windows coated in blackout material transformed looking into a privileged act. Hence, Elizabeth Taylor and Patrick Hamilton provide extensively detailed descriptions of the temporary wartime living situations in which their characters found themselves; this descriptive technique provides bearings even as it captures disorientation. More than ten years later, MacInnes's novels have the sociological or touristic quality that emphasizes the physically visible attributes of people, buildings, or neighborhoods that can be observed, classified, and understood so that they might become more socially visible in the midst of imperial devolution and economic reinvention. Vision becomes a powerful humanistic social tool in reconstruction fiction, as it has the ability to reveal and witness injustice, neglect, or as yet unseen value, and therefore to set the stage for changing present conditions. Second, even as reconstruction fiction accounts for what is visible, it does not offer a false sense of closure or comprehension. In its representation of recognizable worlds, it also accounts for what is invisible or missing. Bowen's *The Little Girls,* for example, represents the demolished country house not through direct narration but indirectly through various tropes of absence: an empty time capsule, a half-full cave museum, a bomb site, abortive dialogue. Similarly, the limits of hospitality, dead telephone lines, and an unsettlingly open-ended plot figure in Greene's spy novel, *The Human Factor,* to show what cannot be accommodated in the late-1970s Cold War safe house and in the late Welfare State narrative.

---

30. Certainly, this interest in the visible also can be explained partly by the rise of cinema and documentary culture in the interwar years. Thomas Davis makes this argument in *The Extinct Scene: Late Modernism and Everyday Life,* and he coins the phrase "the outward turn" to describe "late modernist" attention to the visible and quotidian. Tracing this through line creates aesthetic continuity between the pre- and postwar years, which adds credibility to the term "late modernism" as a phenomenon that extends beyond the war. I would argue, however, that the war marks a significant turning point in this developmental link between cinema, documentary, and literature: namely, that the physical exigencies of wartime life made the attention to visibility more of a material and social necessity than a politically inflected aesthetic choice.

31. Bowen, "Calico Windows," 186.

Third, the realism of reconstruction fiction demands a response to history as writers are compelled to ask: what will be preserved, what will be demolished, and what will be left behind in the era of reconstruction? Is it more important to maintain historical continuity or to clear room for new voices? Some texts answer to history formally in terms of literary lineage or genre. Elizabeth Taylor repurposes prewar country house Gothic novels like *Jane Eyre* and *Rebecca* with her ironic, anti-nostalgic iteration in *Angel* (1957). She employs realistic techniques to enable an older, more romantic form to more directly engage with transformed contemporary material and social conditions. Fourth, and finally, reconstruction fiction also engages with the present. Not only thematically, but formally and stylistically, these texts often produce an affectively realistic representation of the contemporary conditions that make it difficult to build or reinvent. As a result, the reader or viewer experiences a discomfort or isolation that mirrors the experience of the characters. In an early work of reconstruction fiction, *The Slaves of Solitude* (1947), Patrick Hamilton makes use of focalization to reproduce the anxiety surrounding participation in wartime communities, and at the other end of the period, in Doris Lessing's *The Good Terrorist* (1985), real-time narration prevents the reader from settling comfortably into an established literary tradition or narrative space. In this important sense, reconstruction fiction does not provide a false sense of security or stability through its realistic mode; rather, it clarifies conditions.

With the context of rebuilding in mind, then, the realistic mode of reconstruction fiction can be interpreted productively not as stylistically reactionary but as an imaginative necessity for reestablishing and reevaluating British society at key moments of transition throughout postwar history. My attention to reconstruction as a broad cultural phenomenon born out of the war and the immediate postwar decade allows for a new way of considering how postwar fiction takes up "the task of imagining the present and future" that Marina MacKay and Lyndsey Stonebridge identify as central to midcentury fiction.[32] The realist representations of reconstruction fiction, I argue, offer more than thematic and mimetic representations of history; they actively contribute to its construction as much as town plans, architectural models, builders, and government policies.

Graham Greene's 1954 short story, "The Destructors," is a demonstrative piece of reconstruction fiction in its realist mode and in its thematic focus on housing and the legacy of the war. Greene is also a writer whose career spans the entire postwar period (in addition to the interwar years) and whose work

---

32. MacKay and Stonebridge, *British Fiction after Modernism*, 2.

consistently engages with the most pressing social and political issues of the Welfare State, often capturing the social and aesthetic complexity inherent in key moments of transition—or "reconstruction." "The Destructors" is therefore a useful example to dwell on briefly here. The story demonstrates the tension between domestic values that emphasize a stable connection with the past—prewar aesthetics—and those that embrace a future-oriented modernity and social mobility. Greene uses the destruction of a house whose design was inspired by Christopher Wren, one of Britain's canonical architectural figures, to pit tradition and history against modern engineering skills and a mobile postwar youth. The teenage boys who make up the Wormsley Common gang—Blackie, Summers, Mike, and T.—are against everything in the built environment that refers to a time before they existed: glorified Georgian interiors, Victorian collections and decoration, Palladian façades. They despise these things because they represent a past in which they find neither value nor use and because they obscure and complicate the appearance of things. These boys value transparency.

Rather than mourn the homes lost in the blitz or glorify those homes that survived, the boys take the destructive historical moment as their starting point; the blitz cuts off the past and presents a new basis for power and purpose. Establishing a new postwar ritual, the gang meets every morning at "the site of the last bomb of the first blitz," but "no one was precise enough in his dates" to point out to Blackie that he could not possibly have heard the first bomb fall, as he claims, because he would only have been one year old "and fast asleep on the down platform of Wormsley Common Underground Station."[33] Blackie was born into the acute mobility of wartime Britain; each night during the blitz, he moved with his family to an underground shelter. Whereas the forced mobility of the war disrupted the safe, stable home held as an ideal by an older generation, Blackie's generation feels "at home" when they are on the move. The boys value contingency and risk: they prefer the future to the past, the open outdoors to the protected indoors. They meet in "an impromptu car-park" and plan to "disperse in pairs, take buses at random, and see how many free rides could be snatched from unwary conductors."[34] With mobility and disruption as some of their most prized values, they are indifferent, if not directly opposed, to architectural preservation and the social status afforded by owning historical artifacts. Greene thus represents not only what this generation values but also what is missing from its worldview: an

---

33. Greene, "Destructors," 226.
34. Greene, 226, 228.

appreciation for physical stability, the ability to comprehend and memorialize the losses of the war.

The gang condemns the practice of architecture as an authoritative, middle-class exercise in taste and heritage formation. T.'s father is a former architect, and T. uses his architectural knowledge not to reinforce a traditional aesthetic appreciation of buildings but to create a plan for their demolition. It is his understanding of the industrial engineering of the house—its layout, plumbing, building materials, electrical wiring—and not his ability to theorize its beauty that gives T. authority within the gang. Initially, Blackie distrusts T. because he seems to be praising Old Misery's house, which T. recognizes as a Wren building, for its beauty; he tells the group about its wood paneling and free-standing, two-hundred-year-old staircase held up by opposite forces.[35] "It was the word 'beautiful' that worried him [Blackie]—that belonged to a class world that you could still see parodied at the Wormsley Common Empire by a man wearing a top hat and a monocle, with a haw-haw accent."[36] Blackie, in other words, links conventional notions of "beauty" with socioeconomic and even political treachery. But T.'s suggestion that they pull the house down methodically from the inside rather than break in and steal things gains popularity with the group as a total rejection of the past. The act of demolition becomes a more ironic affirmation of a dismantled modernity when the narrator explains that Old Misery had once been a builder and decorator, but that he had no knowledge of plumbing; he had to use an outdoor lavatory once the pipes had been damaged in the blitz. Old Misery's lack of modern home-building knowledge puts him at an ironic disadvantage when the boys lock him in his lavatory as they complete the demolition by turning on the taps and flooding the house.

T. is a planner without attachment to the past or architectural canon. As such, he works against not only the nostalgia of the prewar generation but the postwar preservationist ethos promoted by influential figures such as architectural historian John Summerson and National Trust Secretary James Lees-Milne. T.'s vision requires the use of modern techniques—a gut rehab—to remove any historically resonant sense of "home" from the structure. When the other boys suggest that they leave after having gutted everything within the walls, T. protests that they haven't finished, and he emphasizes the importance of the exterior: "'Anybody could do this—' 'this' was the shattered hollowed house with nothing left but the walls. Yet walls could be preserved. Façades were valuable. They could build inside again more beautifully than before.

---

35. Greene, 226.
36. Greene, 229.

This could again be a home."³⁷ Demolition, for T., requires elimination of all historical referent; an outdated attachment to history would perpetuate an outdated idea of "home." Old Misery's house, from the perspective of the gang, epitomizes the persistence of obsolete history. It is the only house to have survived the bomb blasts on its street; it "literally leant," and it "stuck up like a jagged tooth and carried on the further wall relics of its neighbour, a dado, the remains of a fireplace."³⁸ As they destroy the house, they reject nostalgic efforts of preservation as well as the profit-driven reappropriation and redevelopment of old buildings by contemporary builders: the boys would rather burn the money they find in Old Misery's mattress than become inheritors of tainted capital. For T., the signs of a middle-class domestic life have become completely stripped of their ability to confer meaning. "There's only things," he tells Blackie, "and he looked round the room crowded with the unfamiliar shadows of half things, broken things, former things."³⁹ For Greene's teenagers, total demolition that leaves a clean slate is the only antidote to a world populated by things and buildings that have no meaning for a new generation. "The Destructors" is narrated with an ironic edge that critiques the older middle-class generation for its over investment in "useless" appearances and aesthetics, but it also does not let the boys off scot free. Their power is completely of the moment and, given their lack of precise historical knowledge, fleeting and pointlessly destructive. In the ambivalent architectural conflict between these two generations, Greene's story emphasizes the persistent existential questioning inherent in postwar reconstruction.

CRITICAL CONVERSATIONS

Reconstruction Fiction: Housing and Realist Literature in Postwar Britain addresses itself to critics working in twentieth-century British literary and cultural history as well as those with interests in realist narrative and in the built environment. As a critical term, "reconstruction fiction" brings a new set of contextual parameters to twentieth-century British literary and cultural studies, which traditionally has been defined by categories of modernism, postmodernism, and postcolonialism. Unlike these categories, "reconstruction fiction" specifically accounts for the undeniable impact of the war and the creation of the Welfare State, and it foregrounds formal questions about realist writing. In these ways, it offers an alternative to dominant scholarly assess-

---

37. Greene, 238.
38. Greene, 226.
39. Greene, 236.

ments of the period that frequently return to World War I or modernism in order to assign literary or cultural value.⁴⁰ Recent work treating the midcentury period in this way by Jed Esty, Marina MacKay, Lyndsey Stonebridge, Patrick Deer, Leo Mellor, and Thomas Davis—among others—has been indispensable in reframing scholarly understanding of wartime and postwar texts within cultural, political, and broadly historical circumstances.⁴¹ In *Modernism and World War II*, for instance, MacKay helpfully foregrounds the stakes of political and civic engagement in wartime and immediate and postwar literature by identifying an alignment of "the renovation of the public sphere in [World War II] Britain with the aesthetic discourses that had anticipated its necessity and came to record it in the process of taking shape."⁴² Davis also productively identifies an "outward turn" and a focus on the everyday that began in the 1930s and extends into the postwar period as "specifically a late modernist form of attention."⁴³ Without considering the central importance of "realism," these contributions still dovetail with my own attention to the way in which wartime and postwar literature confronts the social world. *Reconstruction Fiction*, like Gill Plain's *Literature of the 1940s*, is a rejoinder to Jed Esty's book, *A Shrinking Island*. Esty begins with the formal starting point of high modernism to take up "the question of late modernism and imperial contraction between 1930 and 1960" in order to "address the blank space or interregnum between modernism and postmodernism, between empire and welfare state."⁴⁴

As this introduction has made clear, I begin from the premise that World War II is anything but a "blank space," "interregnum," or even a continuation of modernism in a "late" form, as MacKay and Davis would have it. Through the concept of "reconstruction fiction," therefore, I intervene most significantly by moving the conversation away from modernism as the decisive term of value.⁴⁵ Like Phyllis Lassner, Gill Plain, Petra Rau, Victoria Stewart, and

---

40. As Gill Plain argues in *Literature of the 1940s: War, Postwar and 'Peace,'* literature of the 1940s in particular has often been neglected because of "the long-ingrained practice of reading the twentieth-century through the formal trajectory of modernism and after, into which the 1940s disappear as afterthought or hiatus" (5).

41. See Jed Esty's *A Shrinking Island: Modernism and National Culture in England* (2004), Marina MacKay's *Modernism and World War II* (2007), Marina MacKay's and Lyndsey Stonebridge's *British Fiction after Modernism* (2007), and Patrick Deer's *Culture in Camouflage* (2009), Leo Mellor's *Reading the Ruins: Modernism, Bombsites, and British Culture* (2011), and Thomas Davis's *The Extinct Scene: Late Modernism and Everyday Life* (2016).

42. MacKay, *Modernism and World War II*, 4.

43. Davis, *Extinct Scene*, 4.

44. Esty, *Shrinking Island*, 4.

45. In this respect, "reconstruction fiction" aligns with Kristin Bluemel's term "intermodernism" and with Middlebrow Studies, both of which have resisted the expanding timeline of

others, I maintain that the war is a culturally generative moment in its own right, and I add to their insights that the war calls for a specific realist literary idiom that begs more nuanced investigation.[46] The significance of reconstruction fiction, moreover, is most evident not through the work of the canonical high modernists whose later careers continued into this period, as Esty has argued for T. S. Eliot and Virginia Woolf, but through emerging voices of a younger generation that has remained comparatively neglected by scholars in more conventional works of literary history that are eager to extend modernism or make the leap from modernism to postmodernism or postcolonialism.[47] Instead of looking backward to high modernism or World War I, this study looks forward, even as it accounts for historical conditions. In this sense, *Reconstruction Fiction* moves the discussion away from debates about "the end of modernism" toward a more open historical analysis of realist techniques since World War II, thus encouraging a different way of thinking about mid-century and postwar literature.[48]

---

the New Modernist Studies and insisted on the need for categories other than "modernism" to fully appreciate twentieth-century literature and culture. See Bluemel's volume *Intermodernism: Literary Culture in Mid-Twentieth-Century Britain* (2009) and Erica Brown and Mary Grover's volume *Middlebrow Literary Cultures: The Battle of the Brows, 1920–1960* (2011), for example.

46. Some of the most important ground clearing for further work on the literature and culture of World War II came from feminist scholars in the 1990s who examined the significance of the war for women's lives, often as expressed through the work of middlebrow writers. Several rich examples of this intervention include Phyllis Lassner's *British Women Writers of World War II: Battlegrounds of Their Own* (1998), Gill Plain's *Women's Fiction of the Second World War: Gender, Power and Resistance* (1996), and Karen Schneider's *Loving Arms: British Women Writing the Second World War* (1997). In more recent years, Victoria Stewart's *The Second World War in Contemporary British Fiction* (2011) and Petra Rau's edited volume *Long Shadows: The Second World War in British Fiction and Film* (2016) treat the continued significance of the war not only throughout the Welfare State period but beyond as well. As Rau notes in her introduction, the persistence of World War II in British cultural memory is extraordinary, calling for scholarly collections like hers and monographs like Stewart's and my own: "Few countries attribute as much importance to the Second World War and its memory as Britain; nowhere else has this conflict developed such longevity in cultural memory and retained such presence in contemporary culture. . . . The phrase 'the war' suggests that the war in question is the determining conflict in the lives of those who participated in it" (3).

47. In this sense I again follow Plain when she argues, "There is no doubt that many [wartime and postwar] writers continued to be influenced by a modernist aesthetic," but in scholarly terms, "'modernism' is a distraction for the 1940s, and its deployment risks obliterating the very diverse voices and literary developments of the period. The Second World War really does change everything" (*Literature of the 1940s*, 5).

48. This book can be understood as contributing to what Jed Esty and Colleen Lye have described as "a 'new realist turn' in criticism. Such a term would designate a range of disparate projects that register the lapsing of the linguistic or cultural turn that had once installed literary studies in the hub of interdisciplinary influence" ("Peripheral Realisms," 276). Interestingly, Esty's turn to realism seems in part to be a direct reaction against the dominance of a modernist framework for twentieth-century and postcolonial writing, a framework he has been instrumental in reinforcing it.

In addition to recent critical discussions of modernism, war literature, and postcolonialism, postwar British literature has long been taken up productively by scholars interested in cultural materialism, sociological questions, and the place of class relations within the Welfare State. Alan Sinfield's work, beginning in 1989 with *Literature, Politics and Culture in Postwar Britain*, has been enormously influential in shaping the field of inquiry for postwar literature in these ways. Sinfield's cultural materialist approach contextualizes literature within various determining cultural, social, economic, and political relations in order to identify ways in which subcultures might resist dominant and oppressive institutions and structures of authority. His understanding of stories as historically generative aligns with my own assumptions about the productive nature of realist reconstruction fiction. As he puts it, "Societies have to reproduce themselves culturally as well as materially, and this is done in great part by putting into circulation stories of how that world goes."[49] Writing within a Marxist tradition, particularly influenced by Adorno, Sinfield further understands these stories dialectically and ideologically in terms of their relationship with various historical forces. He argues,

> It is through such stories that ideologies are reinforced—and contested, for subordinate groups struggle to make space for themselves, and attempts to legitimate the prevailing order have to negotiate resistant experience and traditions. Literary texts raise complex questions of cultural affiliation and appropriation, while engaging with the most sensitive issues of our time.[50]

The materialist model that Sinfield promotes has encouraged scholars working on postwar British literature to foreground questions of social conformity and resistance with the ultimate leftist political goal of identifying "positive cultural strategies for dissident intellectuals and for subcultures."[51] While *Reconstruction Fiction* undoubtedly is indebted to Sinfield's materialist work, the dominance of such a framework within studies of postwar literature is now a limiting force in its own right that obscures insights that are possible when taking a different, more formalist critical perspective. My focus on realism and reconstruction thus depends on Sinfield's basic assumption that stories are

---

49. Sinfield, *Literature, Politics and Culture in Postwar Britain*, 2–3.
50. Sinfield, 2–3.
51. Sinfield, 4. See, for example, John Brannigan's monograph, *Literature, Culture, and Society in Postwar England, 1945–1965*, which is keen to identify the relative political merits of postwar writing, especially with regard to the Angry Young Men. Such politicized projects following Sinfield are also apparent in the scholarship I cite throughout the book in relation to particular texts.

generative of real conditions, but it loosens his critical narrative that assigns rigid political implication to interpreting those stories.

Sinfield's cultural materialism intersects with more recent contributions in cultural history and in interdisciplinary studies of the postwar period—several of which are particularly relevant precedents to this book in their attention to the built environment. Peter Kalliney's rich study of twentieth-century British literary culture and national identity in relation to the urban environment, *Cities of Affluence and Anger: A Literary Geography of Modern Englishness* (2006), combines Marxist and postcolonialist approaches to literature, geography, and national identity. Doing so allows him to posit literary texts as discursive sites through which class differences were renegotiated as a by-product of colonial decline, thereby creating a unifying national discourse.[52] Kalliney's methodology and his way of understanding the relationship between literature and history is an important precedent for the argument made here, although, as chapter 1 explains, my own approach is not so thoroughly committed to interpretive models that insist on linking specific textual meaning with the abstractions of global capitalism.[53] Richard Hornsey's *The Spiv and the Architect: Unruly Life in Postwar London* (2010) also offers a compelling and immensely useful account of the historical culture of reconstruction, claiming that one can only understand the parameters of postwar identities—specifically, for his argument, queer identities—within the context of architectural and planning discourses that attempted to "reorganize everyday space and time within postwar London."[54] This line of inquiry follows Sinfield in its attention to the relations between dominant and subcultural groups, but more directly, it adopts a Foucauldian approach to culture that ultimately understands identity as subject to disciplinary powers exercised through discourse, a view that stands somewhat in tension with what I argue are the humanizing effects of realist writing. To these interventions, which are both ultimately concerned with the construction of a unified postwar national culture, this book adds the more formally oriented framework of "reconstruction fiction." This framework insists that the realistic world building of midcentury fiction deserves special attention when considering a historical moment in which the actual world was being rebuilt in original and, literally, concrete ways.

---

52. Kalliney, *Cities of Affluence and Anger*, 6.

53. My resistance to such interpretive models echoes Matthew Taunton's position in *Fictions of the City* (2009), in which he usefully notes, "Certain accounts of the development of capitalist modernity—Marxist ones in particular—have tended to paper over . . . differences [in the experience of urban life] in the interests of producing a schematic model. . . . Novelists and filmmakers have often proved to be more sensitive to specifics" (4).

54. Hornsey, *Spiv and the Architect*, 3.

ORGANIZATIONAL PLAN

Reconstruction Fiction: Housing and Realist Literature in Postwar Britain charts the chronological construction of the British Welfare State and dismantling of the postwar consensus through realist fictional interventions. It is organized thematically around different types of housing that best highlight the literary engagement with the task of postwar rebuilding at crucial transitional moments: billets and boardinghouses, innovative and improvised urban dwellings, country houses, and Cold War safe houses and squats. Each of these types of housing, moreover, allows a different aspect of reconstruction discourse to emerge: town planning, demolition and modernization, preservation and heritage, and government housing policy. The fictional texts that I examine are all concerned with environmental instability, with the transience of tables and chairs that Bowen lamented during the war. For some writers, instability and impermanence was cause for celebration, as it made way for innovation and new experiences; for others, it was a threat to basic securities and established socioeconomic circumstances; for many, it was met with ambivalence. In all cases, these works of fiction face up to the conditions of instability by representing transformed or transforming living space and its social implications.

Because my primary aim is to develop a clear picture of the relation between housing and realist writing during the postwar period, I have not prioritized the lives and careers of individual writers, nor have I attempted to offer a complete survey of geographical regions of Britain. Where possible, I have highlighted neglected writers, like Colin MacInnes, or less frequently studied texts by more canonical writers, like Elizabeth Bowen's *The Little Girls* or Graham Greene's *The Human Factor,* in order to contribute to scholarly efforts to increase literary historical nuance and complexity. I have, however, intentionally resisted the model of literary scholarship that relies on personality and reputation as a governing force. Focusing on suburban, urban, and rural housing contexts introduces diverse geographical dimensions to this study, but I do not claim that any of the texts I examine provide fully generalizable examples that apply to all of Britain. This claim is especially true of those texts set in London, which is represented, for the most part, at the expense of any other urban setting (with the exception of a brief discussion of literature from northern cities in chapter 3). In terms of sheer volume, London experienced the most noticeable and dramatic change in terms of housing throughout the postwar period, making it both an ideal case study for considering the fictional and nonfictional engagement with reconstruction as well as an atypical example that has limited application when accounting for

British experience as a whole. I hope that my work invites future contemplation of reconstruction fiction in other regions to continue the work of literary historical recovery.

Similarly, it reasonably may be asserted that other kinds of writing not considered here—poetry, drama—also represent and mediate postwar reconstruction, and that therefore they deserve consideration. There is no doubt that such writing could productively add to efforts to understand the literary engagement with this period, as postwar poetry by writers such as John Betjeman, H. D., and Philip Larkin clearly takes up the domestic scene as a major theme. Terrence Rattigan's plays are similarly one prime example of how the domestic literally takes center stage in wartime and postwar drama. My choice to focus solely on novels relies on a basic assumption that, unlike other genres, novels formally invite writers and readers to inhabit a total world through language and representation in a way that poetry and drama do not. This way of thinking about novels as inhabitable echoes Henry James's 1881 conception of "the house of fiction" with its innumerable windows[55] or, more recently, Zadie Smith's claim, "The novels we know best have an architecture. Not only a door going in and another leading out, but rooms, hallways, stairs, little gardens front and back, trapdoors, hidden passageways, etc."[56] In a formal sense, then, novels have a deep connection with housing, with real inhabitable spaces. So while I am not offering a study of reading habits and reader response during the postwar years, I am presuming a fundamental historical relation between the acts of creating and encountering the fictional worlds of novels and the perception and shaping of the material world.[57]

As I have already noted, chapter one addresses the theoretical stakes of reconstruction fiction in terms of literary realism. Chapter 2, "Billets and Boardinghouses," assesses the implications of wartime and immediate postwar reconstruction through the relationship between the individual and community in public debates, town plans, and two novels set in shared wartime living space: Hamilton's *The Slaves of Solitude* and Taylor's *At Mrs. Lippincote's*. As real individuals adjusted to a leveled, slowly recovering world with limited space for individualism, literary protagonists adjusted to a similarly restricted kind of realist narrative; the individual-centered development plot of much traditional realism gave way to a more ambivalent set of negotiations among multiple characters and voices. Major reconstruction initiatives such

---

55. James, Preface of *Portrait of a Lady*, n.p.
56. Smith, "Rereading Barthes and Nabokov," 42.
57. This basic theoretical assumption derives from materialist, often Marxist, conceptions of the relationship between literature, history, and the material world, several of which I discuss in chapter 1 as part of my elaboration on realism and its postwar iterations.

as the *County of London Plan* reveal the historical importance of the value of individual living space in Britain while appealing to the spirit of unified wartime sacrifice to justify plans that asked citizens to share living space to a far greater degree than they had before. In the novels by Taylor and Hamilton, this historical reality is critiqued thematically as characters' living space is limited by the billet or boardinghouse setting, but it is also expressed as a structural limitation as characters compete with minor characters and heavy-handed narrators rather than emerging as the fully developed individuals of nineteenth-century realist novels.

Chapter 3, "Mobile Housing," explores how increased geographic and social mobility in the late 1950s were experienced with varying consequences by teenagers, emigrants, and the working classes in British cities. This chapter considers how Colin MacInnes's trilogy of London novels, but especially *Absolute Beginners*, reinvents the realist tradition from a peripheral perspective that foregrounds the experience and implications of increased mobility. MacInnes in particular shares with the New Brutalist architects who emerged during this period an explicit commitment to "reality," with emphasis on actual social conditions, and to creating art and living spaces that express and confront this often messy, even violent, reality. In this sense, they reconstruct the postwar environment and its culture yet again with their renewed turn to material conditions.

Chapter 4, "Country Houses," shifts to the rural postwar setting and examines the effects of Welfare State land reform and middle-class consumer culture on country houses and country house novels by Elizabeth Taylor and Elizabeth Bowen. After the war, as many country houses were sold, repurposed, or demolished, they were no longer active and dominant sites of sociopolitical power for the landed classes; instead, their main purpose became historical preservation and display directed toward middle-class consumers. Taylor's *Angel* and Bowen's *The Little Girls* offer differently classed perspectives that highlight the critical role of narrative in this transition. Taylor's novel uses the mode of realistic historical fiction and the character of a popular romance novelist to reveal the ambivalence of middle-class upward mobility, notably critiquing ahistorical treatments of both fiction and country houses. Bowen's novel, on the other hand, rejects nostalgia as it represents the unsettling gap between what has been lost historically and what is preserved through heritage culture.

Finally, chapter 5, "Safe Houses," measures the legacy of the postwar consensus and its deconstruction under the rise of conservative power in the late 1970s and under the Thatcher Government through the fictional desire for safety and hospitality in the built environment. In Graham Greene's *The*

Human Factor and Doris Lessing's *The Good Terrorist*, resurgent realism responds to the largest sociopolitical paradigm shift in Britain since the 1940s. As with 1940s realist texts, these novels face head-on destabilizing conditions and adopt narrative techniques that force the reader to affectively experience the restlessness of life in a Britain in which the possibility looms that, as Thatcher infamously put it, "there is no such thing as society."[58] As the postwar settlement unravels and privatization becomes the new rule for the housing industry, individualism, rather than social welfare, becomes the predominant ideology. *The Human Factor* and *The Good Terrorist* expose the violent consequences of this ideology for Britain's most vulnerable.

Each chapter supports the more global aim that presents this book's contribution to modern literary and cultural history: to bring fictional and nonfictional discourses into constellation with each other in order to better understand how the need and desire for postwar reconstruction operated throughout various layers of human experience. "Reconstruction fiction" introduces a new framework for twentieth-century British culture that helps to recover the nuances and significance of realistic postwar fiction and that allows the most important social issues of the Welfare State to come to the foreground. The writers I examine felt the urgent necessity of their fictional task, and *Reconstruction Fiction* attends to this urgency.

---

58. Thatcher, Interview for *Woman's Own* ("no such thing as society") with Douglas Keay, n.p.

CHAPTER 1

An Urgent Invitation

Theorizing Postwar Realist Writing

POSTWAR REALISM needs reevaluation. Recent critiques have begun to emerge of dominant modernist and poststructuralist claims that realism, at any time in literary history, is naïvely mimetic, and that twentieth-century realism in particular is residual. This book adds to those critiques. In midcentury Britain specifically, realist writing responds to the demand for reconstruction. It acts as an assertive interruption that seeks to clarify and transform—and to communicate that transformation to others through an inviting aesthetic mode. Postwar realism intervenes in the perception of the world after war—physical disorder, political upheaval, the effects of bombing, mass genocide—with an effort to counter alienating fragmentation and abstraction. As it signifies individual experience in relation to social and material conditions, the realist mode asserts the possibility of reconceiving a world marred by dehumanizing events. In rejecting or reformulating the comforting narrative patterns of genre fiction, moreover, postwar realism interrupts an escapist mode of readerly perception. Whether in relation to the actual world or imagined narrative, postwar realism calls for attention to be reoriented.

This argument dialogues with recent attempts to rethink realism in literary theory and literary history. In the preface to Matthew Beaumont's 2007 edited volume, *A Concise Companion to Realism,* Rachel Bowlby immediately establishes realism in general as something in need of critical defense and rehabilitation: "Poor old realism. Out of date and second-rate.... When realism does get mentioned it is usually in the form of a passing, knee-jerk dismissal of it as something self-evidently without interest, not to say a bit dumb."[1] Bowlby rightly locates this trend of dismissal in scholarship that privileges the modernist call to "make it new." In his introduction, Beaumont draws on Terry Eagleton to add, "Postmodernism, defined in telegraphic form as 'the contemporary movement of thought which rejects totalities, universal values, grand historical narratives, solid foundations to human existence and the possibility of objective knowledge,' has made an impatient or apathetic attitude to realism seem acceptable."[2] As a rejoinder to the on-going project of the New Modernist Studies to claim increasing geographic and temporal territory[3] as well as the long wave of postmodern and poststructuralist theoretical dominance, Beaumont claims that his volume "represents an intervention in a field of intellectual debate that has for some time been shaped by an anti-referential, an anti-realist consensus" ("Reclaiming Realism," 10). With this project in mind, the collection proceeds to take for granted that the nineteenth century was the high point of realism, although it does include a number of essays that work to complicate the assumption that realist epistemology goes away with the rise of modernist experimentation.[4] It also takes a generous view of the disciplinary category of realism, putting the literary iteration into dialogue with essays on realism in painting, photography, cinema, and philosophy. This strategy productively opens up new ways of thinking about realism in terms of a set of epistemological and ontological questions that persist. And yet, no contributions in this collection consider the fate of realist aesthetics after early twentieth-century modernism in more contemporary literature or other arts. So, while the volume goes a long way to rejuvenating critical interest in the realist canon (almost every literary scholar included cites George Eliot's *Adam Bede* as a primary example), it stops short of considering what to make of realist art after World War II.

---

1. Bowlby, Foreword to *A Concise Companion to Realism*, xiv.
2. Beaumont, "Introduction: Reclaiming Realism," 2.
3. In their influential 2008 PMLA article, "The New Modernist Studies," Douglas Mao and Rachel Walkowitz sought to define the new era of modernist studies primarily in terms of its expansiveness: "Were one seeking a single word to sum up transformations in modernist literary scholarship over the past decade or two, one could do worse than light on expansion" (737). In the wake of their assertion, numerous modernist critics have pursued the kinds of expansion that Mao and Walkowitz enumerate, with the most temporally and spatially radical being Susan Stanford Friedman's *Planetary Modernisms: Provocations on Modernity Across Time* (2015), which considers texts from before 1500 through the twenty-first century as instances of modernism.
4. See essays in Beaumont's collection by Esther Leslie, Laura Marcus, John Roberts, and Brandon Taylor.

The evolutionary model of literary history, which informs the majority of Beaumont's volume as well as other, more global interventions, such as Jed Esty and Colleen Lye's theory of "peripheral realism," remains a major obstacle for thinking productively about postwar realism in the European context. *Reconstruction Fiction* challenges this model by establishing the historical value of midcentury realism and investigating its interruptive potential. This chapter situates postwar British realism within the critical terrain surrounding the term realism. Three main interrelated issues are at stake in debates surrounding this term: geographical determinants, periodization, and aesthetic definition. Since the mid-twentieth century, there has generally been a move from thinking about realism in broad European terms toward more strictly defined national and then local traditions, and, more recently, back outward again to a more global framework. In almost all accounts, the nineteenth century, with its capitalist and nationalist obsessions, remains central to periodizing and contextualizing efforts. Defining realism aesthetically, meanwhile, has always drawn scholars, to varying degrees, into literary debates about the nature of representation and the cognitive processes of reading and interpretation, philosophical discussions of epistemology and ontology, as well as impassioned arguments about the relationship between literature and social and political realities. For postwar British realism and for reconstruction fiction as a concept, this last line of inquiry is especially relevant in advancing a new critical direction for twentieth-century literary studies.

•

Marxist, feminist, and narrative theories of realism help to explain the interruptive and reconstructive potential of postwar British realism. Since the mid-twentieth century, critics working within a Marxist tradition have most consistently studied and defended the social value of literary realism.[5] In short, Marxist frameworks give critics a way to comprehend literary representation not as passive mimesis but as integral to the production of the real world or, "the real." Georg Lukács, the most influential Marxist to have theorized and promoted realism, defined it as a modern European and Russian tradition epitomized by Honoré de Balzac in France, Thomas Mann in Germany, and Leo Tolstoy in Russia. Lukács influentially argued that realism is the single necessary literary tool that has the power to bring individuals into history,

---

5. One reason for this preoccupation with realism is that Marx's own career coincided with the conventionally understood dominance of European realism in the mid-to-late nineteenth century. Another reason is that Marx directly theorized literary and cultural production as part of his extensive analysis of capitalism and the dialectical "laws" of historical progress.

repairing or reversing their alienation from social and political forces, which he recognizes as acute in the aftermath of two World Wars and the terrors of Fascism. In *Studies in European Realism* (1948), he considers recent modern developments in what he describes as extreme naturalism (e.g., Emile Zola) and extreme subjectivity (e.g., James Joyce), and he asserts that realism

> is not some sort of middle way between false objectivity and false subjectivity, but on the contrary the true, solution-bringing third way, opposed to all the pseudo-dilemmas engendered by the wrongly-posed [sic] questions of those who wander without a chart in the labyrinth of our time. Realism is the recognition of the fact that a work of literature can rest neither on a lifeless average, as the naturalists suppose, nor on an individual principle which dissolves its own self into nothingness. . . . True realism thus depicts man and society as complete entities, instead of showing merely one or the other of their aspects. Measured by this criterion, artistic trends determined by either exclusive introspection or exclusive extraversion equally impoverish and distort reality.[6]

With this formulation, Lukács articulates a crucial foundational assumption for Marxist literary scholarship that privileges realism as a genre that has the potential symbolically to resolve real material contradictions through its balanced representation of individual humans in relation to the social forces of their time, thereby contributing to the forward progress of history itself. Fredric Jameson, focusing on French and British writers, would echo and develop this formulation, most notably in *The Political Unconscious: Narrative as a Socially Symbolic Act* (1981), as would Raymond Williams and Terry Eagleton throughout their careers. Jameson, for instance, took Lukács's idea about the content and style of realism and extrapolated it into an argument about "the ideology of form." His theory was influential in clarifying how literature—and he privileges nineteenth-century realism as well through chapters on Balzac, George Gissing, and Joseph Conrad—and "the real world" are not separate spheres, but rather dialectically interconnected realms that construct each other ideologically through language.[7] Thus, following Lukács, Jameson offers

---

6. Lukács, *Studies in European Realism*, 6.

7. According to Jameson in *The Political Unconscious: Narrative as a Socially Symbolic Act*: "The literary or aesthetic act therefore always entertains some active relationship with the Real; yet in order to do so, it cannot simply allow 'reality' to persevere inertly in its own being, outside the text and at [a] distance. It must rather draw the Real into its own texture, and the ultimate paradoxes and false problems of linguistics, and most notably of semantics, are to be traced back to this process, whereby language manages to carry the Real within itself as its own intrinsic or immanent subtext. Insofar, in other words, as symbolic action . . . is a way of

a persuasive way to think about realism not as a static reproduction but as a generative literary form (which is part and parcel of content) that transforms the reality in which and through which it is produced. Drawing on Lukács's and Jameson's insights, postwar realism should not be understood as a hermetically sealed mimetic escape. In reaching out to the real world through representation, it automatically intervenes in real conditions and in the perception of those conditions.

Marxist theories of literature are compelling for theorizing postwar reconstruction fiction because they maintain that literary language and narrative is enmeshed in dialectical relationships with physical realities. Marxist social geographers, moreover, including David Harvey and Henri Lefebvre, have elaborated the spatial implications of the Marxist model to deliberately link literary realism with the potential to transform real environments and geographical perception. Harvey, for instance, has argued that a politics of justice "needs a firmer grounding of the material conditions of peoples' existence in a concrete historical and geographical world. Of all literary forms the realist novel is most suited to facilitate this kind of geographical understanding. It typically grasps the individual not just as an identity located in space but as 'a juncture in a relational system without determined boundaries in time and space.'"[8] Postwar British reconstruction fiction exemplifies Harvey's understanding of the dynamic, two-way relationship between humans and their environments: it represents the effects of the environment on individual subjectivity and also the ways in which individual agency resignifies that environment. This is most apparent in Elizabeth Taylor's postwar fiction, which presents individuals who are at the mercy of their environments (Julia, in *At Mrs. Lippincote's*) as well as those who dramatically reshape the spaces they inhabit (as in the eponymous Angel). In both novels, an intersubjective rela-

---

doing something to the world, to that degree what we are calling 'world' must inhere within it, as the content it has to take up into itself in order to submit it to the transformations of form. The symbolic act therefore begins by generating and producing its own context in the same moment of emergence in which it steps back from it, taking its measure with a view toward its own projects of transformation" (81).

8. Harvey, *Spaces of Hope*, 144. Similarly, Lefebvre theorizes the abstract conjunction of real and imagined experience in what he terms the "social production of space," which accounts for the spatially homogenizing effects of capitalism. Drawing on Lefebvre, Josephine McDonagh helpfully identifies how "thinking about literary realism in terms of abstract space is a useful critical maneuver. For instance, it allows us to see the extent to which the 'sense of place,' . . . for which realist fiction comes to be admired, is a projection onto the homogenous regularity of abstract space. It is not the link to the 'real' place—the index to reality—which it appears to be. Rather it is a supplement, an added accessory that punctures the evenness of homogenous space with a flash that *gives the effect of* familiarity or recognition" ("Space, Mobility, and the Novel," 60).

tionship between individual and built environment emerges that is central to the narrative. Taylor's fiction also demonstrates the productive effects of realist intervention by evoking the narrative formulas of genre fiction—the romance, the Gothic—only to derail the expectations conjured by those formulas. This realist strategy forces readers, then and now, to reorient themselves to the particulars of the relationship between individuals and the social and material conditions in which they live. Marxist conceptions of space and literary representation thus help to theorize how postwar realism itself has the power to intervene in and shape real spatial experience.[9]

Three main aspects of the Marxist tradition, however, are limiting for the postwar context. First, the totalizing and teleological model of historical progression underwriting Marxist literary analysis privileges nineteenth-century realism as the epitome of the genre, which enables critical dismissal of later realisms as residual and conservative. This position is reductive and problematic for a number of reasons, not least its Eurocentrism. Second, the rejection of immanent meaning and the insistence on symptomatic interpretive methods, particularly by Jameson, can be understood as subordinating the literary text to historical context in limiting ways—a point of view expressed most recently by Stephen Best and Sharon Marcus in their special issue of *Representations* on "Surface Reading," to which I will return later. Third, as the primary examples cited by Lukács and Jameson (Balzac, Mann, Tolstoy, Gissing, Conrad) indicate, the Marxist tradition for evaluating literary realism is dominated in its formative works by an almost exclusive focus on male writing—a problem that is now so apparent it hardly needs stating, and one that quickly becomes obvious when considering the English tradition on its own. This blind spot in canonical theoretical appraisals of realist writing is especially significant for the subject of reconstruction fiction, which prioritizes the material and imaginative engagement with the domestic. It means that the Marxist approach to realism has historically failed to recognize domestic experience and home building, from the smallest to the largest scale, as not merely a part of "history" that relates indirectly to the more "public" social world but as central to its unfolding.

Where the Marxist approach is limited, feminist critics, theorists of the novel, and New Historicist approaches have emerged to further explain and complicate realism. In the English context, feminist criticism has provided the much needed corrective to Marxist conceptions of realist narrative and

---

9. Mikhail Bakhtin's notion of the chronotope offers a further model for theorizing the literary relation between individual experience and space and time. Reconstruction fiction has the potential to be considered a chronotope, but Bakhtin's ultimate emphasis is more on embodied experience than on the social and material engagement of literary representation.

to Ian Watt's highly influential historical account of the development of the English novel (*The Rise of the Novel*, 1957), which also focuses solely on men: Defoe, Richardson, and Fielding. Most notably, Elaine Showalter's *A Literature of Their Own* (1977) and Jane Spencer's *The Rise of the Woman Novelist* (1986) emphasized the foundational role of middle-class women, particularly Jane Austen, the Brontës, and Elizabeth Gaskell, in establishing the realist tradition in England. Nancy Armstrong's *Desire and Domestic Fiction* (1987) added to this invaluable recovery work the New Historicist argument that the construction of female subjectivity in literature by writers of any gender and across cultural documents and institutions was central to the rise of the English middle class and therefore the English novel. Feminist literary history and critical perspectives connect realist representation with the demands and opportunities afforded by the home as setting, plot device, and driver for characterization. The feminist approach also theorizes the home as a discursive site for broader historical circumstances, even if those circumstances are not as explicitly represented as they might be in the realist historical novels of Balzac, Stendahl, or Walter Scott, which have been so valued by the Marxists. Feminist scholarship on women's World War II writing by Phyllis Lassner, Gill Plain, Victoria Stewart, and others, while not specifically limited to realist texts, has persuasively elaborated on the historical and political centrality of the home front.

More recent feminist work in cultural history has refreshed the relationship between realism and domesticity by putting pressure on the strict conceptual divisions that have sustained much critical discourse surrounding gender and space. In *Apartment Stories* (1999), for instance, Sharon Marcus challenges conventional treatment of the separate spheres ideology and identifies how the "apartment plots" of nineteenth-century realism in both France and Britain mediated a generative relationship between complexly gendered private and public spaces. Unlike earlier feminist critique, moreover, she resists the oversimplification of binary oppositions, which she rightly claims "still have scholarly currency."[10] *Reconstruction Fiction* draws on the substantial tradition of feminist literary criticism in its insistence that material changes to the home—building, rebuilding, redecoration, and demolition—matter deeply as historical experience and as literary trope. Like Armstrong and Marcus, I find significance in writing by both men and women, and I follow Marcus

---

10. Marcus asserts persuasively, "By refusing to collapse theoretically autonomous domains, I seek to make visible the relationships that separate-spheres frameworks occlude and to question totalizing claims . . . that create oppositions between men and women, public and private realms, and exterior and interior spaces, then conflate the opposing terms of each pair" (*Apartment Stories*, 7).

in resisting reliance on oversimplifying binaries as a way of conceptualizing domestic space and its realist representation. It must be noted, however, that all of the works I have cited as key examples of the feminist engagement with literary realism focus primarily on eighteenth- and nineteenth-century traditions. Modernist experimentation, as in the case of Virginia Woolf, whose work gives Showalter her book's title, is understood as a kind of outer limit for theorizing the realist genre.[11] Postwar realism emerges at a moment when the material changes to the domestic environment take center stage in an unprecedented way, and it should therefore play a major role in feminist conceptions of literary history. In Britain, women's central role in the wartime workforce, the dissolution of the servant class, the further decline of aristocratic power, and postcolonial immigration made the stakes of postwar realist representation more broadly egalitarian than ever before. If the nineteenth-century realist mode is understood as crucial to the mediation of separate spheres and class-based hierarchies, postwar realism must be understood in terms of reconstructive interventions that affect a range of identities and political positions.

Franco Moretti has influentially reinforced the idea that modernism provides a periodization limit for the novel, arguing that, after the first "scandalous" successes of high modernism (he cites Mann's *Mephisto* as his example), it doesn't "take long for European literature to discover that it has nothing left to say."[12] Moretti is one of a number of theorists of the novel, including Armstrong, D. A. Miller, Susan Stewart, and Alex Woloch, who have defined realism as interconnected with the simultaneous development of the novel, the nation state, and the increasing dominance of the bourgeoisie (and bourgeois institutions) within globalizing capitalism.[13] Influenced by Derrida, Foucault, and the New Historicism, these critics value realism not for being liberating, as Lukács, Jameson, and some feminist critics would have it; they value realism for its ability to reveal, through formal analysis, how things work within the capitalist paradigm. In *On Longing* (1984), for example, Stewart defines

---

11. As I noted in the introduction, feminist work on the literature of World War II has been a major precedent for my own project. In many cases, even though this work is not limited to considering realism as such, it takes realist texts as primary examples because of their more explicitly politically engaged content. My aim is to connect this ground-laying work with broader, more formally driven accounts of realism.

12. Moretti, *Distant Reading*, 33.

13. See Nancy Armstrong's *How Novels Think: The Limits of British Individualism from 1719–1900* (2005), D. A. Miller's *The Novel and the Police* (1988), Susan Stewart's *On Longing: Narratives of the Miniature, the Gigantic, the Souvenir, the Collection* (2007), and Alex Woloch's *The One vs. the Many: Minor Characters and the Space of the Protagonist in the Novel* (2003).

realism in a way that captures poststructuralist conceptions of history and literature as fundamentally linguistic and predetermining:

> As genres approach 'realism,' their organization of information must clearly resemble the organization of information in everyday life. Realistic genres do not mirror everyday life; they mirror its hierarchization of information. They are mimetic in the stance they take toward this organization and hence are mimetic of values, not of the material world. Literature cannot mime the world; it must mime the social. It cannot escape history, the burden of signification borne by language before literature takes it up.[14]

With their primary interest in literary form, theorists of the novel like Stewart and Moretti help to explain how postwar realist reconstruction works. Moretti describes how Austen's free indirect style was crucial to establishing a robust historical relationship between the bourgeois individual and social communities.[15] In their novels set in wartime billets and boardinghouses, Patrick Hamilton and Elizabeth Taylor capitalize on the ironic effects of Austenian free indirect style to reveal the postwar tenuousness of that historical relationship. Following Stewart's insistence on realism's reproduction of social information, reconstruction fiction should be understood as expressing the historical *desire* for transparency that informs experience of the real postwar world. The formal and often Foucauldian approach to the novel as a distinct form or genre opens up room for readings that are not tied to particular ideologies or political positions, and yet, they are often just as totalizing, and therefore just as limiting, as the Marxist approach.

Following Sharon Marcus, I foreground the formal qualities of literary texts and the details of historical context without submitting these elements to a totalizing explanation, particularly one that relies ultimately on the mechanisms of late or global capitalism. This strategy aligns my work with one ver-

---

14. Stewart, *On Longing*, 26.
15. Moretti analyzes free indirect style as a crucial new technique that was integral to the emergence of the novel, Austen's realism, and the socialization process of her era that solidified middle-class hegemony: "Emotions, plus distance: it is truly a peculiar mix, free indirect style, but its composite nature was precisely what made it 'click' with that other strange compromise formation which is the process of modern socialization: by leaving the individual voice a certain amount of freedom, while permeating it with the impersonal stance of the narrator, free indirect style enacted that *veritable transition de l'objectif dans le subjectif* which is indeed the substance of the socialization process. And the result was the genesis of an unprecedented 'third' voice, intermediate and almost neutral in tone between character and narrator: the composed, slightly resigned voice of the *well-socialized individual*, of which Austen's heroines— these young women who speak of themselves *in the third person*, as if from the outside—are such stunning examples" (*Distant Reading*, 82).

sion of "surface reading" outlined by Marcus and Stephen Best, in which they define surface "as the location of patterns that exist within and across texts."[16] In taking this approach, it is not my intention to avoid making a political claim for the value of literature or realism but to attend more carefully to the interruptive workings of realism in periods of postwar transition and transformation without the analytical constraint of foregone political conclusions. Marcus and Best describe this methodology as open and attentive, two words that aptly describe the realist mode of reconstruction fiction itself:

> Surface reading, which strives to describe texts accurately, might easily be dismissed as politically quietist, too willing to accept things as they are. We want to reclaim from this tradition the accent on immersion in texts (without paranoia or suspicion about their merit or value), for we understand that attentiveness to the artwork as itself a kind of freedom. . . . To some ears this might sound like a desire to be free from having a political agenda that determines in advance how we interpret texts, and in some respects it is exactly that. We think, however, that a true openness to all the potentials made available by texts is also prerequisite to an attentiveness that does not reduce them to instrumental means to an end and is the best way to say anything accurate and true about them.[17]

Historicized formalism is thus central to my method, but at the same time, I move away from the dominant Marxist and Foucauldian grand narratives that have accompanied such methods in the past. The pattern of interruptive realism in postwar British fiction, while uniformly interested in clarifying and reconstructing social conditions, is not limited to a particular political agenda or social position, as the varied investments of writers like Bowen, Lessing, and MacInnes make clear. Reading reconstruction fiction alongside housing discourse foregrounds the formal workings of realism and the dynamic, rather

---

16. Best and Marcus, "Surface Reading," 11.
    Marcus and Best further define this kind of surface reading in contrast to symptomatic interpretive methods such as those promoted by Jameson: "This notion includes narratology, thematic criticism, genre criticism, and discourse analysis. Symptomatic reading looks for patterns in order to break free of and reach beyond them to a deep truth too abstract to be visible or even locatable in a single text. Jameson thus urges interpreters to sketch the ideological rectangles that structure texts only in order to move toward what lies outside them. Surface readers, by contrast, find value in the rectangles them-selves [sic] and locate narrative structures and abstract patterns on the surface, as aggregates of what is manifest in multiple texts as cognitively latent but semantically continuous with an individual text's presented meaning" (11–12).

17. Best and Marcus, 16.

than fixed, relationship between literature and culture. As a result, a diverse range of social positions and visions emerge.

•

The range of critical perspectives I have addressed so far share one major limitation that my own work seeks to redress. To varying degrees, they adopt a linear or evolutionary conception of literary history that makes little room for considering realism and realist techniques since modernism and the turn to poststructuralist theory following World War II. Even critics like Marcus, who are less invested in teleological linear development, still locate the nineteenth century as the crucial point of attention for theorizing realistic narrative. Such formulations have supported scholarly perspectives that understand any twentieth-century realism as a residual, conservative, uninventive alternative to the newer and more progressive modernism.

Jed Esty and Colleen Lye reconsider and reframe contemporary realism in their 2012 special issue of *Modern Language Quarterly*. Esty and Lye coin the term "peripheral realisms" to explain and claim the continuing significance of realist writing in a global context.[18] This intervention helpfully suggests a way to combine scholarly interests in postcolonial and realist writing.[19] Importantly, though, they assert that realism is thriving only in economically and politically developing regions or "peripheries" that have been understood by postcolonial studies as subaltern or oppressed. Rather than envisaging a linear progression and a necessary one-way transfer of realist practices (or modernist ones, a binary opposition they maintain) from Europe to the rest of the world, they

> venture a new schematic built on the old decking: Where classical realism maps national space as a working social totality, and where modernism (including the late modernisms of minority and postcolonial magical real-

---

18. Their concept of "periphery" within a "world-system" is based on Moretti's and Wallerstein's tripartite concepts of core, periphery, semi-periphery, which Moretti outlines in his *Distant Reading* chapter, "Conjectures on World Literature."
19. They build on the Foucauldian model of cultural history that identifies the totalizing operations of global capitalism in local examples, and they also take up Moretti's call to reconceptualize literature after modernism in terms of a "world-system" (a term that Esty and Lye also use) instead of using the more conventional scholarly framework of the national tradition, which Moretti argues is now no longer the determining sociohistorical context for novelistic production. Unlike Moretti, however, who understands realism as an eighteenth- and nineteenth-century European invention that is extinct in the grand evolution of world literature, Esty and Lye propose that realism continues to thrive.

ist writing) stylizes, even heroicizes, its baked-in failure to map the global system (projecting the latter as abysmal antimatter to literary description itself), peripheral realisms approach the world-system as partially, potentially describable in its concrete reality. But, recognizing the historicity of both subjects (their own style as part of an enduring literary modality) and objects (global capitalism as a moving target of representation), they invite their publics to grasp the world-system, via its local appearances or epiphenomenal effects, and not to imagine it as a foreclosed or fully narrativized entity.[20]

Much of their theory is compelling, particularly the final notion here that postwar twentieth- and twenty-first-century realism is by definition open and incomplete, rather than naïvely all-encompassing. Realism, in other words, can be ambiguous and fragmentary. They also usefully describe peripheral realism as a mode of writing that seeks to represent general conditions without universalizing them. These two ideas help to "package" realism in a way that skirts challenges from poststructuralist and postmodernist critics. Reconstruction fiction certainly fits this characterization, but rather than emphasize how it shies away from totality, I argue that it is important to attend to the overt ways in which reconstruction fiction deliberately invites readers into realistic worlds. In other words, while reconstruction fiction may deploy varying degrees of ambiguity and fragmentation in its narratives and characters, as in Elizabeth Bowen's *The Little Girls* or Doris Lessing's *The Good Terrorist*, it avoids extreme stylistic ambiguity, intentional difficulty, or insularity that would prevent accessibility. Esty and Lye seem to be aware that this quality is important, as they describe peripheral realisms in terms of how they "*invite their publics to grasp the world-system*" (emphasis mine), but I argue that this "inviting" quality is central in moments of historical upheaval. This invitation, moreover, is not a simple point of access to the world-system of late capitalism; it effectively pauses and redirects perception of the relationship between individual subjects and the material and social world they encounter.

My theory of realist reconstruction fiction responds to two main aspects in Esty and Lye's paradigm. First, they implicitly endorse Moretti's evolutionary model by locating the most significant examples of contemporary realism outside of Europe and North America. Postwar British realism, their framework thus implies, is defunct. This hypothesis is borne out by Esty's earlier work in *A Shrinking Island,* in which he delineates the midcentury decline of British literature, through the high modernist examples of Woolf and Eliot,

---

20. Esty and Lye, "Peripheral Realisms," 285.

alongside the collapse of the British Empire. Despite the increasingly global nature of capitalism, however, nations clearly continue to matter after World War II in complex and important—and not just residual—ways: politically, economically, socially, and culturally. Second, Esty and Lye rely on a totalizing relationship between realism and the "world-system" of global capitalism, a relationship that limits the generative powers of realist writing before the fact, as it were. The critical insistence on such dominating, all-encompassing explanation is, ironically, at odds with the open realist techniques they are claiming to identify and champion. In this sense, the model they provide is overdetermined and limits interpretive possibilities for postwar realism. My analysis of reconstruction fiction throughout this book shows how realist writing in postwar Britain does more than simply lie in wait for global capitalism to make its mark. This is not to say that capitalism and globalization do not matter for postwar British literature and culture; obviously they do, specifically in the contexts of decolonization and Welfare State economic reforms. Colin MacInnes's *Absolute Beginners* most overtly demonstrates the relevance of global socioeconomic forces in his representation of immigrant culture and Americanized consumerism in 1950s London; indeed, I argue in chapter 3 that MacInnes can be read productively as a peripheral British realist. The critical burden of always returning to the operations of capitalism in theorizing literature, however, occludes other possibilities for meaning and interpretation.

These other possibilities are best captured in light of two final strands of thinking about realism: the midcentury humanist tradition and British socialist literary criticism. Erich Auerbach's work provides a major humanistic precedent for considering realist aesthetics beyond the totalizing model of literary history that renders European "Realism" an extinct historical category.[21] While Auerbach's *Madame Bovary* chapter is often cited to support the continued critical preoccupation with nineteenth-century realism and "the serious imitation of everyday life,"[22] he actually locates the roots of realist writing in two distinct forms at the beginning of Western literary culture: in *The Odyssey* and the Bible.[23] At the other temporal end of Auerbach's study, in contrast

---

21. Auerbach's *Mimesis* (1948) went out of favor in the latter portion of the twentieth century for its philological methods, its unquestioned commitment to "humanism," and its central reliance on the concept of mimesis, which clashed with the postmodern theoretical resistance to referential aesthetics. But there is renewed investment in Auerbach's work. Beaumont, for one, describes Auerbach as a sorely neglected and valuable champion for reviving discussions of realism, and several of Beaumont's contributors praise and rely on *Mimesis*.

22. Auerbach, *Mimesis*, 482.

23. In *The Odyssey*, he finds the roots of immanent realist representation; Homer's style presents a world in concrete detail that hides nothing (all "foreground"). The Bible, meanwhile (he focuses on the story of Abraham and Isaac) represents real human spiritual struggle, but

with the current critical models that oppose nineteenth-century realism with twentieth-century modernism, he finds the current of realist representation still running strong in Virginia Woolf's *To the Lighthouse* with its impressionistic filtering of time through individual consciousness.

The bookends of *Mimesis* suggest a way of reconceiving realism as not solely tied to bourgeois capitalism. This is not to claim that realism, or literature in general, is universal or that it exists in an ahistorical vacuum. Rather, it is to consider realism as a set of epistemological assumptions or questions and as a set of aesthetic techniques that can be present at any time, modified by historically particular circumstances. This way of thinking about realist writing is inspired by Auerbach's boldly open framework, which in turn points back to Aristotle's notion in *Poetics* that all art is imitation and, further, that realistic imitation is an especially edifying and valuable kind of representation:

> Imitation is natural to man from childhood, one of his advantages over the lower animals being this, that he is the most imitative creature in the world, and learns at first by imitation. And it is also natural for all to delight in works of imitation. The truth of this second most is shown by experience: though the objects themselves may be painful to see, we delight to view the most realistic representations in art, the forms for example of the lowest animals and of dead bodies. The explanation is to be found in a further fact: to be learning something is the greatest of pleasures not only to the philosopher but also to the rest of mankind, however small their capacity for it; the reason of the delight in seeing the picture is that one is at the same time learning—gathering the meaning of things, e.g. [sic] that the man there is so-and-so; for if one has not seen the thing before, one's pleasure will not be in the picture as an imitation of it, but will be due to the execution or colouring or some similar cause.[24]

For Aristotle, realistic representation turns outward toward "the thing," whatever that thing may be, and it assembles the meaning of those things that are apprehended. In the postwar period, after the high modernist rejection of turning outward, to make that turn again, that effort of gathering meaning from the outside in, is not only aesthetically bold but humanistically so.

Indeed, Auerbach and Aristotle encourage us to consider realistic representation as intentionally humanist. Although the term "humanism" may be

---

does so not through the concrete description of everyday life but through spare detail and pregnant omissions that compel readerly interpretation (all "background")—a mode of interpretation dependent on Judeo-Christian revelation that, later, Paul Ricoeur would theorize in a secular framework, vis-à-vis Freud, as a "hermeneutics of suspicion."

24. Aristotle, *Poetics*, 1457–58.

passé for all matter of understandable reasons, not least its anthropocentrism, it is necessary to claim that, unlike other kinds of writing that may be more syntactically experimental, on the one hand, or have more formulaic plots or characters, on the other, realist writing believes in the value of perceiving, shaping, and communicating the experience of being human in the physical world.[25] Pam Morris defines realism aptly in a similar way as something that extends beyond the nineteenth-century pigeon hole to a more broadly humanist category: "The epistemology that underwrites all uses of realist representation is the same: the need to communicate information about the material, non-linguistic world. Thematically and formally, realism is defined by an imperative to bear witness to all the consequences, comic and tragic, of our necessarily embodied existence."[26] Morris's emphasis on realism as a mode of witnessing is especially relevant to the postwar moment in which European humanism itself was in desperate need of ethical reconstruction. Rachel Brenner describes the wartime breakdown of "Enlightenment humanism" in her work on Polish Holocaust diaries, arguing,

> The Holocaust challenged the very foundations of . . . liberal intellectuals' formative, humanist *Weltanschauung*. Staunch believers in humanity's enlightened progress, they were now confronted with a world which no longer endorsed the humanist universals of human dignity and the sanctity of human life, a world in which the capacity for empathy, which enables human beings to recognize each other's mental and emotional sameness, had been shattered.[27]

Realism emerged as a tool to witness the traumas of recent historical experience and to rebuild the humanist worldview.

Not incidentally, both Auerbach and Georg Lukács developed their theories of realist literature out of their experiences in forced exile. Both were Jewish and barely managed to escape from genocidal regimes. Auerbach left Nazi Germany for Istanbul in 1935, while Lukács fled Stalin's Great Terror in Tashkent. As threatened Others, both theorists understood realism as especially well suited to attest to moments of historical crisis, upheaval, and transition that call for remaking humankind. "In such critical, transitional periods," Lukács argued in 1948, "the task and responsibility of literature are exception-

---

25. The term "humanism" has been problematic since the latter third of the twentieth century for its association with Enlightenment thinking. Such thinking has been shown to be deeply problematic, particularly in political ways that privilege the experiences and ontologies associated with white European men of at least a middle-class social position.

26. Morris, *Realism*, 44.

27. Brenner, *Ethics of Witnessing*, 3–4.

ally great. But only truly great realism can cope with such responsibilities."[28] Most compellingly, he moves from abstract ideas about literature and history to the particular transition facing Europe after the War and the Holocaust, as he was completing *Studies in European Realism*, uprooted, in Budapest. In this moment of postwar reconstruction, he identifies a unique opportunity for realist engagement: "With the collapse and eradication of Fascism a new life has begun for every liberated people. Literature has a great part to play in solving the new tasks imposed by the new life in every country."[29] And he concludes with an urgent plea that speaks to the basic optimism—even utopianism—of the Marxist conception of realist narrative:

> Never in all its history did mankind so urgently require a realist literature as it does today. And perhaps never before have the traditions of great realism been so deeply buried under a rubble of social and artistic prejudice. . . . The practical road to a solution for the writer lies in an ardent love of the people, a deep hatred of the people's enemies and the people's own errors, the inexorable uncovering of truth and reality, together with an unshakable faith in the mark of mankind and their own people towards a better future.[30]

Lukács's rhetorical passion here is symptomatic of wartime and immediate postwar calls for renewed cultural and political vision. Recall Elizabeth Bowen's more muted but still hopeful prediction that when the war is over "we shall look out through glass."[31] Auerbach also, completing *Mimesis* in exile in Istanbul, seems to be aware of the historical poignancy of his work on realism. The Epilogue concludes with a call for the construction of a postwar readerly community: "Nothing now remains but to find him—to find the reader, that is. I hope that my study will reach its readers—both my friends of former years, if they are still alive, as well as all the others for whom it was intended. And may it contribute to bringing together again those whose love for our western history has serenely preserved."[32] Hence, realist reconstruction fiction should be understood as urgently needed within its own historical situation as a response to recent material, political and social atrocities. In this sense, postwar realist interventions have an ethical dimension.

Building on Lukács's commitment to realism as a humanistic mode of writing that was necessary in postwar Europe, Raymond Williams and Doris Lessing articulate the need for realistic literature, also from a Marx-

---

28. Lukács, *Studies in European Realism*, 10.
29. Lukács, 17.
30. Lukács, 19.
31. Bowen, "Calico Windows," 186.
32. Auerbach, *Mimesis*, 557.

ist or socialist perspective, in the particular context of the British Welfare State. Writing around the same time, at the turn of the 1960s, both deplore the current state of English literature and envision a realistic antidote. In *The Long Revolution* (1961), Williams argues, "There is a formal gap in modern fiction, which makes it incapable of expressing one kind of experience, a kind of experience which I find particularly important and for which, in my mind, the word 'realism' keeps suggesting itself."[33] He echoes Lukács and anticipates Jameson in outlining realism as a mode of writing that creates a balanced representation between the individual and society. In doing so, he argues, realism "offers a valuing of a whole way of life, a society that is larger than any of the individuals composing it, and at the same time valuing creations of human beings who, while belonging to and affected by and helping define this way of life, are also, in their own terms, absolute ends in themselves. Neither element, neither the society nor the individual, is there as a priority."[34] In "A Small Personal Voice" (1957), Lessing similarly diagnoses her contemporary literary and political moment as one of false consciousness, fear, and the avoidance of responsibility. Like Williams, she calls for balanced literary representations that confront, rather than retreat from, the existential uncertainties of the postwar era:

> It is a balance [between the individual and the collective] which must be continuously tested and affirmed. Living in the midst of this whirlwind of change, it is impossible to make final judgements or absolute statements of value. The point of rest should be the writer's recognition of man, the responsible individual, voluntarily submitting his will to the collective, but never finally; and insisting on making his own personal and private judgements before every act of submission.[35]

She further defines this "committed" approach to writing as necessarily "humanist."[36] And yet, Lessing is anything but naïve in her call for humanistic realism. She directly acknowledges the challenges that postwar writers face in setting out to craft realistic representations:

> If there is one thing which distinguishes our literature, it is a confusion of standards and the uncertainty of values. . . . Words, it seems, can no longer be used simply and naturally. All the great words like love, hate; life, death; loyalty, treachery; contain their opposite meanings. Words have become so

---

33. Williams, *Long Revolution*, 304.
34. Williams, 304.
35. Lessing, "Small Personal Voice," 12.
36. Lessing, 6.

inadequate to express the richness of our experience that the simplest sentence overheard on a bus reverberates like words shouted against a cliff. One certainty we all accept is the condition of being uncertain and insecure. It is hard to make moral judgements, to use words like good and bad.[37]

Postwar realism, for both Lessing and Williams, has the potential to be boldly referential in spite of the knowledge that language has been damaged or destabilized. Contemporary theoretical and critical engagement with twentieth-century literature needs to be more attentive to this sense of inherent risk in realist representation that is not always apparent at the level of syntax.

THE INVITATION OF POSTWAR REALISM

Reconstruction Fiction defines realism as a persistent set of queries and techniques associated with world-building that takes on unique qualities at any given historical moment. Rather than delimiting or championing "realism" as a static genre or period of literary history, I understand realist writing as a mode that intervenes in moments of historical transformation to call for rebuilding and reconfiguring both physical and imaginary sites. In postwar Britain, these moments include immediate postwar stock taking and planning, increased social and economic mobility, decolonization and migration, reframing cultural heritage, and the breakdown of postwar consensus. As the ensuing chapters will explore, realist engagements with these historical moments act as interruptions that intentionally draw attention to social conditions in order to further illuminate the way things are and the ways they might be changed. Considering realism not as direct mimesis but as a bold invitation to attend to the real world aligns with Esty and Lye's extrapolation of Lukács: "A realistic mode of representation is meant not to reproduce reality but to interrupt the quasi-natural perception of reality as a mere given."[38] At a time when the critical treatment of twentieth-century aesthetic interruption is almost always narrowly associated with modernist experimentation, emphasizing the interruptive potential of realist writing provides a major opportunity to see postwar literature anew. The realist interruptions of postwar reconstruction fiction assert urgent textual invitations in the midst of an inhospitable referential context. This book affirms and accepts those invitations.

---

37. Lessing, 5.
38. Esty and Lye, "Peripheral Realisms," 277.

CHAPTER 2

Billets and Boardinghouses

Shared Space and the Reconstruction Novel

WORLD WAR II fundamentally disrupted the historical association between the British novel and the individual.[1] Despite the frequent rejection by interwar novelists like Joyce and Woolf of the stylistic conventions of traditional realism, the modernist probing of consciousness and subjectivity nevertheless reinforced the deep connection between the art of the novel and primacy of the individual in British social and cultural life. It was the historical conditions of World War II that made this connection more difficult to take as a given. With the demands put on domestic life by the war, a necessary asymmetry emerged within national life, favoring public responsibilities over individual desires, a dramatic change for a culture

---

1. Ian Watt's formulation in *The Rise of the Novel: Studies in Defoe, Richardson and Fielding* (1957)—itself a key reconstruction text for postwar British literary culture—names the individual and the process of individuation as central developments within European prose literature and philosophy since the Enlightenment. Although Watt's theory has been revised, complicated, and challenged since then, it remains influential among theorists of the novel. Nancy Armstrong, for one, claims in *How Novels Think: The Limits of British Individualism from 1719–1900* (2005) that the "ideological core" of the novel has not fundamentally changed since the eighteenth century, even given iterations of the novel and novelistic criticism that emphasize fraught identity politics. She identifies this ideological core as "the presupposition that novels think like individuals about the difficulties of fulfilling oneself as an individual under specific cultural historical conditions. Whether this involves resistance, complicity, mimicry, or hybridity does not alter the basic fact that new generations of novels in English . . . are by definition reproducing modern individuals wherever novels are written and read" (10).

centered around liberal humanist values. The Emergency Powers (Defence) Act of 1939 legislated that individual citizens subordinate their needs to the state in the name of the war effort; housing, food, and clothing, among other basic provisions, became subject to rationing regulations and military necessity. The socialist policies of the Welfare State and the physical rebuilding resulting from its reconstruction initiatives continued to emphasize the needs of the collective after the war, directing desire away from the promise of individual advancement toward visions of socioeconomic leveling. As a military and political tactic, the Defense Act was intimately linked to the British household, as many individuals were obligated to subordinate their attachment to private personal space as they took in evacuees, lent houses to billeted military personnel and their families, or faced evacuation and billeting themselves due to bombing dangers. Thus, World War II changed the relationship between individuals and the political, architectural, and, as this chapter argues, fictional spaces they inhabited.

Narratives set in wartime boardinghouses and billets offer particularly keen examples of these new relationships. Novels such as Elizabeth Taylor's *At Mrs. Lippincote's* (1945) and Patrick Hamilton's *The Slaves of Solitude* (1947) depend dramatically on the problem of shared space. In using the always public wartime billet or boardinghouse as a setting, these texts highlight the changing relationship between the British individual and community while also reframing expectations for the realist novel in terms of character and plot development. They respond to the fact that the war insisted on the normalcy of makeshift communities and shared housing instead of "proper" nuclear families and private space, which effectively made every house a potential billet and every individual a potential boarder. No one was permanently at home, and this enforced transience disrupted the basic rules of hospitality that structured social interactions as well as narrative expectations. Although wartime and midcentury narratives make use of many of the same conventions characteristic of the nineteenth-century realist novel, they frustrate characters and readers alike in terms of expectations for development. As Pam Morris notes in her discussion of realism, "Many critics have come to see the human desire to impose meaning on the chaos of existence as the impulse underlying the ubiquity of narrative in all times and places. It is the strong desire for order which keeps us turning the pages, hurrying onwards to the resolution of all mystery and confusions promised at the end of the tale."[2] Reconstruction culture has the disruption of order and the challenge to progressive mobility at its core in an explicitly material sense.

---

2. Morris, *Realism*, 110.

Despite the utopian rhetoric of the 1942 Beveridge Report, building and planning documents, and the 1945 Labour campaign and election victory, reconstruction was not a swift transition to functional, thriving peacetime, and novels set in shared living space from the period often capture this less idealistic, more ambivalent scenario. In reality, reconstruction was a lengthy and laborious undertaking that necessitated first and foremost a realistic assessment of the effects of wartime destruction and instability. Reconstruction efforts had to account not only for destroyed housing but for general residential disruption: over the course of the war 60 million changes of address were registered for a civilian population of 48 million.[3] Responding to the housing crisis with emergency efforts to rebuild, moreover, created further destabilization. Mollie Panter-Downes observed in 1944 for the *New Yorker*, "The armies of workmen who were recruited from the provinces to do these rush jobs have created a housing problem themselves. They are being lodged in rest centres and air-raid shelters and fed from canteens that were hastily set up in such queer places as the Chinese section of the Victoria and Albert Museum."[4] Such layers of displacement and spatial repurposing generated fatigue and disorientation. As one woman who housed numerous evacuees over the course of the war described the transition to peacetime in 1945, it was a time when "the old landmarks had disappeared and the new ones were not yet clearly defined."[5] *At Mrs. Lippincote's* and *The Slaves of Solitude* are representative of wartime and immediate postwar novels that contribute to reconstruction culture not by cultivating an avant-garde abstraction or by forecasting a utopian or dystopian future but by realistically fleshing out the experience of shared household space that unromantically defined wartime life for many and would continue to shape it going forward.

In these texts, it is clear that the effects of wartime life and the literary legacy of modernist experimentation challenge conventional realist expectations of character and plot development. And yet, there is an unmistakable yearning for a traditional, more straightforward representation of the individual within society. Characters such as Taylor's Julia or Eleanor and Hamilton's Miss Roach desire growth into social positions that were once unquestionably meaningful (friend, love interest, wife, mother, political activist), but these positions, and traditional narrative pathways toward them, are not easily attainable, if at all; private personal space has been made scarce by the war, and the goal of upward mobility for the individual has diminished historical and narrative relevance. The boardinghouse as a constraining realist backdrop

---

3. Calder, "UK: Domestic Life, War Effort, and Economy," 885.
4. Panter-Downes, *London War Notes*, 422.
5. Hartley, *Hearts Undefeated*, 280.

allows these writers to assess the leveling effects of the war and reconstruction in which individual desire is being recalibrated according to collective needs. Character development—or the lack thereof—and ironic narration ultimately suggest that individualistic fantasies have become untenable as a result of the war. These texts are demonstrative examples of the immediate postwar decade in which realist fiction and the individual, conventionally understood, are in ruins and on the brink of reconstruction.

THE INDIVIDUAL AND HOUSING IDEALS IN INTERWAR CULTURE

Postwar, community-oriented reconstruction should be understood as a significant turn away from the desire for individual privacy that characterized Victorian and modernist sensibilities. In the nineteenth century, the goal of upward mobility became central to British social and cultural life, especially for the middle classes. Property ownership was one of the major avenues for pursuing this aim. Those aspiring to middle-class or upper-middle-class social positions counted the occupation of a single-family home and its tasteful interior decoration as one of the more important signs of successful upward mobility. Social historian Deborah Cohen explains the importance of the home and household possessions for developing a social identity in late Victorian England:

> The Victorian preoccupation with possessions reflected an age in which once-rigid distinctions of class and rank seemed to be rapidly eroding. The question, as late nineteenth-century observers noted, was no longer merely who you were, but what you had. For aristocrats, of course, land and title still guaranteed a privileged status. Among the middle classes, whose numbers more than tripled in the second half of the nineteenth century, possessions became a way of defining oneself in a society where it was increasingly difficult to tell people apart.
>
> Homes . . . became flexible indicators of status, which could be exchanged for better accommodation as fortunes allowed. Taste, viewed in the eighteenth century as a largely innate quality reserved for the well-born, was now a trait to be cultivated, available to all.[6]

---

6. Cohen, *Household Gods*, xi.

Good taste in homes and household goods was best expressed by the Victorian single-family home. The ideal home prized individual privacy, as the architectural features and partitioning of space for specific uses indicate: rooms with lockable doors, nooks for reading and writing, separate rooms for children and parents, clearly distinguished public and private rooms. With the support of a nuclear family, the individual in the single-family, middle- or upper-middle-class Victorian home had a built-in socializing experience that allowed the individual to learn how to negotiate the demands of public life—represented by parents, siblings, and properly received guests—with the needs of private development.

Modernist writers such as Virginia Woolf and George Orwell emphasized the continued importance of the single-family home, private individual space, and the desire for upward social mobility in their 1930s writings. In 1929, when Woolf associated women's intellectual liberation with the ability to have a room of one's own, her prescription tacitly required private property ownership and the possibility of being surrounded by one's own possessions. In her 1937 chronicle of the Pargiter family, *The Years*, working-class characters identify with their employers' houses and things, rather than their own space and possessions. This displaced attachment prevents working-class characters from advancing socially and from gaining more prominent roles as literary characters. When the family house, Abercorn Terrace, is sold after Colonel Pargiter's death, Crosby, the long-time housekeeper, moves into a house that has been subdivided into flats. She relocates to "her little room," which merely echoes the upper-middle-class interior of which she had been part and parcel:

> Her room was at the top, and at the back, overlooking the garden. It was small, but when she had unpacked her things it was comfortable enough. It had a look of Abercorn Terrace. Indeed for many years she had been hoarding odds and ends with a view to her retirement. Indian elephants, silver vases, the walrus that she had found in the waste-paper basket one morning, when the guns were firing for the old Queen's funeral—there they all were. She ranged them askew on the mantelpiece, and when she had hung the portraits of the family—some in wedding-dress, some in wigs and gowns, and Mr Martin in his uniform in the middle because it was her favourite—it was quite like home.[7]

Quite like home, but not home. Crosby needs more than a room of her own filled with other people's things in a converted single-family home to be

---

7. Woolf, *Years*, 190.

socially, intellectually, and narratively liberated. As a servant within the Pargiter home, Crosby cannot fully claim her own domestic space, supporting Victoria Rosner's point that the late Victorian and modernist home "does not proffer its protection equally to all household members, nor does its protection invariably extend autonomy to those who dwell within its doors."[8] In theory, late Victorian interior design and decoration, as influenced by reformers like William Morris and John Ruskin, were a primary avenue of individual expression within the home. In practice, however, personalized room décor and, therefore, individuality itself, was limited to the upper- and middle-classes who had the means to acquire possessions that had no clear function. Crosby, as live-in housekeeper and not home-owning homemaker, can only mimic the decorative taste of her upper-middle-class employers. If, as Rosner asserts, the modernist home was a site of social experimentation for Woolf,[9] that experimentation required working-class characters to remain minor at the expense of the development of other characters, revealing the reality that bourgeois individualism was not universally accessible in the modernist paradigm.

A more socioeconomically radical figure than Woolf, George Orwell made working-class people his main focus in *The Road to Wigan Pier* (1937). But even as he critiqued the conditions facing the working classes, he held fast to the promise of personal living space and its middle-class trappings that defined life for Woolf's Pargiter family. *The Road to Wigan Pier* confirms the idea that sharing interior space would not enable the development of strong, personal intellect for the working classes. Orwell laments the stagnant social and intellectual position of individuals forced by economic need to inhabit slum-like boardinghouses. By starting his study with a detailed description of what he calls a "fairly normal" lodging-house of industrial areas,[10] Orwell foregrounds the problem of shared housing as against the ideal single-family home of the Victorian and Edwardian periods:

> There were generally four of us in the bedroom, and a beastly place it was, with that defiled impermanent look of rooms that are not serving their rightful purpose. Years earlier the house had been an ordinary dwelling-house, and when the Brookers had taken it and fitted it out as a tripe-shop and lodging-house, they had inherited some of the more useless pieces of furniture and had never had the energy to remove them. We were therefore sleeping in what was still recognizably a drawing-room. Hanging from the ceiling there was a heavy glass chandelier on which the dust was so thick

---

8. Rosner, *Modernism and the Architecture of Private Life*, 5.
9. Rosner, 5.
10. Orwell, *Wigan Pier*, 13.

that it was like fur. And covering most of one wall there was a huge hideous piece of junk, something between a sideboard and a hall-stand, with lots of carving and little drawers and strips of looking-glass, and there was a once-gaudy carpet ringed by the slop-pails of years, and two gilt chairs with burst seats, and one of those old-fashioned horsehair armchairs which you slide off when you try to sit on them. The room had been turned into a bedroom by thrusting four squalid beds in among this other wreckage.[11]

For Orwell, the lodging-house is a degenerate space because it prohibits privacy and therefore cannot sustain an individual sense of purpose or identity. This spatial crowding is compounded temporally, as the lodgers are transient: "a succession of commercial travelers, newspaper-canvassers and hire-purchase touts who generally stayed for a couple of nights."[12] Like the Pargiter home for Crosby, the lodging-house does not enable individual development for residents because rooms and their furniture and decoration no longer signify individual ownership and middle-class social status, as they had been intended to do when the building was an "ordinary dwelling house."[13] The publicizing of private space, impermanence, and the disruption of room-use specification, Orwell's study suggests, underlie the problem of working-class poverty and stagnation in the 1930s. Without a permanent, private, "properly" decorated room of one's own, how could workers become the enfranchised, enlightened citizens that liberal humanism calls into being? Interwar housing ideals in literature as well as in social and architectural discourses recognized that traditional individualism was at once desirable and not attainable for everyone, yet the desire remained strong as a structuring device for narrative, personal, and social development.

PLANNING AND THE INDIVIDUAL IN RECONSTRUCTION CULTURE

The wartime shift to socioeconomic leveling and the challenges to individual privacy that concerned interwar writers were expressed in nonliterary reconstruction discourse through debates about planning. As architectural and urban planning historians have observed, the idea of national planning and planning in general came to dominate all fields of life in Britain during the 1930s. In architectural circles, the comprehensive planning ideal, with the

---

11. Orwell, 3.
12. Orwell, 4.
13. Orwell, 3.

survey as its central tool, reached its peak of influence during World War II through reconstruction initiatives. In 1941, still in the early days of the war, Louis MacNeice observed the cultural dominance of planning questions; as he put it, "the new division, the vital division, in this country [after the war] will be between Planners and Non-Planners (or Anti-Planners)."[14] In this way of conceiving built space, according to architectural historian Michiel Dehaene, "the planner-intellectual takes centre stage," which allows for a gradual "transition from an architecture-based planning tradition to a more technocratic style of planning, . . . merging the expert's voice with the artist's vision of the architectural design."[15] Wartime reconstruction and planning thus combined the aesthetic priorities of modernist architecture of the 1930s with more practical aims of technological progress and social reform. The challenge inherent in British reconstruction plans was to preserve a long tradition of individual-centered, humanizing architecture within scientifically grounded plans to rebuild quickly and efficiently.[16]

---

14. MacNeice, *Selected Prose of Louis MacNeice*, 114.
15. Dehaene, "Surveying and Comprehensive Planning," 44.
16. One of the most influential voices in midcentury debates about planning, architecture, and their social implications was that of Lewis Mumford. Although his impact was most evident in the United States, his 1938 book *The Culture of Cities* remains a cornerstone for the international history of architecture and urban planning. In this volume, he sets out a universal humanist vision that merges modern technological efficiency with an emphasis on individual development. He locates the basis of this revolutionary architecture—"biotechnic planning," as he calls it—in the design of the family home. For Mumford, the family home is, above all, a space for human reproduction and child-rearing. The most important design factor, he argues, is the clear demarcation of private space for children and parents:

> The child is no less entitled to space than the adult: he must have shelves and cupboards for his toys, room for play and movement, a place for quiet retreat and study, other than his bed. No housing standard is adequate that provides only cubicles or dressing rooms for the child, or forces him into the constant company of adults. . . . At the same time, every part of the dwelling must be arranged equally with an eye to sexual privacy and untrammeled courtship. Private rooms alone are not enough: soundproof partitions are equally important. (432)

For Mumford, a dedication to using birth control combined with a loving devotion to one's children, if practiced within the nurturing environment of the biotechnically planned houses and urban communities, would lead to a flourishing civilization. This civilization would value the regenerating life cycle instead of valorizing the "false" permanence of stone monuments erected by previous "great" civilizations. Instead of stone, which gives "a deceptive assurance of life," Mumford names glass and synthetic materials as "valid symbols of this more vital and more enlightened social sense" (443). Mumford's vision foreshadows the work of British wartime and postwar planners in its effort to reconcile the desire for individual identity, individual space, and the nuclear family—values expressed by Woolf and Orwell—with a transparent and fluid relationship between individual and community. Mumford's modernism is rooted in a domestic architecture that bridges private housing and public planning.

Concerns about the desire for efficiency were not new in the 1940s; they had been an integral part of interwar culture. As Evelyn Cobley argues in *Modernism and the Culture of Efficiency*, "Although efficiency became an issue in the nineteenth century, it was during the first three decades of the twentieth that it generated a host of cultural anxieties."[17] Cobley reads British modernist novels as dramatizing a broad ideological preoccupation with efficiency: "These novels reflect, in various registers, an almost imperceptible cultural slide from the desire for the perfectibility of machines to the perfectibility of society."[18] The modernist desire to perfect society—a desire that Cobley characterizes as "the lure of a perfectibility remaining always out of reach"—translated into greater systemization of the materials and processes shaping the environment, including housing, with the proliferation of suburbs and prefabrication techniques in the 1930s.[19] These more efficient approaches to technology and production brought with them anxieties about how such changes would affect citizens' daily lives: would the benefits of efficiency and mass production outweigh the potential limitations on individual expression?

With the threat of autocratic totalitarianism in mind, the planning ethos that dominated Britain during the war was balanced by a consistent strain of skepticism in the name of individual freedom.[20] In his 1944 book *Building and Planning*, one example of many such wartime publications, economist G. D. H. Cole summed up the ambivalence and anxiety about the implications of large-scale planning initiatives:

> Are we to plan? If so, what are we to plan, and what are the essential instruments for making our plans and for carrying them into effect? And, first and foremost, what is planning, and how much substance is there in the allegation that it is inconsistent with liberty? . . . Would it mean less real and tangible freedom for ordinary people, or would it mean an enlargement of the kinds of freedom that most people want and value?[21]

---

17. Cobley, *Modernism and the Culture of Efficiency*, 5.
18. Cobley, 5.
19. Cobley, 8.
20. Alan Jacobs notes a similar preoccupation among writers and thinkers, including C. S. Lewis, T. S. Eliot, and W. H. Auden, who were reevaluating the role of the Christian tradition during wartime. In *The Year of Our Lord 1943: Christian Humanism in an Age of Crisis* (2018), he explains how such thinkers envisioned a new approach to spiritual education in the postwar world. Jacobs observes, "That a putatively, but not actually scientific model of the human being would transform us into animals trained 'for the utility of the state' is a constant theme of writers in this period" (124). Spiritual intellectuals faced the same challenge that urban planners did in imagining a rebuilt world after war and after modernist alienation. For additional insights into spirituality and faith during and after the war specifically in Britain, see Allan Hepburn's *A Grain of Faith: Religion in Mid-Century British Literature* (2018).
21. Cole, *Building and Planning*, 38.

Cole's questions point to the cautionary attitude toward planning expressed by Mass-Observation in a 1943 article for *Town and Country Planning*. M-O resists the possibility of a totalitarian bureaucracy in which individual lives lose value:

> Mass-Observation's job is to provide the link between expert and amateur, planner and planned-for, the democratic leader and the democrat. In the increasing complexity of modern civilisation the specialist's job tends to become more specialized and he to become more remote from the people in whose interests he is working. In this article we have tried to suggest some of the lines along which experts in housing might stiffen their knowledge a little, in order to ensure that the houses they plan are not only beautiful, hygienic and convenient, but also lived-in, lived-for and demanded.[22]

Planners are reminded, in an official capacity, that houses must be built for individual human beings in a democratic, community-oriented society, not for sweeping principles of technological efficiency or aesthetic vision. And yet, Louis MacNeice, for one, saw no conflict between efficient planning and political integrity. He argued in 1941 that "it is possible to become more efficient at the same time as, *and by reason of*, becoming more democratic."[23] It is this ideal expressed by MacNeice that was one of the fundamental goals not only of architectural reconstruction but the Welfare State as a whole.

As reconstruction plans began to take shape, efficiency was put to work with overtly democratic aims. Utopian visions of a community in harmony with the individual dominated, from the New Town to the suburban style city council estate to the tower block. The *County of London Plan* (1943) and New Towns Act (1946)—major examples of official planning documents—lobbied for reconstruction that would happen at a community level. Both within large cities like London and in more suburban locations, a combination of single-family homes and blocks of flats were arranged within neighborhood units with the explicit goal of socializing inhabitants to an entire lifestyle centered on the defining institutions of "little England": pubs, churches, and pedestrian shopping areas. The *County of London Plan*, devised by Patrick Abercrombie and J. H. Forshaw for the London County Council, made a strong case for carefully planned reconstruction—as opposed to quick, cheap, haphazard building to solve the immediate shortage crisis. The argument for

---

22. Mass-Observation, "File Report 1622," 7.
23. MacNeice, *Selected Prose*, 112.

well-planned but more costly and slower paced building was based on a philosophical commitment to long-term community planning that serves human needs and improves living conditions but that also requires continued sacrifice by citizens facing restriction on every front:

> Houses are needed to replace those destroyed by enemy action or condemned as unfit for human habitation. Are they to be built on isolated sites picked up from time to time, perpetuating an antiquated street net, or are they to build up into a general community plan, which the inhabitants can see gradually realised before their eyes? Does a translation of blocks of housing into real societies of men and women in a planned form in fact cost more than haphazard building?[24]

As this example indicates, reconstruction documents were more than functional blueprints; they were opportunities for the cultivation of sociopolitical vision, for articulating utopian ideals that invested architecture with a new symbolic significance for the postwar era.

The *Plan* reinforced the single-family home ideal, but it also sought to balance this ideal with the realistic demands of the housing shortage. It definitively states, "A good house with all the amenities necessary for a full and healthy life, is a primary social need for everyone and must be the constant objective."[25] Although the *Plan* contends that houses are preferable to flats because they have private gardens and "fit the English temperament, . . . houses would provide for only a quarter or a third of the present population."[26] In order to meet its sociopolitical mandate of providing housing for all, non-single-family homes had to be built—or created through conversion—and incorporated into the ideal of utopian, planned community. For a density of one hundred people, the *County of London Plan* put fifty-five percent in houses and forty-five percent in flats.[27] Unlike works of literature, documents like the *County of London Plan* had to be functional as well as economically and philosophically persuasive. But like works of fiction, such documents created imagined environments and worlds. With its neighborhood maps and building elevations, the *County of London Plan* calls a particular world into being: one in which individuals live in harmony with their local and national communities, where citizens are "ready and alive" to "the opportunity that [is]

---

24. Abercrombie and Forshaw, *County of London Plan*, 18.
25. Abercrombie and Forshaw, 74.
26. Abercrombie and Forshaw, 77.
27. Abercrombie and Forshaw, 74, 83.

before London, as before the world, to create an environment that is worthy of our sacrifices."[28]

Five years later, the 1951 Festival of Britain contributed to realizing and promoting the vision of harmonious individual–community relations put forth during the war. The Festival was conceived by *News Chronicle* editor Gerald Barry and Labour deputy leader Herbert Morrison as a "tonic for the nation," which continued under strict rationing conditions until 1954. Innovations in home and community planning were a key component of the Festival. A "live architecture" exhibition, Lansbury Estate, was created in the heavily bombed East End as an example of urban and New Town reconstruction initiatives. According to the Museum of London,

> Catering for the whole community [of Lansbury Estate], houses, flats, churches, schools, an old people's home, a pedestrianised shopping centre (first in London, sets trend for postwar towns and New Towns) and covered market place, pubs and open spaces were all carefully laid out and linked by footways. There was even a block of flats and a special garden with sheltered seats tailored specifically to the needs of older inhabitants who were not yet ready to move into the old people's home. Particular effort was paid to ensuring that the centre of the neighbourhood would be a focus for social life. The use of traditional materials such as London stock bricks and Welsh slates countered the modern architecture and layout, making the neighbourhood seem new, clean and fresh and yet in some ways reassuringly familiar.[29]

The Festival of Britain, like the *County of London Plan,* promoted transparency of planning and design initiatives that at once sympathized with the needs of the individual and demanded continued sacrifice of personal needs to national socioeconomic recovery. Alongside public exhibitions like the Festival, pamphlets, articles, and books related to housing and intended for consumption by the general public were generated in vast quantities. Publications such as *Homes for the People* (1946), put together by the Association for Building Technicians, promoted community-oriented building and planning while also clearly laying out the desire for individual living space as one of the most important facets of postwar building initiatives: "No part of the housing problem is so obvious as this: that there are not enough houses. *Very large numbers of the British people have no dwelling to themselves*" (emphasis original).[30] With the experience of wartime living conditions and postwar austerity measures in

---

28. Abercrombie and Forshaw, 19.
29. "The Festival of Britain," Museum of London website, n.p.
30. Association of Building Technicians, *Homes for the People,* 18.

the forefront of the public mind, community-based living would have signaled continued deprivation just as much as, if not more than, utopian promise. As Mollie Panter-Downes observed in 1945, Britain was by that point an "island of tired people."[31]

Building initiatives after the war tried to recast the idea of the collective so that it was not primarily associated with totalitarian or socialist regimes but with neighborhoods that emphasized groupings of nuclear families as well as individuals. With nearly a decade of wartime rationing ahead, British citizens of the immediate postwar period were encouraged to recalibrate their sense of individual identity to accommodate the needs and desires of others. *Homes for the People* emphasized to the general public that a balanced view of the debate about housing in single-family buildings versus housing in flats "requires not only a consideration of how the advantages and disadvantages of houses and flats affect (a) the individual at home, but also how they affect (b) the town as a whole with its citizens."[32] The town, city, and nation were to be aligned with, not pitted against, the individual. The Association of Building Technicians assured the public that its ultimate goal was not to eliminate the individual and spatial privacy: "We cannot be content, our standards will not be really civilized, until every unmarried person other than a young child can have a separate bedroom."[33] Postwar architects and planners imagined a society in which the possibility of consequence for individual lives would be reinstated in the community-centered living space, and postwar fiction set in wartime billets and boardinghouses created a critical space for assessing this postwar vision.

INDIVIDUALITY AND NOVELISTIC SPACE: MINOR POSTWAR PROTAGONISTS

Responding to the war, writers explored the connection between individual citizens and various collectives through fictional meditations on the transformed relationship between individuals and homes that were no longer private. Domestic interiors took center stage during the war; they were disrupted and exposed through bombs, evacuation, and billeting, which laid bare to strangers the most intimate corners of personal space. In her 1945 essay "Opening Up the House," Elizabeth Bowen describes the dramatic potential inherent in this disruption of interiors; she reflects on "those unnumbered

---

31. Panter-Downes, *London War Notes*, 435.
32. Association of Building Technicians, *Homes for the People*, 21.
33. Association of Building Technicians, 27.

human beings who came and went . . . [who] have left something behind them, something that will not evaporate so quickly as the smell of unfamiliar cigarettes."[34] Given the historical value placed on domestic privacy and permanence in British life, the forcible opening up of the house was a major turning point that at once exposed the fear of losing individual privacy while also creating a new imaginative space for fiction. Writers took up the displaced individual and shared living space for diverse ends and using various narrative approaches. Evelyn Waugh satirizes the responsibility of billeting evacuated children in *Put Out More Flags* (1942), with Irish neutrality as his hidden target. While evacuees generally "were tolerated now as one of the troubles of the time," the Connolly children were housed in one place for no longer than ten days and for as little as an hour and a quarter. "Everyone agreed that the only place for the Connollys was 'an institution.'"[35] The surreal quality of an air raid is captured in James Hanley's experimental *No Directions* (1943), not through focusing on a single individual's harrowing experiences within a family home but through a multivocal narrative that represents a string of flat-dwelling characters seeking shelter in the basement of their London building. Betty Miller's *On the Side of the Angels* (1945) places a nuclear family plus one sister, as in Taylor's *At Mrs. Lippincote's*, in a countryside billet to foreground the particular effects of the war on women. The displaced veteran was the subject of Henry Green's *Back* (1946), narrated in Green's signature fragmented prose, which places wounded vet Charley in a rented room upon his return to explore the dislocation, trauma, and challenges inherent in demobilization and reintegration. As these brief select examples suggest, writers were preoccupied with the consequences of shared living space on everything from national politics to personal identity, emotion, romance, and aesthetics.

The housing crisis suggests a common formal problem for postwar literature and planning discourse in terms of the use of space and the distribution of inhabitants. The novel as a literary form, like the architectural form of the house, is challenged by the war to reconsider the necessity of individual space for social success. Protagonists in realistic wartime billeting novels like Taylor's *At Mrs. Lippincote's* and Hamilton's *The Slaves of Solitude* cannot find enough—or the right kind of—household and literary space to emerge as traditionally developed individual protagonists. As they struggle with the communal exigencies and responsibilities of wartime living, they become occasions for narrators to call into question the largely middle-class literary fantasies of individual identity, marriage, and single-family home occupa-

---

34. Bowen, "Opening Up the House," 132–33.
35. Waugh, *Put Out More Flags*, 82.

tion. These fantasies historically depended on the potential for upward social mobility and narrative progress—both of which became unavailable within the wartime context. Against characters' aspirations for social and personal advancement as well as readers' expectations for such advancement, the setting and the narration have a leveling effect, similar to that of centralizing planners, who limit the desired development of any single character. The tension between aspiration and reality creates ambivalence within the texts that ultimately serves to critique historical denial, especially denial of the war and its consequences, while also acknowledging the difficulty of facing up to a world without the comforts of past, individual-centered traditions.

Alex Woloch's spatially oriented work on character in the nineteenth-century novel, *The One vs. the Many* (2003), helps to theorize the unique narrative attributes of these mid-twentieth-century reconstruction novels that rework nineteenth-century conventions. Alongside Woloch, Nancy Armstrong's discussion of the novelistic individual offers a way of understanding narrative not as abstract or isolated but as socially and historically productive in its generation of social codes that shape how readers understand unique individuals within complex societies. According to Woloch's conception of narrative, literary characterization emerges from what he calls a distributional matrix in which the "discrete representation of any specific individual is intertwined with the narrative's continual apportioning of attention to different characters who jostle for limited space within the same fictive universe."[36] Individuals, in other words, emerge through novels because the narration gives more space and thus demands that readers give more attention to certain characters (protagonists) at the expense of others (minor characters). This way of thinking about fictional narrative dovetails with established theories of the novel going back to Ian Watt's 1957 formulation that centered on the significance of the bourgeois individual, but it adds to this body of theoretical work by emphasizing that such individuals emerge only as long as minor characters, especially those of lower social positions, do not take up too much space. In Woloch's words, "The space of a particular character emerges only vis-à-vis the other characters who crowd him out or potentially revolve around him."[37] Within the wartime and immediate postwar context, the problem of crowding is very real and not selective according to class, as it was in the nineteenth century; everyone is forced to share space. As a result, in novels set in shared wartime living space, protagonists emerge in the negative: in their fraught and ultimately futile desire to crowd others out. In *The Slaves of Solitude* and *At*

---

36. Woloch, *One vs. the Many*, 13.
37. Woloch, 18.

Mrs. Lippincote's, in particular, middle-class female characters feel the effects of wartime crowding most acutely, which highlights the unique wartime and midcentury challenges faced by middle-class women on the home front, whose domestic landscapes were transformed by billeting and evacuation as well as the departure of servants and husbands. Such departures meant that the war crucially opened up new spaces for women to contribute to public life and express their unique subjectivities, as feminist scholars of World War II literature have importantly demonstrated. However, my readings of novels by Taylor and Hamilton reveal the complex, often highly ambivalent reality of encountering such new openings in the midst of a war that leveled, and thus crowded, social experience.

Representations of these fictional wartime experiences should not be understood as isolated within literary history but as active contributions to reconstruction culture, as the anxieties about individual identity and shared space across literary, architectural, and planning histories suggests. Nancy Armstrong helps to frame the active cultural contribution of novels theoretically by identifying the role of the novel in determining the relationship between individuals and societies. Drawing on Watt, she charts how, since the eighteenth century, a mutually constitutive relationship has existed between British novelists, their protagonists, and their readers that hinges on the notion of a modern, middle- or upper-middle-class subject with a self-contained and internally coherent identity. "Once formulated in fiction," Armstrong contends,

> this subject proved uniquely capable of reproducing itself not only in authors but also in readers, in other novels, and across British culture in law, medicine, moral and political philosophy, biography, history, and other forms of writing that took the individual as their most basic unit. Simply put, this class- and culture-specific subject is what we mean by "the individual."[38]

Characterization, for Armstrong, is not isolated within the bounds of novels, but rather depends upon the reader's willingness to understand a character as an implied human individual and, by implication, to further understand that individual as someone who inhabits a greater narrative and larger social context. As characters in wartime billeting and boardinghouse texts struggle to develop as individuals due to spatial constraints, so, too, the reader experiences the breakdown of conventional, individual-centered narrative and social progression. Using nineteenth-century novels as her evidence, Armstrong

---

38. Armstrong, *How Novels Think*, 3.

argues that in order to "qualify [as a protagonist] a character had to harbor an acute dissatisfaction with his or her assigned position in the social world and feel compelled to find a better one."[39] The promise of upward mobility, in other words, was crucial to nineteenth-century narrative. Again, in the wartime context, this "law" of narrative development came into sharp relief, as characters like Taylor's Julia or Hamilton's Miss Roach certainly feel dissatisfied with their predicaments, but unlike in the nineteenth-century novel, these characters have nowhere to go, both narratively and architecturally. In the planned environment of reconstructed Welfare State Britain, whether architectural or narrative, characters relate to each other on lateral terms. In the literary context, this environment renders all characters potentially minor, which puts pressure on expectations for traditional novelistic development.

Reconstruction fiction by Patrick Hamilton and Elizabeth Taylor exposes the space of the novel and the role of the individual protagonist as thoroughly fraught. They use ironic and invasive narrators, comically biting description, and an unromantic realist mode to explore the consequences of the sacrifices and responsibilities with which the postwar individual is charged. Protagonists in *The Slaves of Solitude* and *At Mrs. Lippincote's* are caught between conventional desires and the realities of wartime life, and their antidevelopment plots reveal the horizontal operations of the reconstruction novel. Confounding the anticipation of linear advancing plotline and the emergence of a transformed individual protagonist, these novels specialize in bringing character and plot development to a standstill. They achieve this at the level of dialogue by preventing characters from communicating and therefore from entering into meaningful narrative relations with others. Romance plots and political plots are initiated only to be cynically aborted. Narrators reinforce the isolation and dislocation of characters by emphasizing their mistakes and lack of self-awareness. All of this, of course, is expressed against the backdrop of the unique wartime setting. As characters are forced to inhabit borrowed and shared spaces, room décor and house plans do not translate logically to self-knowledge and family security that would allow for growth. At times a Gothic sensibility emerges through the claustrophobia of the physical and sensory environment: crowds literally drown out and impede the assertions of any given individual, and sounds emanate—often, it seems, without a source—without clear or logical signification for characters. The result, for these reconstruction novels, is that something other than the individual development of a single protagonist constitutes their *raison d'être*. Armstrong argues sweepingly that "new varieties of novel [after the nineteenth century] cannot help

---

39. Armstrong, 4.

taking up the project of universalizing the individual subject. That, simply put, is what novels do."[40] In the analysis that follows, I offer a more nuanced rejoinder to Armstrong's claim: an examination of shared living space in realist reconstruction fiction does not simply reaffirm the existence of a universalized, modern individual. It reveals the simultaneous power and fragility of this construct within the unique context of World War II.

AT MRS. LIPPINCOTE'S AND THE LIMITS OF THE POSTWAR PROTAGONIST

Elizabeth Taylor's *At Mrs. Lippincote's*,[41] written during the final years of the war, reworks traditional realist conventions and reveals the limitations of various narrative traditions in the wake of the war. The novel features two female characters, Julia and Eleanor, who are narratively and architecturally limited, or overcrowded, as a result of the shared household spaces they inhabit. The novel dramatizes the unromantic circumstances of evacuation and billeting for the middle-class Davenant family: Roddy and Julia, their son Oliver, and Roddy's cousin, Eleanor. This nuclear family plus one is evacuated out of London and billeted in the country, close to Roddy's RAF base. They move into Mrs. Lippincote's house, a Victorian structure complete with a locked tower attic—an allusion to *Jane Eyre* that is quickly rendered ironic as the Davenants' living situation is revealed to be anything but romantic or even excitingly Gothic. To accommodate the military family, Mrs. Lippincote has been relocated to a nearby hotel. Her move is another in a series of evacuations that destabilizes the relationship between individual and household, and acts as a reminder that the challenges of evacuation are shared by all and not unique to Julia, the ostensible protagonist of Taylor's novel. Surrounded by Mrs. Lippincote's things, furniture, and décor, the Davenants are depicted as struggling to find clear roles within the household, and their positions within the narrative itself are therefore destabilized. Middle-class property, in the case of the wartime billet, is stripped of its historic power to confer social standing and to signify character development. Without its properly ordered and personally owned possessions, Taylor's novel suggests, the British middle classes in particular are without physical as well as fictional space. N. H. Reeve reads the novel similarly in terms of the problem of ownership for the Davenant family, characterizing it as "an intricate study of dispossession, of losing what

---

40. Armstrong, 10.
41. References to Taylor's *At Mrs. Lippincote's* will use in-text citations.

one owns, or finding one may never really have owned it, and of the mixture of damage and opportunity such losses can afford."[42] As reconstruction plans for the Welfare State promise to tether the individual to the community in an unprecedented way, the exigencies of the wartime billet and the dispossession that Reeve identifies loom as a new reality.

The wartime billet, as opposed to the permanent home, has to accommodate material possessions that belong to multiple occupants, and rooms once designated as servants' spaces become storage compartments for miscellaneous items that do not logically belong together. The Davenants cannot make a proper home in the billet partly because Mrs. Lippincote's things simply take up much of the available storage space. Julia "went to the bureau and opened the drawers one after another. All full: knitting-needles, playing-cards, paper-patterns, photographs . . . , some black-edged visiting cards and letters. . . . She felt burdened by Mrs. Lippincote's possessions. 'We shall never make a home of this,' she cried" (*Mrs. Lippincote's*, 13). When Julia asks Roddy, "Where did you put all the rubbish?" he responds, "In the maid's room along with the dressmaker's dummy and the fishing rods" (73). As Taylor depicts the Davenants' comically frustrated attempts to make themselves at home in the midst of cluttered rooms and full drawers, she exposes a central task of middle-class fiction in the reconstruction period: to reassess the relationship between middle-class individuals and their living spaces.

Taylor develops a critical assessment of this relationship by highlighting a conflict between past cultural traditions—nineteenth-century realism, romance, modernism—and present day demands. In doing so, she recalls E. M. Forster's critique in his 1939 essay on Jan Struther's "Mrs. Miniver" columns. For Forster, romantic attachment to past aristocratic traditions prevents the middle class from "build[ing] itself an appropriate home," literally and metaphorically:

> That . . . is the trouble with Mrs. Miniver and with the class to which she and most of us belong, the class which strangled the aristocracy in the nineteenth century, and has been haunted ever since by the ghost of its victim. . . . [It] has never been able to build itself an appropriate home, and when it asserts that an Englishman's home is his castle, it reveals the precise nature of its failure. We who belong to it still copy the past. The castles and the great mansions are gone, we have to live in semi-detached villas instead, they are all we can afford, but let us at all events retain a Tradesman's Entrance. The Servants' Hall has gone; let the area-basement take its place. The servants

---

42. Reeve, *Elizabeth Taylor*, 21.

themselves are going; Mrs. Miniver had four, to be sure, but many a suburban mistress batters the registry office in vain. The servants are unobtainable, yet we still say, 'How like a servant!' when we want to feel superior and safe. Our minds still hanker after the feudal stronghold which we condemned as uninhabitable.[43]

Taylor depicts Julia as battling with this "ghost" of past traditions that are no longer appropriate for postwar society. For example, Julia is initially nostalgic for the Edwardian world of Mrs. Lippincote, in which social positions and material life were more stable:

She looked at Mrs. Lippincote on her wedding day as she was often to look at her in the future. Nothing of her security, in these days. What would she have said to this? No home of one's own, no servant, no soup tureen, no solid phalanx of sisters, or sisters-in-law, to uphold her; merely—she glanced at Eleanor—merely an envious and critical cousin-in-law. (*Mrs. Lippincote's*, 12).

Julia's wistful daydream romanticizes the prewar possibility of a middle-class "home of one's own" while alluding ironically to Virginia Woolf's "A Room of One's Own." The Woolfian tradition of modern female liberation through having one's own private space to think and work cannot be realized easily in the wartime billet for women or for men. Indeed, surrounded by artifacts of Mrs. Lippincote's life, Julia resembles Crosby from Woolf's *The Years* more than she does the empowered feminist inspired by Woolf's essay. The unavoidable realities of wartime living become more apparent as Julia continues to imagine Mrs. Lippincote's wedding day: "But it was only something which perished very quickly, the children scattered, the tureen draped with cobwebs, and now the widow, the bride, perhaps at this moment unfolding her napkin alone at a table in a small private hotel down the road" (*Mrs. Lippincote's*, 10). For Taylor, modernist prescriptions for women's liberation have become romantic middle-class fantasies that must be revealed as such in the context of a war that has altered the relationship between the individual and the space she inhabits.

Julia's approach to domestic life—marriage, sex, parenting, cooking—reveals the wartime middle-class housewife as caught between a romantic, comfortable past and a present that demands practical responses. As a counterbalance to her nostalgic daydreams about Mrs. Lippincote's wedding and marriage, Julia looks to popular books for guidance such as *Happy Marriages*,

---

43. Forster, "Mrs. Miniver," 299.

How to Make, Maintain, and Endure Them (*Mrs. Lippincote's*, 10). When Oliver asks where babies come from, she awkwardly attempts to explain through drawings, according to advice "she had read once in a pamphlet on sex-instruction" (68). After Oliver tells her, "I was dreaming I was killing you," Julia says to Eleanor, "I don't believe in all that nonsense about Freud. . . . Dreams just happen—any old nonsense comes out of the tangle. It doesn't *mean* anything" (78, emphasis original). Despite the fact that she claims to understand Freud only to reject his theories, and that she gets her cooking inspiration from *Villette* and *To the Lighthouse*, Julia's day-to-day life is "not quite so much like Emily Brontë learning German grammar while she kneaded bread as Julia liked to suppose" (99). Julia looks to past literary and intellectual models—Freud, Woolf, the Brontës—to bolster her sense of identity as wife and mother, but Taylor consistently undercuts any suggestion of high-brow sophistication or romantic fantasy through the comic irony of the narration. As a result, Julia emerges not as a Romantic heroine or modernist feminist, but as a minor protagonist of midcentury realism. In this realist mode, social limitations and material constraints are foregrounded as the free indirect narration emphasizes Julia's alienation.

In the spaces of the billet, Julia is forced to eschew prewar practices for new responsibilities. She cannot assume the role that Mrs. Lippincote once played in her home with the help of servants, and at the same time, she is not fully prepared to take on the duties associated with servants' rooms: sculleries, maids' quarters, tower attics. As Julia hesitantly moves from kitchen to scullery to dining room, Taylor depicts the challenge faced by many middle-class women as they found themselves unexpectedly in someone else's domestic world without help:

> Through an archway hung with plush, she came into the kitchen. It was like the baser side of someone's nature. Beyond the plush curtains, the house put aside all show of decency. Here, there was no doubt about the suggestion of damp. . . . This room, she supposed, represented what was fitting for the working class. On this side of the arch, varnished deal was preferred, wallpaper of brown and pink flowers, a brown tablecloth reaching to the floor and a plant with thick grey velvety leaves. Then down a hollowed stone step into a brick scullery where a refrigerator whirred and water dropped bleakly and with regularity into a bowl. She opened a cupboard and was frightened by a soup tureen the size of a baby's bath. In another cupboard a dozen meat dishes of very slightly varying sizes, white with a wreath of inky flowers, the glaze traced with faint sepia cracks. 'That is how Mrs. Lippincote set up house,' she told herself. (8–9)

Julia's ambivalence and discomfort in someone else's kitchen, without the help of servants, is typical of postwar novelistic depictions of middle-class domestic life.[44] As Phyllis Lassner, Gill Plain, Karen Schneider, and other feminist scholars have discussed extensively, women's lives were dramatically transformed during the war as they served in military organizations or worked in factories supporting the war effort.[45] The relative freedom and independence that women experienced on the home front was abruptly challenged in the immediate postwar decade. Alison Light explains that the virtually complete dispersal of the servant class during the war put the average, middle-class housewife in a newly limited position in the postwar period: "The well-off woman of the 1930s could indeed be far freer than her Victorian grandmother, wrestling with the Angel in the House, or her daughter in the 1950s suburb, servantless."[46] After the war, many middle-class women like Julia went into the kitchen, as it were, for the first time. Lassner has interpreted Julia's ambivalent female position as a "first step toward the possibilities for change in British domestic society."[47] With the context of the wartime billet and reconstruction plans in mind, this ambivalence can also be interpreted as Taylor's critique of middle-class attachment to outdated values. Julia is nostalgic for a prewar relation to household space and objects, and she is resistant to unfamiliar domestic work. When the narrator describes Julia comically as being "frightened by a soup tureen," Taylor creates a critical gap between the life that Julia fantasizes for herself and the real conditions that demand her participation.

Julia is not the only object of the narrator's critical gaze. Eleanor is also depicted as having a frustrated relationship to conventional household space and literary development. She vacillates between plot lines that never quite get beyond the fantasy stage: she is a minor character, in Alex Woloch's sense of the concept, who is repeatedly prevented from becoming anything more "major." Her doomed romantic attachments—to her married cousin and to a soldier whom she has never met—will never become marriage plots. She has

---

44. In *One Fine Day* (1947), for example, Mollie Panter-Downes tells the story of a woman much like Taylor's Julia who sits in her empty, postwar house thinking nostalgically of her servants from the prewar period: "What had happened? Where had they gone? The pretty, hospitable house seemed to have disappeared like a dream back into the genie's bottle, leaving only the cold hillside.... They would never come back into the tame house again. Everyone said so" (19).

45. See Phyllis Lassner's *Women Writers of World War II: Battlegrounds of Their Own*, Gill Plain's *Women's Fiction of the Second World War: Gender, Power, Resistance*, and Karen Schneider's *Loving Arms: British Women Writing the Second World War*.

46. Light, *Forever England*, 121.

47. Lassner, *British Women Writers of World War II*, 186.

a romantic view of marriage, which is made even more unrealistic by her particular wish to marry Roddy, whose infidelity behind Julia's back makes him a less than worthy object of desire: "'If I had Roddy,' thought Eleanor, 'my greatest happiness would be to go out with him to meet the other wives.' . . . She could not forgive Julia for wanting more than her own dearest dream" (*Mrs. Lippincote's*, 11). Taylor emphasizes Eleanor's misguided romanticism when the narrator describes the grim reality of Julia's marriage and identity as a wife: "having no life of her own, all she [Julia] could hope for would be a bit of Roddy's" (20). Although Eleanor tries "not to behave like a spinster in a book," Taylor mockingly limits her to precisely this minor literary position by "what Roddy called her 'little ways,' by which he meant the trivial comforts, consolations, cups of tea and patent medicines, small precautions against draughts and a gentle fussing" (20).

Taylor depicts Eleanor as being limited politically as well as romantically. She is curious about communism but conducts her explorations in secret and ultimately remains politically ambivalent. She attempts to find a sense of empowerment and belonging outside the billet, in which she has no clear role beyond that of a spinster, but her one-night move into a house shared by a group of unmarried communists does not provide the narrative mobilization she needs to emerge as a strong political character. Instead, her "adventure" reads like a comic set piece. Upon entering the house, Eleanor immediately scans the room and feels, rather absurdly, alienated by the shabby décor: "two sash windows there were, not clean, a fawn, characterless wall paper, a deal table covered with a typewriter, a duplicator; then, the worn moquette sofa and an empty grate littered with cigarette ends and toffee papers. A breakfast cup full of faded dog-roses stood on the mantelpiece and a large clock with a brass plate" (*Mrs. Lippincote's*, 64). The unkempt and unfamiliar décor prompts Eleanor to confront her lack of secure individual identity as she lies awake on the sofa where she has been invited to sleep: "'Everything so strange,' she thought. 'Who am I? Lying here, under this coat, which is heavy but certainly not warm. It is not I. Or is it, at last, I, myself? The adventurer, the liar, the hypocrite?'" (127). Like the neighborhood units and blocks of flats mapped out in the *County of London Plan,* this house explicitly depends on property relations that privilege the community over the individual, and this proves troubling for the middle-class single woman. As Taylor narrates Eleanor's exaggerated squeamishness in the space, she satirizes both the communist ideology of communal property as well as Eleanor's middle-class approach to defining herself through the things that surround her. Not quite part of the Davenant family, Eleanor is also not part of the communist collective. As an unmarried middle-class woman at the end of the war who still clings to prewar ideas about self and society, she can be accommodated peripherally in the shared spaces of fiction, billets, and communes only as a minor and alienated spinster.

In *At Mrs. Lippincote's*, the literary consequences of shared living space and limited individual ownership that characterize wartime life and reconstruction initiatives are made clear by the identity crises experienced by both Julia and Eleanor, which are rendered somewhat ridiculous and yet also retain a seriousness. These characters cannot find solace in outdated literary or social identities that require secure middle-class property ownership and the possibility of upward mobility, and as a result, they can both be considered as minor protagonists, positions which reveal the desire for, but unattainability of, traditional individual development. Although Julia tries to determine whether she will be "a Madame Bovary" or "a good mother, a fairly good wife," the comic representation of her struggle devolves into a less funny reality: she ultimately does not have the luxury to make such a choice (*At Mrs. Lippincote's*, 204). Despite the presence of the narrative components of romance, she does not have an affair with the Wing Commander and take up the romantic role of the bourgeois adulteress (204). Without the physical or literary space to return to prewar conventions, characters like Julia emerge from a moment in which the middle-class novel is forced to reconsider the significance of the individual within literary and domestic structures in the postwar period. Julia's qualities—jealousy, vanity, nostalgia, cruelty—are not those of a Romantic heroine or a modern feminist, but those of a middle-class housewife coming to accept that she will be neither Jane Eyre nor Madame Bovary nor Lilly Briscoe, as she fantasizes; those models no longer work. As the narrative unfolds, nostalgia for prewar traditions is ultimately discarded in exchange for an often-reluctant willingness to reconstruct middle-class identities as Britain transitions to the Welfare State. Plans dominated by neighborhoods that include mixed housing types introduces an environment in which the dividing lines between middle- and working-class identities are more difficult to identify. The anxieties of reconstruction, both architecturally and narratively, thus point to uncertainty about what a more hybrid experience of socioeconomic space and identity might look like.

By taking up the scenario of makeshift families and domestic impermanence, *At Mrs. Lippincote's* lays the foundation for a novelistic question that occupied Taylor throughout the 1940s and 1950s: what defines the idea of "home," and what is the role of this idea in fiction? In *At Mrs. Lippincote's*, Oliver associates home with the idea of return after walking back to the billet: "It has made it seem more like my home, because I am coming back to it" (149). Taylor's subsequent fiction tests and ultimately undercuts the possibility of a peaceful, postwar return. Her late 1940s novels, *A View of the Harbor*, *Palladian*, and *A Wreath of Roses*, are tragedies—not comedies—of domestic reorganization. Love affairs break up marriages only to lead to further disillusion within the household. Children die. Men commit suicide or suffer from mental illness. Following the pattern established in *At Mrs. Lippincote's* but taking it to existentially bleaker territory, characters in these novels cannot find solace in private domestic space or prewar domestic conventions. In *Palladian* (1946), for instance, Taylor depicts the decline of a Victorian household once upheld by servants and governesses. The death of prewar social traditions plays itself out in the decay of the estate house at the center of the novel:

> The fewer people were in the house, the less it seemed able to support its existence. The sound of voices, of doors slamming, seemed to have prolonged its life beyond what was natural and to be expected. But as the life was gradually withdrawn, the house became a shell only, seeming to foreshadow its own strange future when leaves would come into the hall, great antlered beetles run across the hearths, the spiders let themselves down from the ceilings to loop great pockets of web across corners; plaster would fall, softly, furtively, like snow, birds nest in the chimneys, and fungus branch out in thick layers in the rotting wardrobes. Then the stone floor of the hall would heave up and erupt with dandelion and briar, the bats wing up the stairs, and the dusty windows show dark stars of broken glass. As soon as grass grows in the rooms and moles run waveringly down passages, the house is not a house any more, but a monument, to show that in the end man is less durable than the mole and cannot sustain his grandeur.[48]

Taylor's depiction of the decaying, servantless house resembles that of a house that has been bombed: plaster falling, the floor erupting open, glass breaking. Man-made "civilization" has destroyed itself by ruining the very concept of "home" over the course of the war. In the wake of this destruction, according to Taylor's novelistic vision, the wilderness, rather than the architect or town planner, reasserts itself. In literary terms, the romantic and Gothic traditions of the past can be conceived of within midcentury fiction only as monuments that are no longer capable of producing and sustaining human life. Indeed, *Palladian* concludes when the young boy who would inherit the house is killed by a statue on the estate grounds. For Taylor, the exigencies of wartime and immediate postwar life have made past definitions of "home" nostalgic, unavailable, or at worst, fatal.

---

48. Taylor, *Palladian*, 234.

Published in the last year of the war, *At Mrs. Lippincote's* is an example of the complexities of early reconstruction fiction. While on its stylistic surface the novel appears to fit quietly within the tradition of women's comic domestic fiction, its narrative ambivalence to romantic character development and conventionally realistic plot progression marks it out as a work of reinvented realism that interrupts the instability of its historical moment with its sustained narrative attention to present conditions. The individuals of Taylor's novel emerge as such only through the ultimate irony of their desires. It is an uncomfortably open-ended narrative that, as a whole, expresses a kind of existential anxiety for the realist novel as a form. Two years later, Patrick Hamilton's *The Slaves of Solitude* takes this existential anxiety even further to reveal the extensive ramifications of wartime transformation and denial.

THE SLAVES OF SOLITUDE AND NARRATIVES OF INCONSEQUENCE

Like Elizabeth Taylor, Patrick Hamilton was a writer for whom domestic space mattered a great deal. Born in 1904, he was an upper-middle-class writer who acutely felt the effects of transitioning from a world of fairly stable domestic conditions to one defined by disruption and transience. The spaces that he shared with family, servants, schoolmates, and strangers deeply influenced Hamilton personally, and it was shared and reconstructed living spaces in particular that came to dominate his fiction, including *Twenty-Thousand Streets under the Sky* (1935), *Hangover Square* (1941), and the subject of my analysis here, *The Slaves of Solitude*. Hamilton's biographer, Nigel Jones, finds significance in the fact that his birthplace in Sussex went from being a secure sign of Victorian England to one of destabilized, modernized England: "Dale House was a mid-Victorian, rambling, gabled affair, overlooked by the South Downs and containing in its grounds a wood, a stream, a lake with islands, as well as lawns, stables, summer-house and kitchen garden. The building was demolished in the 1930s to make way for those Hamiltonian symbols—a cinema, a garage and housing estate."[49] In addition, Hamilton's family moved frequently during his childhood. The domestic instability that defined Hamilton's childhood expressed itself later in his simultaneous disdain for and attachment to transient spaces and living conditions that offered no clear sense of identity or belonging for the individual. This attitude emerges in his reflections on one of his other childhood residences in Hove, Sussex:

---

49. Jones, *Through a Glass Darkly*, 17.

> I myself can only say that it [the house] is quite unlike anything else I have ever seen on earth. The grey, drab, tall, treeless houses leading down to the King's Gardens and the sea convey absolutely no social or historical message to me. They are not even funny, or ostentatious, or bizarre, or characteristic, so far as I know, of any recognized form of taste.[50]

In other words, Hamilton felt an acute sense of alienation from his childhood homes. These personal struggles with environmental and existential alienation were also pervasive motifs of his fiction. Friend and admirer J. B. Priestley found Hamilton's attention to his characters' relationships to living space to be crucial for understanding his novels, especially their sense of existential crisis. Priestley described Hamilton as having "a suspicion from which his chief characters are exiled. It is a deep feeling that there are no real homes for his homeless people to discover. It is a growing despair that dreads the way our world is going."[51]

Hamilton's personal and fictional preoccupation with existential homelessness should also be considered alongside his political investigations, which were motivated by a desire to overcome the alienation he felt and observed around him. Like George Orwell as well as many British writers and intellectuals during the 1930s, including Elizabeth Taylor, Hamilton became fascinated with the struggle between Fascism and Communism, read Marx extensively, and became committed to socialist ideas. For a short time during the war, Hamilton held the "unofficial post of play-reader to the Soviet embassy, advising the Russians on what British works would be ideologically suitable for translation and distribution in the USSR."[52] His attention to the lack of meaningful individual space in modern and wartime Britain combined with his persistent interest in Marxist socialism, with its privileging of the collective over the bourgeois individual, helps to justify the unconventional reading of *The Slaves of Solitude* that follows. As I will show, Hamilton relies on a number of literary strategies both to emphasize sympathetically the lack of individual privacy in wartime and to mock the overvaluation of the desire for privacy so prominent in English culture. Most critics, notably Jean-Christophe Murat and Mark Rawlinson, read Hamilton's narration as sympathetic to Miss Roach as an innocent and thoroughly English victim of foreign and fascist forces, and there is no doubt that the characters of Mr. Thwaites and Vicki Kugelmann are brilliant instances of Hamilton's ability to render the frankly

---

50. Qtd. in Jones, 21.
51. Qtd. in Jones, 251.
52. Jones, 268.

sadistic, even evil, forces at work in Nazism and Fascism.[53] However, given the necessary demands of wartime life, Hamilton's Marxist sympathies, Miss Roach's own capacity for violence, and her determined ahistorical, apolitical attitude toward the war, it is also revealing to read Miss Roach's alienation as ironic and her innocence as not so clear cut. While the narration allows for her to be seen, at times, as a harmless and endearingly uptight spinster, similar to Taylor's Eleanor, ultimately her closed-mindedness and frustrated attempts to both protect and assert herself within the boardinghouse are sent up as futile, pitifully naïve, and even destructive. In attending to the setting of the wartime boardinghouse in developing a reading of the novel that goes against the grain, my work aligns with Eluned Summers-Bremner's view that Hamilton "seems less interested in merely showcasing the content of expressions of wartime domestic hatred than he is in larger structural questions about how latent tendencies towards aggression and self-aggrandizement, anxiety and victimization can become exacerbated in the war's makeshift domestic contexts."[54] On the whole, I argue, Hamilton's novel is a complex, often ambivalent examination of the effects of war on the individual and British society, carrying with it the haunting suggestion that no one is constitutionally safe from the violent impulses of Fascism nor from the effects of alienation.

Thierry Labica, Alan Munton, Jean-Christophe Murat, and Mark Rawlinson have debated the extent to which *The Slaves of Solitude* should be read as a war novel. Labica observes that *The Slaves of Solitude* is "generally seen (when seen at all) as a good documentary novel about war and evacuation."[55] He offers a rejoinder to this perspective by arguing that the novel "rehearses a non-strictly contextual tradition of literary experience of the city (and more particularly that of London); and that indeed *The Slaves* is a war novel, but a war novel in which war-as-context is the metaphor of a non-contextual issue, that of conversation."[56] Labica's essay ultimately explains away the war in order to get to what he thinks is the most important aspect of the novel: a theory of language and linguistics. More recent interpretations, including my own, have insisted on the centrality of the war for the novel. Murat argues, for instance, that although the novel should not be read as a documentary account of the war, its polyphonic language "fully conveys the intensity and complexity of the

---

53. Interestingly, Bill Rust, editor of the *Daily Worker*, said of Hamilton's previous novel, *Hangover Square* "that it was the general opinion of the comrades that nobody could possibly reproduce so exactly the manners, speech, outlook, and behaviour of a Fascist who had not been or did not have the most intimate connections with the Blackshirts" (qtd. in Jones, 269).

54. Summers-Bremner, "Drinking and Drinking and Screaming," 83.

55. Labica, "War, Conversation, and Context," 74.

56. Labica, 74–75.

war in people's minds."[57] Rawlinson has seconded this position, arguing that "the book is clearly of the war," and that the suburban scene of Thames Lockdon should be understood as a "front line of total war, a place subjected to occupation and invasion."[58] My argument, while assuming that the war is central to the fabric of *Slaves of Solitude*, moves beyond the debate about whether or not the novel is a "war novel" as such to ask what it can tell us about the complexity of wartime life and its literary and social implications for the postwar period in which it was published.

The Slaves of Solitude[59] chronicles the daily wartime experiences of Edith Roach, unmarried former headmistress of a boys' boarding school and current boarder herself at the Rosamund Tea Rooms in the fictional suburb of Thames Lockdon. Forced to evacuate her London home due to bombing, Miss Roach (as the narrator calls her, with a characteristic hint of mockery) finds herself in too-intimate proximity with a misfit group of fellow boarders. By setting his novel in a boardinghouse, an always public living space that subordinates the tenant to the standards of the house, Hamilton is able to explore the consequence of individual life in the wartime and postwar community. Hamilton dramatizes this common wartime scenario by depicting Miss Roach's attempt to maintain her sense of self while also entering into meaningful relations with other characters. Her desires, thoughts, and actions are limited on every front: by the type of building she lives in, by an authoritarian landlady, by what she fears the other boarders will think of her, by her frustrated attempts to know others, and ultimately by the war and history itself, which she stubbornly blocks out of her consciousness. Throughout, the narration intensifies the ambivalence of Miss Roach's predicament by consistently establishing her desire for individual assertion and affirmation, and then foreclosing on this desire by pointing out that she never has the right information at the right time in the right order.

"Consequence" and "inconsequence" are key terms for thinking about the relationship between individual and community in this text. The narrator often uses the word "inconsequence" to describe the way Miss Roach thinks of people, as when she decides on "inconsequence" as the characteristic that best describes the American Lieutenant (*Slaves*, 36). The narrator emphasizes the limits of Miss Roach's individualism by directly undermining her efforts to piece together meaning about the events that unfold around her: the social consequence of what she perceives is never clear to her, and therefore, the narrative consequence of particular characters and relationships remains elusive

---

57. Murat, "City of Wars," 330.
58. Rawlinson, "*The Slaves of Solitude* and the Second World War," 260.
59. References to Hamilton's *Slaves of Solitude* will use in-text citations.

for the novel as a whole. As she refuses to acknowledge the full significance of the war, she struggles with consequence on a daily basis in the smallest ways. These minor struggles amount to her alienation from the individualized plotlines of traditional development novels, such as the marriage plot, that rely on linear, logical progression—in other words, narrative consequence. Against readerly expectations, for Miss Roach, every action remains inconsequential. The disconnect between a character's self-awareness and the events that unfold around her is the stuff of comedy, and indeed this novel is funny, but in the wartime context this is the blackest of humors, with comedy gradually receding as violence and existential angst move to the foreground. Hamilton's representation of existential helplessness in the character of Miss Roach clearly has Kafka's "The Metamorphosis" as an intertext—signaled not least of all by her name. But where Kafka's story captures the absurd, the surreal, the tragic fate of the alienated, Hamilton's tale is more cynical: it seems to ask, is the sense of loss experienced by the English middle classes really the stuff of tragedy? Is it to be taken seriously, given the gravity of the war and its global implications?

Miss Roach's difficulties with consequence are exacerbated by the boardinghouse itself. If, as Orwell would have it, the boardinghouse is a degenerate living space, then, the boardinghouse narrative can be similarly understood as wanting in terms of individual novelistic development. Hamilton's narrator observes that "nearly all who lived in the boarding-houses of Thames Lockdon were conscious of having descended in the world, of having arrived where they were by a pure freak of fate" (*Slaves*, 74). Rather than housing those with lofty expectations and life goals arrived at through lengthy introspection and deep exploration of one's interior self, the boardinghouse caters to those who lack agency and self-awareness. In the context of World War II, the boardinghouse setting mirrors the subordination demanded of individuals within the national community of Britain, but without political purpose. Historically, boardinghouses had always limited the desires and actions of each resident through their transparent labor economics and house rules, as well as their regulated furnishings and décor. The twentieth-century boardinghouse featured in *The Slaves of Solitude* has its roots in the nineteenth-century tension between home and work. As historian Wendy Gamber explains, "In an era dominated by powerful—if often illusory—dichotomies between home and market, public and private, love and money, boardinghouses emerged as unsavory counterparts to idealized homes."[60] In those idealized middle-class homes, women's homemaking work was taken care of by servants or went

---

60. Gamber, *Boardinghouse*, 2.

unpaid. The boardinghouse, on the other hand, made the work of managing a home and the financial transactions of tenancy overt. Moreover, as Gamber notes, "Women's labor stood at the heart of this social equation, for boardinghouse keeping was women's work."[61] The seediness associated with boardinghouse life suggests that, in the ideal middle-class home, women's housework has no cache and is at its best when it is invisible—an increasingly difficult task in the interwar and postwar periods with the servant class disbanding. In Hamilton's novel, Mrs. Payne, the owner of the Rosamund Tea Rooms, is a Dickensian caricature of the profit-hungry landlady: "This active, grey-haired, spectacled, widowed woman had no interest in knowledge, only in gain" (*Slaves*, 4). In agreeing to be her paying tenants, boarders consent to her rules and the overarching goal of profitability, which the war inadvertently helps to serve by forcing evacuations from London. This goal often directly challenges boarders' desires for personal privacy and individual expression.

Already forced into undesirable intimate proximity with other residents, boarders are at the mercy of Mrs. Payne, "whose love of gain over-rode all other considerations, [and who] did not hesitate, when the occasion arose, to inflict her regular guests with the company of strangers at meals" (*Slaves*, 156). Profit is put into direct tension with any sense of "home" that a boarder might derive from living at the Rosamund Tea Rooms. Individual comfort and expression are strictly limited by boardinghouse rules: "All innovations were heralded by notes, and all withdrawals and adjustments thus proclaimed. Experienced guests were aware that to take the smallest step in an original or unusual direction would be to provoke a sharp note within twenty-four hours at the outside, and they had therefore, for the most part, abandoned originality" (5). Mrs. Payne seems to be in her element as enforcer of blackout regulations, announcing curtly that "*Visitors will be held personally responsible for completing their own black-outs in their bedrooms*" (5, emphasis original). Even personal actions within personal space are subject to strict regulation. With the architectural history of private space in mind, such close "public" monitoring of individual rooms calls into question the very possibility of individual subjectivity within the boardinghouse community and indeed suggests it could be a space with fascistic tendencies. Recall the uneasiness felt by many about threats to individual freedom during wartime debates about the nature and value of planning. Through the comic nature of Mrs. Payne's characterization, however, Hamilton also pokes fun at the obsession with private space and fear of community-oriented reconstruction plans. While it might not be everyone's first choice to share meals with strangers, it is hardly the stuff of

---

61. Gamber, 7.

totalitarianism. If the boardinghouse seems like a metaphorical space for fascist allegory, Hamilton's comic approach complicates any attempt to take such an allegory seriously.

The mocking continues with Miss Roach's reaction to Mrs. Payne's regulation of furnishings and décor. As the narrator describes Miss Roach taking in the bleak attributes of her personal room, her sense of alienation from both her surroundings and herself become humorously apparent:

> [She] saw her room in the feeble light of the bulb which hung from the ceiling in the middle of the room and which was shaded by pink parchment. She saw the pink artificial-silk bedspread covering the light single bed built of stained-oak—the pink bedspread which shone and slithered and fell off, the light bedstead which slid along the wooden floor if you bumped into it. She saw the red chequered cotton curtains (this side of the black-out material) which were hung on a brass rail and never quite met in the middle, or, if forced to meet in a moment of impatience, came flying away from the sides; she saw the stained-oak chest of drawers with its mirror held precariously at a suitable angle with a squashed match-box. She saw the wicker table by the bed, on which lay her leather illuminated clock, but no lamp, for Mrs. Payne was not a believer of reading in bed. She saw the gas-fire, with its asbestos columns yellow and crumbling and its gas-ring. She saw the small porcelain wash-basin with Running H. and C. (the H. impetuously H. at certain dramatic moments, but frequently not Running but feebly dripping—the C. bitterly C. yet steadfastly Running). She saw the pink wall-paper, which bore the mottled pattern of a disease of the flesh; and in one corner were piled her "books," treasures of which she had saved from the bombing in London, but for which she had not yet obtained a shelf. (*Slaves*, 5–6)

This passage, one of Hamilton's many humorous and keenly detailed descriptions of the boardinghouse setting, emphasizes Miss Roach's distance from, and acute dislike of, the things around her in a way that recalls Taylor's description of Julia making her way through Mrs. Lippincote's house or Eleanor's self-reflection in the communist house. Miss Roach's only action in this passage, if it can be called action, is to see, but not, it seems, to fully comprehend or accept, the things she observes. In fact, the narrator comically shuts down the only opening for agency by noting the missing bedside lamp, which would have been useful for the only objects in the room that are demonstrably hers: her "books." Presented in quotation marks and at the very end of the passage, the books are only half capable of expressing her individuality, comically undermining Miss Roach's attachment to them as her "treasures." Syntactically, every time the narrator begins a new sentence with the repeated phrase "she saw," Miss Roach's lack of individual agency within the space grows more obvious. In a concluding jab that recalls the positions of Taylor's Eleanor and Julia, the narrator refers to the space as "a room of her own at the top" (*Slaves*, 7), mocking the pretension to believe that she could derive the sort of personal intellectual development from this room that Woolf's "room of one's own" promised. Although this room undoubtedly is not the most inviting, the irony in the narration makes it difficult to take the threat to Miss Roach's sense of self entirely seriously. From the very beginning of the novel, it is thus clear that the wartime boardinghouse is an ambivalent space that both calls up and shuts down individualistic desires. The comic treatment of Miss Roach's predicament further suggests a critique of individuals who take themselves so seriously that they forget the more important wartime emergency unfolding around them.

Ambivalence seems to be built into the very structure of the building itself, which is architecturally incongruous. The "Rosamund Tea Rooms (which were not Tea Rooms any more, but a boarding-house)" is a converted building, and its name no longer properly describes its function (*Slaves*, 2). In this respect, the Rosamund Tea Rooms recalls other shared living spaces, such as flats or bed-sits, which were created in the modern period by partitioning Victorian or Georgian houses that had become too large or unprofitable.[62] The drama of ambivalent dislocation is at its peak within the public spaces of the architecturally reappropriated boardinghouse, which require a constant balancing of private life and public performance. As tenants "courteously but condescendingly [act] a part in front of their fellow-boarders," possible identities and meanings proliferate, reinforced at the level of signification by indeterminate sights and sounds (74). Individual desire and action are always mediated by a concern for how the other boarders will interpret what has happened, which means there is a persistent gap between private and public experiences. For Miss Roach, it is difficult to locate "real" information about people and events,

---

62. Hamilton is not the first to use the reappropriation of architectural space to lay the foundation for a modern literary comedy of errors: things do not add up spatially or logically as property comes under increasing pressure from middle-class trends and buying power. In one of the more memorable precursors to Hamilton's novel, Evelyn Waugh's *A Handful of Dust* (1934), reappropriation and redecoration become the catalyst for the darkly comic breakdown of Tony and Brenda Last's aristocratic marriage. Brenda moves out of their overly large country house and takes up residence in a room in a Belgravia house that an interior decorator with wildly modern tastes (she lines the walls of their country house with white chromium plating) has divided into six flats. In Waugh's novel and in Hamilton's, a distinctly modernist redecoration coincides with secrets, deception, and the tragicomic alienation of those who reside within the repurposed domestic structures.

and she becomes increasingly overwhelmed by the constant spying, eavesdropping, overhearing, guessing, gossiping, and performing that characterizes her environment. The narrator intensifies the gaps in Miss Roach's knowledge by remaining pointedly limited in omniscience, frequently contributing variations of the phrase, "it was very difficult to ascertain how much precisely was known about last night" (182). Offered such limited omniscience, moreover, the reader comes to occupy a boarder-like position, hoping for a recognizable narrative thread that will create some forward momentum for Miss Roach, but feeling increasingly alienated from traditional narrative expectations.

The residents of the Rosamund Tea Rooms don't express themselves sincerely; they perform roles in order to generate the least amount of gossip and sensation within the always public living space.[63] But these roles are under constant pressure from others who seek to uncover private lives in the most scandalous way possible. The boarder most able to maintain a sense of privacy is the actor and minor character Mr. Prest. Ironically, in this space that requires continual performance it is the actor who is most successful in keeping "himself very much to himself" (*Slaves*, 75). One evening, when he enters the dining room, "A silence fell . . . and people found themselves staring at him, seeking to discover his secret" (75). Each individual presents an exaggerated narrative mystery within the boardinghouse, and even those who seem most transparent, such as Mr. Thwaites, the boardinghouse "bully," frustrate others' desires to reveal the unknown (12). In the case of Mr. Thwaites, it is a proliferation of unintelligible nonverbal sounds that persist in frustrating the other residents in their pursuit of knowledge: he "left the Lounge and went into his bedroom, in which he was heard walking savagely about for at least half an hour—or at any rate what seemed at least half an hour to his fellow-boarders. What was he *doing* in there? This mystery, repeated relentlessly each morning, but never clarified, hung like a sullen cloud over the Rosamund Tea Rooms at this time of day" (70, emphasis original). As with the ironic representation of the obsession with individual privacy, Hamilton's narrator uses exaggeration to satirize the complementary desire at the other end of the spectrum: the desire to know everything about everyone. Indeed, whether Miss Roach feels alienated from herself or from someone else, her sense of

---

63. Gossip and talk in this novel also have clear intertexts with the wartime work of Mass-Observation, which listened in on and observed the daily lives of Britons during the war, documenting the topics and registers of conversation. Thierry Labica briefly discusses the M-O context in relation to the novel in his article, "War, Conversation, and Context in Patrick Hamilton's *The Slaves of Solitude*." John Mepham also provides an illuminating relevant discussion of language and linguistics in his essay, "Varieties of Modernism, Varieties of Incomprehension: Patrick Hamilton and Elizabeth Bowen."

individualism as a governing principle is frustrated as a result of the highly performative nature of boardinghouse social life.

Boardinghouse gossip also fuels the widening gap between public and private realms. Mrs. Payne contributes by knowingly keeping the house telephone in her own room. When Miss Roach receives a call from the American Lieutenant stationed in town, the seed for frivolous scandal, rather than the seed for a meaningful romance plot, is planted. The narrator describes this telephone call, meant to be private, as "a boarding-house sensation": "The residents of the Rosamund Tea Rooms were not telephone-using animals. Mrs. Payne was in the room, and did not see any reason to leave it" (*Slaves*, 39). Miss Roach's sense of self is increasingly threatened by this kind of "scandal" but also, and even more so, by *assumed* gossip, or suspicion. Her anxious suspicion reaches its peak when she presumes that Mr. Thwaites and the German boarder, Vicki Kugelmann, have bonded over teasing Miss Roach behind her back:

> To gain the knowledge that she had been talked about at all by two people was shock enough for Miss Roach (such knowledge is always a shock of a kind to any human being, unless it is at once followed and compensated for by the news that the talk is of a highly favourable nature): but to learn that two people of this sort had been talking about her, and in this way—she believed it was more than she could stand. . . . And she betted your life they had talked! If she knew anything about them, they had talked and talked and talked. (178–79)

Already self-victimized by the possibility that she is the subject of gossip, Miss Roach is further teased by the narrator in this passage with the ambiguous use of the word "if": "*If* she knew anything about them" (179; emphasis added). Colloquially, the phrase affirms the fact that she is right in what she suspects, but taken literally, the word "if" undermines her ability to know anything at all with certainty. Even if her assumption about their gossiping is accurate, moreover, that assumption allows her to conclude merely that they have talked—but about what, precisely, she remains ignorant. The consequence of her suspicion is elusive, an irony that underscores the comparative significance of the valid wartime suspicion of actual Nazi spies.

Along with gossip, spying and eavesdropping within the boardinghouse amount to seeing and hearing without apparent consequence for Miss Roach as an individual. There is a kind of indeterminate white noise that forms the sensory backdrop of residents' interactions. The narrator draws attention to this noise in describing the half-overheard conversations that take place between the cooks and servers on either end of the dumbwaiter in the dining room:

> Enquiries, comments, and sometimes remarks of a censorious nature being hurled down from above in the hearing of the guests, and appropriate rejoinders from below feebly making their way to the surface amidst the rumbling of the lift. In the long pauses, when no one was talking, the guests listened, in a hypnotized way, to these back-stage noises and manoeuvres. (13)

When someone sees something through a cracked door or hears something through a thin wall, that seeing or hearing is not integrated as part of a meaningful interaction with the person who generates the sound or sight. As Miss Roach gathers superfluous intelligence instead of paying attention to intelligence about the war, which really matters, she accumulates excess knowledge that was never meant to circulate. In the Rosamund Tea Rooms, such excess knowledge is sometimes redistributed as gossip, but it does not enable narratively fruitful connections among individual characters, despite the intense proximity of the forced wartime community. Miss Roach is so invested in this inconsequential excess knowledge that she continually imagines overhearing or glimpsing something in order to confirm conclusions that will bolster preconceived ideas about others but that have no impact on agency. Upon returning to the boardinghouse one evening, for example, she hovers on the first floor landing "outside the 'Lounge,' from behind whose closed door she could hear (she was now aware that she had been hearing it in anticipation all the way back from the station) Mr. Thwaites' voice booming nasally, indefatigably, interminably" (*Slaves*, 5). Her imagined and actual hearing of Mr. Thwaites's incomprehensible voice only reinforces her mounting hatred of him, which in turn increases her sense of alienation from the boardinghouse as a whole. This is not to suggest that Miss Roach's feelings about Mr. Thwaites are unjustified, but rather to emphasize that there seems to be no interpersonal narrative solution for her, whether it be a frank conversation with Mr. Thwaites, which never happens, or a coordinated alliance with the other boarders who also find him infuriating. Instead, everyone remains isolated and frustrated by attempts at successful communication.

Although Miss Roach refuses to think about the war directly, the specifics of the war context also contribute to the accumulation of excess knowledge and inconsequential information within the boardinghouse, since under blackout conditions, "people were muffled from each other" (*Slaves*, 3). The blackout causes half-glances and missed interpersonal connection. While sitting in the dining room, Miss Roach "glanced up at Mr. Thwaites and Mrs.

Barratt, and saw that they were not looking at her. But their way of not looking at her, she observed, was a way of looking" (151). Clandestine looking and paranoid observation establish a nonconnection between Miss Roach and the other boarders. Nothing of narrative significance for Miss Roach comes of this mutually acknowledged, withheld recognition except for an increased sense of isolation and frustration. Near the pitch of her frustration with boardinghouse life, rather than directly knocking on Mr. Thwaites's door one evening to find out what is happening, she spins in circles of eavesdropping and suspicion: "She went on to the landing, listened, went into her room again, came out and listened, and at last, after four or five minutes had passed, went downstairs and listened outside Mr. Thwaites' door" (176). Miss Roach's listening amounts to nothing of consequence. She remains stuck: physically, mentally, and narratively. Hamilton reinforces her position through the ironic repetition of "listened," which parallels the earlier repetition of "she saw" when Miss Roach was trying to take in the décor of her room. As in that earlier scene, she remains unable to piece together the information she perceives in a way that enables her development within the narrative universe of Thames Lockdon. The narrator ultimately reveals the absurdity of her obsessive anxieties when Mr. Prest remains indifferent to her plea, which has no real content: "But you missed something [at the boardinghouse] tonight" (203). Indeed, what exactly has been missed remains unclear to Miss Roach while becoming increasingly more obvious to the reader. As empty, inconsequential content amasses in the boardinghouse, it points inversely and ironically to the most pressing, yet absent, subject of all: the war itself. In this sense, Miss Roach's self-alienation is tied to, if not a direct consequence of, her denial of the war's true significance.

Occasionally, Miss Roach flees the Rosamund Tea Rooms in the hopes of finding an environment better suited to her sense of individual space, but these excursions only end up intensifying the alienation she feels within the boardinghouse. This is because the boardinghouse environment is not at odds with, but an extension of, the wartime context, despite the conspicuous absence of the war from boardinghouse discourse. Like the boardinghouse itself, the war produces its special, spontaneous crowds: compositions of characters that "no imaginable combination of peace-time circumstances could have brought about," which make individuals like Miss Roach feel physically and socially claustrophobic (*Slaves*, 118). "In the war," according to the narrator, "everywhere was crowded all the time. The war seemed to have conjured into being, from nowhere, magically, a huge population of its own—one which flowed into and filled every channel and crevice of the country—the towns, the villages, the streets, the trains, the buses, the shops, the hotels, the inns, the restaurants, the movies" (26). While some people seem exhilarated by the changes brought on by the war, such as the American soldiers stationed in town and their "good time girls," Miss Roach is figured as a victim of the war as "somber begetter of crowds everywhere" (47). The narrator identifies her as sadly out of sync with the world around her, not only inside the boardinghouse, but outside as well, as in the cinema where she "stared at the screen with plain fear on her face—fear of life, of herself, of Mr. Thwaites, of the times and things into which she had been born, and which boomed about her and encircled her everywhere" (27).

Throughout the novel, Hamilton's narrator emphasizes the limits of Miss Roach's individualism by undermining her efforts to piece together meaning about the events that unfold around her. Narrative threads stop and start in her head. She keeps thinking, "it's all over," and then, "it wasn't all over after all!" (*Slaves*, 34, 206–7). She fails, for instance, to understand that the American Lieutenant stationed in town only desires her as a good time girl, not as a potential wife. When Miss Roach does not express her befuddlement through quoted dialogue, the narrator provides it through free indirect discourse, further emphasizing her lack of self-awareness, as when the narrator contemplates her conversation with the Lieutenant: "Or again, had she completely misheard or misunderstood what he had said?" (43). Miss Roach is narratively isolated in her ignorance of other people's needs and desires. "You never knew what people were really like, did you?" (92). The narrator reports variations of this question plaguing Miss Roach throughout the novel: "Though you never knew—you never knew anything about anybody" (203).

The abortive romance plot in the novel, erased by the absent presence of the war plot, most clearly demonstrates Miss Roach's inability to enter meaningfully into narratives of development. Recalling Eleanor's difficulties with romance in *At Mrs. Lippincote's*, Miss Roach struggles to interpret the American Lieutenant's desires and to define their relationship. At first, she imagines that he has brought her fully into the home front, wartime community. "In the last astonishing three weeks it seemed that she had actually acquired her own American—just as every shop-girl, girl-typist, girl-clerk, girl-assistant, girl-anything in fact, in the town, had acquired her own. . . . She felt a sudden, delightful, modest, gin and French pride in her experience as a 1940 Londoner" (*Slave*, 27, 29). The narrator, however, suggests that this feeling of participation is temporary: it only "seemed" that she had become just like all of the other home front London girls. In fact, she is a spinster living in a suburban boardinghouse, where the drama is limited to dining room banter. Her romantic notions about the Lieutenant are abruptly challenged when several other characters intrude while they are having drinks at the pub. Miss Roach's ability to be part of the community is put to the test: "Then, all at once, everything went bad. His friend, Lieutenant Lummis, entered with two girls, and the tête-à-tête was transformed into an awkward yet noisy party of five. . . . She was, in fact, almost completely left out of it, and her sole desire was to go home" (30–31). As a defense against her inability to figure him out, she refuses—or pretends to refuse—to have any interest in or responsibility for how he acts. When he arrives at the boardinghouse, for instance, "She did not like the idea of his going into the Lounge, but," she concludes, "it was not her responsibility or business" (37). Later, contemplating how he might have acted in the Lounge, she again thinks, "It was not her business" (39). Of course, the more frequently she announces that "it was not her business," the clearer it becomes to readers that she is making it hers, and obsessively so. Her compulsive analysis of the Lieutenant leads nowhere narratively, however, as she settles upon "the quality which mainly characterized the Lieutenant—his inconsequence. He was not only inconsequent, as most human beings are, in drink: he was chronically and inveterately inconsequent" (36). Miss Roach cannot comprehend the implications of his actions, as they don't fulfill her romantic expectations, so he appears to her to act without intention. In reality, however, she cannot see that he intends to have her in his life on an inconsequential basis only. She mistakes his advances for the initiation of a romance plot that was never there to begin with.

As the narrative development that Miss Roach desires becomes increasingly unrealistic, her frustration escalates and reveals the fascistic overtones of Mr. Thwaites and Vicki Kugelmann, as numerous critics have discussed in their allegorical readings of the novel and the war.[64] What many have not addressed is Miss Roach's own growing capacity for hatred, passive aggression, and even outright violence. Her hostility toward Vicki is a response to Vicki's assertive behavior, which offends Miss Roach's sense of social conduct and her value of individual privacy. Although it is Miss Roach who initially suggests that Vicki look for lodging in the Rosamund Tea Rooms, Vicki moves in without Miss Roach's help, which enrages her: "And now it had all happened without any bother, had been coolly and calmly fixed up, apart from her. You might almost say it had happened behind her back! The worst part about this feeling was that she not only had to grin and bear it: she had to grin and make a pretence of absolutely adoring it!" (*Slaves*, 60). To Miss Roach's great dismay, Vicki befriends Mr. Thwaites, eagerly becomes chummy with the American Lieutenant and his friends in the pub, and all the while carelessly

---

64. See, for example, Mark Rawlinson's "*The Slaves of Solitude* and the Second World War."

misuses English phrases in a way that amuses her but only underscores her foreignness to Miss Roach. Vicki's assertive otherness always intrudes upon Miss Roach's own sense of self, reaching a crescendo in the symbolically significant space of Miss Roach's "private" room:

> If this woman (thought Miss Roach, as she sat on the wicker-chair and seemed placidly to smoke the last cigarette of the day with her friend) goes on talking about "beans" and "gents": if she makes any further mention of "handling" people or taking people "in hand": if she combs her hair over any more people's photographs, or flops her body on to any more people's beds, or, as she was now doing, flicks her cigarette-ash over any more people's bedside tables, then she, Miss Roach, was at some time in the distant future, or even in the very immediate present, going to start to scream or going to start to hit. But she shows nothing of this, save for a faintly absent minded look in an otherwise cheerful and cordial countenance, and their cigarettes at last came to an end. (99)

Miss Roach's attitude is at once understandable and ridiculous. Hamilton's use of free indirect discourse here creates sympathy for her, even urges her on as she silently observes Vicki's offensive behavior. And yet, Vicki's words and actions alone hardly seem to warrant screaming or hitting.

Hamilton ultimately uses the boardinghouse and the generally claustrophobic wartime environment to put Miss Roach to a test that has political and existential implications beyond Vicki's inability to comprehend English manners and the uncomfortable social theatrics of the dining room. Indeed, from the very first page of the novel, it is clear that Miss Roach will be at a disadvantage in the face of forces greater than her, including the narrator, who specializes in identifying and often mocking the naïveté of those who deny the significance of the war: "The men and women imagine they are going into London and coming out again more or less of their own free will, but the crouching monster [London] sees all and knows better" (*Slaves*, 1). Wartime London has become a Gothic figure here whose presence becomes all the more menacing and threatening to individual agency the more its presence is denied. Miss Roach herself becomes a sort of Gothic victim as she remains stubbornly isolated in her search for secure individuality that is always elusive. Rather than affirming the principles of individualism, her lack of development and narrative mobility affirm only the bleak reality of apolitical modern isolation during wartime—indeed, the novel is aptly named, for she is truly a slave of solitude whose determination to shut out the world around her, and the war in particular, is ultimately at odds with the tenor of the times.

Although Miss Roach tries to bracket the particular version of wartime community experienced at the Rosamund Tea Rooms, the narrator makes it clear that she is more generally in denial about the responsibilities of confronting the historical reality of the war, a war that did not permit people the option of not being cut out for its demands. Whereas in the earlier parts of the novel, the narrator seems to gently tease Miss Roach for her uptight individualism, in the latter half, the narrator describes her sociopolitical isolation directly, without irony:

> About certain things, and about the war in particular, Miss Roach was an ostrich, and purposely and determinedly so.... In pity and horror she didn't want to hear. She hid her head in the sand, and didn't want to have anything to do with it.... As for listening in morning, noon, and night to the wireless ... she hated it, and she would always, if possible, leave the room. (*Slaves*, 165).

Crucially, Miss Roach's denial of the war takes on a spatial dimension that emphasizes the futility of her actions. She leaves the room to avoid confronting the war as part of the wireless community, but as the inevitable wartime crowding caused by bombings, evacuations, and billeting will ensure, this response is ultimately no more than a stopgap. In the final chilling scene, irony returns but without the initial sense of humor. After rejecting the Rosamund Tea Rooms and "escaping" to a hotel room at Claridge's, the narrator undermines her assumption that she is "squaring up" to the war and ultimately indicates the violent consequences of individualistic isolation and determined ignorance of historical reality: "Then Miss Roach, knowing nothing of the future, knowing nothing of the February blitz shortly to descend on London, knowing nothing of flying bombs, knowing nothing of rockets, of Normandy, of Arnhem, of the Ardennes bulge, of Berlin, of the Atom Bomb, knowing nothing and caring very little, got into her bath and lingered in it a long while" (*Slaves*, 242). Although I find Mark Rawlinson's analogy between Miss Roach and the prewar appeasers to be persuasive, my reading directly opposes his ultimate conclusion that "Thames Lockdon is a nightmare from which Miss Roach awakes into history" (268). In this concluding image of Hamilton's novel, Miss Roach remains tied to ways of thinking about herself, others, and history itself that are distinctly anachronistic. If anything, her alienation from historical agency is more pronounced than ever. *The Slaves of Solitude* thus amounts to a nuanced critique of both those who would deny the significance of the war and of wartime novels that do not register the full effects of the war on traditional narrative strategies.

CONCLUSION

At Mrs. Lippincote's and *The Slaves of Solitude* exemplify the ways in which World War II disrupted traditional relations among individuals and the environments and other people they encountered. Novelistically, this disruption translated to an expression of the desire for narrative development and social growth rendered ironically or with ambivalence. It seems that, like bread and milk, character and plot were rationed goods within reconstruction culture. Hamilton's characterization of Miss Roach as ignorant and afraid of the overwhelming forces around her makes her less a protagonist and more a minor character in Woloch's sense of the term, as a character that "is always drowned out within the totality of the narrative."[65] When these examples from Hamilton and Taylor are considered as only two of many wartime texts with similarly stuck "major" characters, the implication is that the war keeps all characters in the minor register. This is not to say that the subjectivities represented by these characters do not matter; indeed, much work has been done, particularly by feminist critics, to show how crucial the political agency of many individuals was during the war.[66] Rather, agency in these novels is shown to be always tied to the war; to deny the significance or demands of the war through escapism or attachment to outdated traditions is to become subject to ridicule with serious implications. These texts are so compelling because they reveal the simultaneous desire for and insufficiency of the individual of various literary traditions after the war. As the Welfare State emerged, such fiction exemplified Raymond Williams's description of realism as "this living tension [between individual and society], achieved in a communicable form."[67] Wartime shared-space novels explored this tension by foregrounding the real challenges to individual identity as well as community solidarity, and they offered a socially attuned approach to narrative as a response.

---

65. Woloch, *One vs. Many*, 38.
66. See Lassner, Plain, and Schneider for exemplary work in this area.
67. Williams, *Long Revolution*, 315.

CHAPTER 3

Mobile Housing

Realizing Movement in 1950s City Fiction

IN THE INTRODUCTION to her book, *Literature of the 1950s: Good, Brave Causes*, Alice Ferrebe notes that the decade has been subject to two persistent stereotypical conceptions that emphasize torpor: "In popular memory, the 1950s function most frequently as a kind of nostalgic shorthand for national consensus, contentment and order (as mobilized by Margaret Thatcher, for example). Alternatively, they are cited as a negative example of the cultural stasis caused by affluence and apathy (by Left-leaners since)."[1] With Ferrebe, this chapter argues that the 1950s were actually far from settled—either positively or negatively, as the dominant stereotypes have suggested. British writers and architects focused on mobility and its effects in order to assert ethical responsibility and claim social value for their crafts. Architectural innovations, from New Towns to the New Brutalism, and literary realism, particularly as written by "peripheral" figures like Colin MacInnes, Shelagh Delaney, and Sam Selvon, embrace mobility thematically and aesthetically to actively interrupt the stasis of postwar recovery and to reconstruct perception of the postwar built environment.

Heightened mobility was, arguably, the predominant characteristic of British life in the late 1950s and into the 1960s. Increasing national wealth, more widespread affluence, and American-inspired consumerism, characterized by

---

1. Ferrebe, *Literature of the 1950s*, 1.

disposability and quickly changing trends that appealed to teenagers, defined the economy. Politically and demographically, the 1948 Nationality Act created the status of "Citizen of the United Kingdom and Colonies," making it possible for colonial subjects to emigrate legally to the UK as citizens. Shortly after the Act passed, the *SS Empire Windrush* departed Jamaica for London, initiating an extensive wave of migration from the Caribbean. This large-scale migration constituted a significant change in racial and ethnic profile for the UK, and it especially transformed the makeup of parts of West and North West London. Demographically, the 1950s and 1960s also witnessed the influx of a substantial Irish emigrant population, with many headed for work in construction.[2] In music and film, these years witnessed the explosion of rock 'n' roll, bebop, and New Wave Cinema, all of which were technologically and stylistically fast moving. The language of popular culture also emphasized mobility. In 1954, the literary editor for the *Spectator*, J. D. Scott, coined the term "The Movement" to define a group of up-and-coming writers that included Kingsley Amis, Thom Gunn, Elizabeth Jennings, and John Wain.[3] And on its April 15, 1966, cover, *Time* magazine picked up on an adjective frequently used in popular culture, "swinging," to describe London.[4] This widespread mobility across cultural discourses and various aspects of society is symptomatic of the fact that, as Ferrebe claims, "the 1950s was a time of genuine sea-change in British experiences and attitudes" as the decade witnessed a "movement from a homogeneous British identity (or its necessary non-contestation during the Second World War) towards far more complex understandings of identity, genealogy and belonging."[5]

---

2. As Clair Wills notes, "During the 1950s over four hundred thousand people left independent Ireland, nearly a sixth of the total population recorded in 1951 and a much greater proportion of the working population. Most left for work in Britain, home to one million Irish-born by the late 1960s" ("Realism and the Irish Immigrant," 374–75). Wills proceeds to offer a compelling analysis of Irish emigrant fiction set in Britain as an instance of "peripheral realism" that makes building and reconstruction central to its narratives (See Jed Esty and Colleen Lye's "Peripheral Realisms"). She observes, "While Irish immigrant narrative mirrors some aspects of British working-class realist fiction and the New Wave films of the early 1960s (particularly in its focus on labor), the rejection of a marriage-and-family plot is a crucial difference. . . . While many thousands of the young, single Irish men and women in British cities by the mid-1950s did couple up, couples did not become part of written narratives, which focused instead on milieu. For the male migrant in particular, building and the landscape of reconstruction were not the background but the very fabric of his narrative. Building sites were at once the migrants' workplace and one location of their community" ("Realism and the Irish Immigrant," 376).

3. Scott, "In the Movement," 399.
4. "London: The Swinging City," n.p.
5. Ferrebe, *Literature of the 1950s*, 2.

Geographically and architecturally, new opportunities for movement abounded, and these opportunities were visually symbolized by the newest addition to the built environment: the high-rise tower block. Tower blocks allowed for an unprecedented degree of literal upward mobility, especially within crowded cities such as London, and they were striking vertical additions to a landscape that had been leveled by bombs, symbolizing a modern Britain that had left behind the strictures of wartime life.[6] In addition to the visually striking promise of future-oriented movement inherent in the tower block, Britain's housing market reflected new opportunities for upward socio-economic mobility. Single-family homeownership transformed in the 1950s and 1960s from the social ideal of wartime reconstruction plans to a viable reality of advancement for many. In 1951, thirty percent of the population of England and Wales owned a home; in 1970, this number had risen to fifty percent.[7] As larger portions of the population gained economic leverage, they moved house, and in doing so, they demonstrated that, socially, they were moving up. Fiction, plays, and films by the Angry Young Men often dramatized the new opportunities for working-class upward mobility in terms of housing. One of the more iconic examples, Alan Sillitoe's *Saturday Night and Sunday Morning* (1958), concludes with the promise of social advancement symbolized by the new housing estate on the outskirts of town, which forms the backdrop as Arthur and Doreen affirm their commitment to each other and to a future of marriage and family life.

While the freedom to move signaled progress and opportunity for some, domestic mobility could also be a threat to the security promised by the Welfare State settlement for peripheral communities. Homelessness persisted throughout the most prosperous years of the postwar period. There had been little public attention to homelessness as a social problem in the first postwar decade, but this began to change in the late 1950s with the 1957 Rent Act. This legislation allowed the decontrolling of rents and opened up a portion of the rental market to private property development via owner-occupation, the seed for the right-to-buy program that was the hallmark of the Margaret Thatcher Government's privatization scheme.[8] Throughout the 1960s, and continuing into the 1970s, long waiting lists, discrimination by landlords, and the decrease of household size were obstacles for immigrants, large families, single women, and gay men looking for residential security. Shelagh Delaney's play, *A Taste of Honey* (1959), is one of many texts from the period focused on the

---

6. In his essay on the tower block in contemporary British cinema, Andrew Burke characterizes the high rises constructed in the 1960s as modernist "primary symbols of the future" ("Concrete Universality," 186).

7. Hanson, *From Silent-Screen to Multi-Screen*, 102.

8. Austerberry and Watson, *Housing and Homelessness*, 54.

precarious position of single pregnant women who are often forced to vacate more stable and comfortable living situations for bed-sits or boarding houses.[9] Set in industrial Manchester, *A Taste of Honey* follows sixteen-year-old Jo, who gets pregnant after a fling with a sailor who is just passing through. Her social-climbing mother abandons her to marry up and out to the suburbs. Jo stays in the city and moves in with Geoffrey, a gay textiles student who takes on a motherly or sisterly role, helping her to prepare for the baby. Jo's future remains entirely uncertain at the end of the play. Similarly, in Sam Selvon's fiction, residential mobility turns into socioeconomic inertia for recent Caribbean and African migrants who settled in large numbers in West London neighborhoods like Notting Hill and Bayswater. In the 1950s, this was one of the few parts of London in which rooms would be rented to nonwhite tenants, if at highly inflated prices. Many newly arrived immigrants became victims of Peter Rachman, a notorious landlord who made millions by acquiring slum properties—he owned 147 buildings in Notting Hill alone—and leasing rooms at extortionate prices to tenants who were intimidated if they complained or could not make payments.[10] The reality of housing in the Welfare State did not always live up to the initial ideals symbolized by the high rise.

Fiction and architecture from this decade express the ideals and limitations of increasing social and spatial mobility. Colin MacInnes pushes the realist novel to its conventional limits in *Absolute Beginners,* with its rambling episodic structure, peripheral perspective, and representation of real-time events like the Notting Hill race riots. Housing projects developed by architects including the Smithsons, James Stirling, Denys Lasdun, and Ivor Smith and Jack Lynn, meanwhile, challenged persistent assumptions that the traditional single-family home was the most appropriate form of dwelling for the mobilizing and modernizing postwar era. MacInnes and the Smithsons, in particular, envision neighborhoods defined by interconnectivity in spite of social difference as a new desirable reality. Instead of turning inward, to individual literary consciousness, to a narrowly defined community, or to the comforts of past styles, they faced the social complexities of the present and envisaged a boldly reconstructed future. The Smithsons capture the essence of the realist literary and architectural imagination of these years in their stated objective for New Brutalist architecture: "To drag a rough poetry from the confused and powerful forces which are at work."[11]

---

9. In addition to Delaney's *A Taste of Honey* and its film adaptation by Tony Richardson, see Lynn Reid-Banks's *The L-Shaped Room* (1962) and its film adaptation by Bryan Forbes, and *Cathy Come Home,* a BBC television play directed by Ken Loach.

10. McLeod, *Postcolonial London,* 49.

11. Smithson and Smithson, "Thoughts in Progress," 113.

In arguing that mobility is central to 1950s realism, this chapter adds nuance to the dominant narrative in twentieth-century literary history. Conventionally, mobility has been associated predominately with interwar modernism and its clear descendants. In *Cities of Affluence and Anger,* for example, Peter Kalliney identifies urban mobility as a defining part of Virginia Woolf's modernist aesthetics in *Mrs. Dalloway* (1925), which he also observes in Sam Selvon's *The Lonely Londoners* (1956) thirty years later. Emphasizing the politically charged reappropriation of London's spaces by postcolonial writers, Kalliney argues that "Selvon's adaptation of high modernism's urban aesthetics" shows that

> metropolitan postcolonial literature abandons neither modernism nor its engagement with urban space but instead uses and transforms them to participate in debates about English national culture. . . . Postcolonial literature seizes the aesthetic territories and material spaces charted by metropolitan modernism. *The Lonely Londoners* is just as fascinated by, and just as ambivalent about, London and Englishness as its forerunner *Mrs. Dalloway*.[12]

Charting a through line from Woolf to Selvon, particularly in terms of urban mobility, ultimately allows Kalliney to claim that postcolonial writers take up the torch of literary modernism in the postwar period, thereby legitimating their art. While Kalliney's reading of Selvon in light of Woolf is convincing, it is also possible to conceive of the mobility that is so central to *The Lonely Londoners* in terms of realism and its relationship to migration.

In "Space, Mobility, and the Novel: 'The spirit of place is a great reality,'" Josephine McDonagh hypothesizes a historical relation between mobility and realist narrative dating to the eighteenth century. Realism, she argues, is a mechanism that counteracts or mediates large-scale movements of population, as in the great urban migrations of the nineteenth century, by strongly investing in a sense of place. According to McDonagh, two ways of thinking about realism as a response to such mass migrations recur throughout the later nineteenth and twentieth centuries: "In one, the presupposition is that the aim of realism is to make people at home in the world; in the other, it is that its object is to explain why people are at odds with the world."[13] Both functions of realism, particularly the second, inform Selvon's novel. As his characters drift from shared flats to train stations to jobs with London transport, the narrator uses a patois style to actively incorporate the environment

---

12. Kalliney, *Cities of Affluence and Anger,* 106–7.
13. McDonagh, "Space, Mobility, and the Novel," 62.

into their new way of being, while also acknowledging the differences that make it impossible for them to fully belong. To read this novel as an expression of metropolitan modernism is to underscore the alienation that these characters experience in postcolonial London. To read it as postwar realism is to emphasize the potential for Selvon's narrative to actively reconstruct the relationship between individual immigrants and the social and spatial conditions they confront. Selvon, like MacInnes, uses the realist mode not simply to react to, but to reshape, midcentury experience in Britain.

FROM THE GARDEN CITY TO "STREETS IN THE SKY": EXPRESSING MOBILITY IN THE POSTWAR ENVIRONMENT

Increased desire for mobility in the 1950s built environment is a direct response to wartime conditions, immediate postwar recovery, and the modernization of British building and design practices. After the instability of the war years, British architects in the late 1940s revived a picturesque style and developed a localized English townscape theory that looked inward to past traditions. These trends reflected the ongoing influence of Ebenezer Howard's late Victorian Garden City movement on British urban planning, architecture, and landscape design, even in the midst and aftermath of widespread modernization. According to architect Hugh de Cronin Hastings, townscape theory favored a picturesque, visual approach to architecture and careful town planning over a conventionally modernist architectural commitment to a more scientific approach that prioritized efficiency and functionality. Recalling the Victorian rooms filled with historical artifacts and trinkets, Hastings's picturesque theory valued the unique and the specific; it was dedicated to "giving every object the best possible chance to be itself."[14] Townscape theory and the picturesque style, like community-oriented reconstruction initiatives discussed in chapter 2, sought to rehabilitate the individual as an indivisible, stable entity rather than as a moving, atomized part of a war machine.

Even as architects, designers, and planners prioritized stability in the 1940s, technological modernization made the demand for mobility an unavoidable factor in conceiving built space. As Elizabeth Darling has persuasively shown in *Re-forming Britain: Narratives of Modernity Before Reconstruction*, by the beginning of the postwar period, architectural modernism, with its emphasis on positive space, clean lines, and circulation, had become hegemonic through nearly three decades of widespread social, political, and aesthetic

---

14. Hastings, "Townscape," 115.

reform. Victorian-influenced trends like English townscape theory were still indebted to and very much embroiled in the British modernist movement. In his discussion of the construction of the M1 motorway in the early 1950s, Peter Merriman echoes Darling in his assessment of the postwar picturesque, explaining that mobility gained a central role in the built environment: "While earlier proponents of the picturesque had presented movement and travel as antithetical to picturesque ways of seeing and experiencing the world, movement lay at the heart of the neo-picturesque formulations of townscape and landscape."[15] Indeed, in the 1943 *County of London Plan*, Abercrombie and Forshaw had predicted that the postwar era would be "the age of mobility," because the war had made many people "mechanically minded"; many cars were to be expected on the roads.[16]

The planning and construction of New Towns such as Harlow and Stevenage signified the "age of mobility" by recasting Howard's Garden City vision through picturesque townscape theory and combining it with modernizing technologies. According to architectural historian Nicholas Bullock, "Harlow, more clearly than anywhere else in Britain, promised a first glimpse of a modern town, a first realization of one of the great hopes of reconstruction."[17] Harlow, north of London, stood out from other New Towns because it mixed picturesque aesthetics with the modernist priority of open space for circulation that had been favored by CIAM (Congrès internationaux d'architecture moderne) in the interwar period.[18] In his plan for Harlow, designer and architect Frederick Gibberd outlined how designing the town would "consist in making a distinct separation between areas for work, homes and play, in connecting those areas by a road pattern free of building in which traffic can flow easily, and in surrounding the whole by a well-defined agricultural belt."[19] Thus, even as planners, architects, and landscape designers aimed to counter excessive and unlimited movement in the immediate decade of postwar recovery, the realities of increased technological mobility and the influence of modernizing aesthetics were omnipresent.

Mobility in postwar reconstruction was also actualized in the process of planned demolition, which the government ordered on a large scale in the early part of the 1950s. The Town and Country Planning Act of 1947, which extended the power of public authorities to acquire and develop land, provided major funds for the clearing of land. Major reconstruction efforts in

---

15. Merriman, "New Look at the English Landscape," 87.
16. Abercrombie and Forshaw, *County of London Plan*, 49, 84.
17. Bullock, *Building the Post-War World*, 131.
18. Bullock, 131.
19. Qtd. in Bullock, *Building the Post-War World*, 132.

London, Coventry, and Plymouth took advantage of the war as an opportunity to demolish overcrowded and dilapidated Victorian slums. Between 1955 and 1974, approximately 1.165 million properties were demolished in England and Wales (an estimated one in ten of all homes in the country), which necessitated the movement of 3.1 million residents, most in established working-class communities.[20] In the *County of London Plan*, planners responded to the long historical tide of "mean, ugly, unplanned building," which "rose in every London borough and flooded outward over the fields of Middlesex, Surrey, Essex, Kent."[21] With "depressed housing" as one of the four major defects identified in the analysis of wartime London, the plan casts the demolition of such housing and the rebuilding of the city as "one of the great moments of history."[22] Slum clearance programs instituted in the early 1950s moved traditional working-class communities out of inner-city areas to newly built two-up, two-down properties on the outer margins of towns. The utopian vision for a rebuilt society inherent in demolition schemes was, of course, not without its disruptive effects on communities with long established ties to particular geographical locations. As planned demolition instigated a new wave of residential mobility that created opportunities for improved living conditions, it allowed the evidence of oppressive living conditions effectively to be erased from historical memory.

Mandates to relocate and rebuild in the 1950s and 1960s also became an occasion for architects to inject new ideas into the built environment. The emerging young generation of British architects, including Alison and Peter Smithson, James Stirling, Denys Lasdun, and Ivor Smith and Jack Lynn, rejected both the picturesque aesthetic of immediate postwar reconstruction lingering in New Towns and the continental approach to totalizing rational urban planning, expressed most directly in Le Corbusier's plans to demolish and rebuild Paris.[23] Instead, they sought to reform CIAM and invent new ways

---

20. *Silent Screen*, 94–95.
21. Abercrombie and Forshaw, *County of London Plan*, iii.
22. Abercrombie and Forshaw, iv.
23. In his 1929 work, *The City of Tomorrow and Its Planning*, Le Corbusier placed the goal of efficiency above all other values when he envisioned a new model for central Paris. He explicitly intended to demolish, cover up, or do away with any remnants of old Paris and to rebuild in a way that foregrounded the principles of architectural circulation rather than humanized scale: "This plan makes a frontal attack on the most diseased quarters of the city, and the narrowest streets: it is not 'opportunist' or designed to gain a yard or two at odd points in over-congested roads. Its aim is rather to open up in the strategic heart of Paris a splendid system of communication. As against streets ranging from 20 to 35 feet in width with cross roads every 20, 30 or 50 yards, its aim is to establish a plan on the 'gridiron' system with roads 150, 250 to 400 feet in width, with cross roads every 350 or 400 yards; and on the vast island sites thus formed to build immense cruciform sky-scrapers, so creating a *vertical* city, a city

to make the increased social and economic mobility defining people's lives a reality in the built environment. Alison and Peter Smithson, as unofficial leaders of this break from recent orthodoxies, described their perspective in *Architectural Design* in 1955, emphasizing the disconnect they observed between contemporary architecture and actual conditions:

> Each generation feels a new dissatisfaction and conceives of a new idea of order. This is architecture. Young architects to-day feel a monumental dissatisfaction with the buildings they see going up around them. For them, the housing estates, the social centers and the blocks of flats are meaningless and irrelevant. They feel that the majority of architects have lost contact with reality and are building yesterday's dreams when the rest of us have woken up in today. They are dissatisfied with the ideas these buildings represent, the ideas of the Garden City Movement and the Rational Architecture Movement.[24]

As a response to prevailing trends, the Smithsons began articulating an alternative approach to architecture, which they called the New Brutalism, that would come to influence much of new British council housing construction in the later 1950s, '60s, and into the '70s. The Smithsons and CIAM Team Ten rejected the idea of separate gridded zones as a basis for urban planning, which had been the principle underlying CIAM since its founding by Le Corbusier and Walter Gropius in 1928. Instead, they argued for a city that more thoroughly promoted organic free circulation, in which boundaries between human activities were fluid or nonexistent, and dwellings were conceived of as "streets in the sky," which would "encourage residents to feel a sense of 'belonging' and 'neighbourliness.'"[25]

The Smithsons themselves had been living in Bethnal Green, a working-class area of East London, and there they had come to appreciate "the web of associations to be found in an established urban community."[26] They sought to reproduce this quality in their architectural philosophy and specific housing plans. In 1952, they submitted a reconstruction plan for Golden Lane, in the heavily bombed area of the Barbican in the City of London, and although

which will pile up the cells which have for so long been crushed on the ground, and set them high above the earth, bathed in light and air." (*City of Tomorrow and Its Planning*, 280, emphasis original)

24. Smithson and Smithson, "The Built World," 185.

25. "Alison + Peter Smithson." "Brutalism" refers to Le Corbusier's preference for raw concrete (*beton brut*), but "New" announces that this next generation of modernist architects were reinventing rather than simply adopting Le Corbusier's methods and philosophies.

26. Bullock, *Building the Post-War World*, 139.

their plan was not ultimately selected for the site, it has come to be iconic for the New Brutalist work of the Smithsons and the groundbreaking ethos of CIAM Team Ten. The plan featured a network of connected, fluidly arranged multistory slabs and cellular clusters (Figs. 1, 2, 3) that "was intended as an attempt to retain the advantages of the traditional city street but in a different form, maintaining the elements, the house and the street, and the relationship between them, to promote the established qualities of community."[27] While this plan for the Golden Lane site was not actualized, the Smithsons designed and built Robin Hood Gardens (Fig. 4) based on many of the same principles in the late 1960s, and Park Hill Estate (Fig. 5), built by Jack Lynn, Ivor Smith, and Frederick Nicklin in Sheffield from 1952–59 was inspired by the Smithsons' vision of a fluid network of streets in the sky rather than a grid of blocks. As the Smithsons' efforts to reform CIAM and introduce their philosophy to the reconstructed London landscape indicate, they conceived of architecture as defined ultimately by social rather than aesthetic concerns. Indeed, they explicitly confirmed this belief when they described the New Brutalism as "an ethic, not an aesthetic."[28]

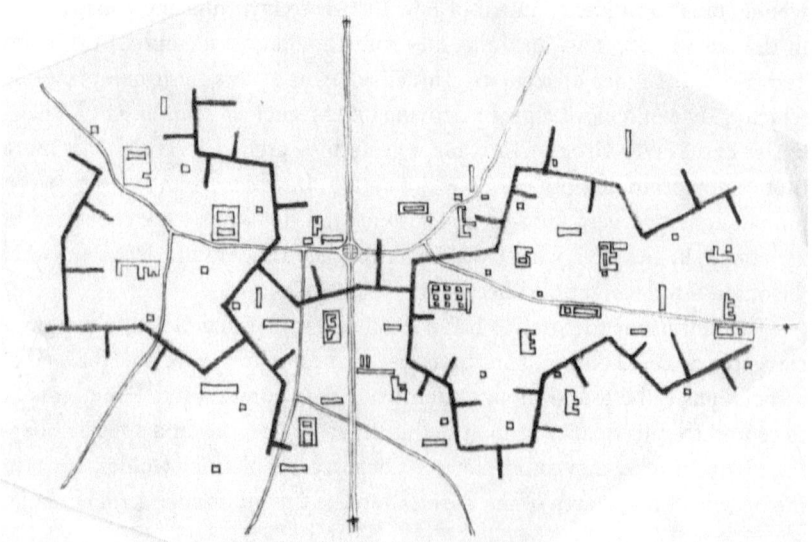

FIGURE 1. Golden Lane Network: explicitly rejects the idea of the modernist grid and instead opts for a single, flowing, cellular network of connected structures. Used with permission from the Smithson Family Library.

---

27. Bullock, 139.
28. Banham, *New Brutalism*, 10.

FIGURE 2. Golden Lane sketch: "streets in the sky." Used with permission from the Smithson Family Library.

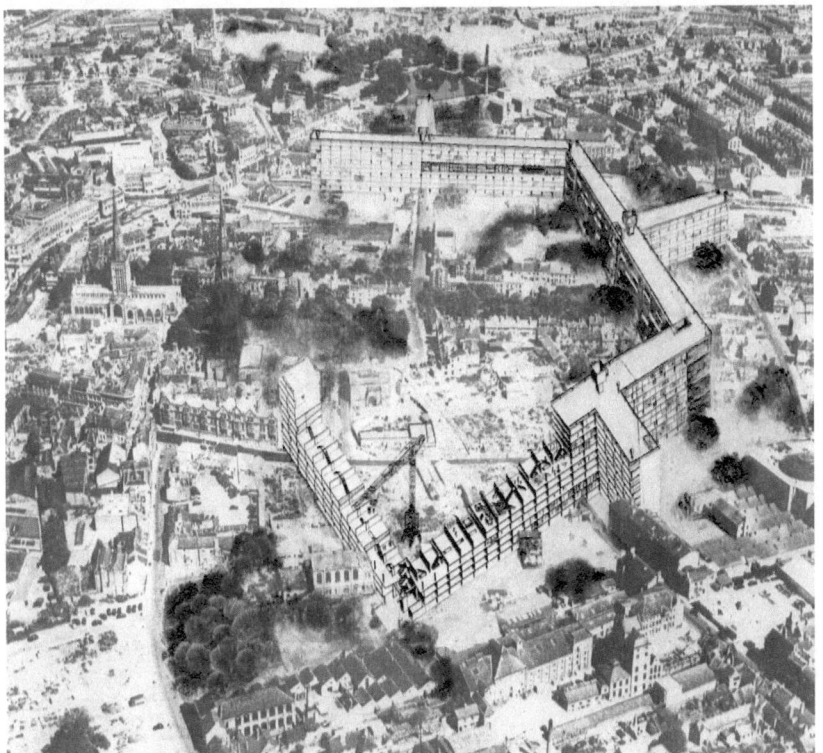

FIGURE 3. Collage view of Golden Lane drawing superimposed on photograph of site (actually Coventry, not London, in photograph). Used with permission from the Smithson Family Library.

FIGURE 4. Robin Hood Gardens, 1972, Sandra Lousada. Used with permission from the Smithson Family Library.

FIGURE 5. Park Hill Estates, Sheffield, aerial view. Built by architects Ivor Smith and Jack Lynn and influenced by the Smithsons' "streets in the sky" housing philosophy. Used with permission from the RIBA Library Photograph Collection.

FIGURE 6. Corridor, or a "street in the sky," Park Hill Estates, Sheffield. Used with permission from the RIBA Library Photograph Collection.

In addition to foregrounding social and ethical demands, the New Brutalism was committed to representing real material conditions in its approach to building. As Peter Smithson wrote in 1957, "Any discussion of Brutalism will miss the point if it does not take into account Brutalism's attempt to be objective about 'reality'—the cultural objectives of society, its urges, its techniques and so on. Brutalism tries to face up to a mass producing society and drag a rough poetry out of the confused and powerful forces which are at work."[29] Aesthetically, this objective translated to the aim of an uninhibited experience of basic contemporary building materials, such as precast concrete, and domestic spaces that rejected the ideal of the single-family home, such as

---

29. Smithson and Smithson, "Thoughts in Progress," 113.

the multistory slab and the tower block, which were intended for everyone, regardless of class, gender, or nationality. "What *is* new about the New Brutalism," the Smithsons explained, "is that it finds its closest affinities not in a past architectural style, but in peasant dwelling forms. It has nothing to do with craft. We see architecture as the direct expression of a way of life" (emphasis original).[30] In its explicit engagement with the social and ethical stakes of architecture as well as its philosophical and aesthetic commitment to facing up to the real conditions of contemporary Britain, we can understand the New Brutalism as having a connection with realist literary innovations in the 1950s and 1960s, even as it used modernist technologies and design techniques. New Brutalist architecture interrupted the visual perception and spatial experience of postwar British life.

1950s REALISM: "JUST THE THING AS IT IS, TAKEN STRAIGHT"

In considering architecture alongside literature from the 1950s, it might seem most intuitive to identify a parallel between the raw, basic building materials of New Brutalist buildings and the similarly raw, stripped-down style and unfiltered content of so much of the kitchen sink social realism by the Angry Young Men that has dominated scholarly attention to the decade.[31] Indeed, the explosion of novels and plays in working-class vernacular, with explicit scenes of drinking, fighting, sex, and abortion was valued at the time for its apparent authenticity, for offering a "direct expression of a way of life," to borrow the Smithsons' description of the New Brutalist architecture.[32] Sillitoe's *Saturday Night and Sunday Morning*, for example, opens with a typical Saturday night scene in working-class Nottingham, which the narrator describes as "the best and bingiest glad-time of the week," when "the effect of a week's monotonous graft in the factory was swilled out of your system in a burst of goodwill."[33] In the very first paragraph, readers are introduced to the anti-hero Arthur and the world he inhabits with an unfiltered description that would have been shocking to middle-class proprieties and sensibilities:

---

30. "New Brutalism," 1.

31. There has been good reason for this critical dominance: the surge of working-class writing and social realist narratives in fiction, theater, and film about working-class lives marked a real turning point in British cultural history. The significance of this "New Wave," however, has been thoroughly accounted for and analyzed by critics across literary, dramatic, and cinematic fields.

32. "New Brutalism," 1.

33. Sillitoe, *Saturday Night and Sunday Morning*, 7.

> The rowdy gang of singers who sat at the scattered tables saw Arthur walk unsteadily to the head of the stairs, and though they must all have known that he was dead drunk, and seen the danger he would soon be in, no one attempted to talk to him and lead him back to his seat. With eleven pints of beer and seven small gins playing hide-and-seek inside his stomach, he fell from the top-most stair to the bottom.[34]

The embodied realities of urban working-class life, rather than a more conventionally manicured aesthetic, take center stage in Sillitoe's novel.

A parallel between the New Brutalism and the Angries would also seem to make sense historically because of the eventual breakdown of the New Brutalist vision and its legacy, which has more often than not been associated with neglect and the failure of socialist Welfare State initiatives in the 1970s and 1980s.[35] The ambivalence and resentment expressed by the Angry Young Men, in hindsight, can be seen to anticipate this architectural legacy. John Osborne's *Look Back in Anger* (1956), for instance, refuses to imagine mobility as a hopeful path to suburban success; instead, he stages the entire play claustrophobically, in a single rented room that seems unable to contain its inhabitants. Jimmy Porter, the eponymous Angry Young Man, would rather stubbornly remain connected to his working-class roots, running a sweet-shop passed down by his mother, than participate in expected middle-class trajectories of relocation, homeownership, and upward mobility. Similarly, the end of Sillitoe's novella, *The Loneliness of the Long-Distance Runner* (1959), presents a working-class "juvenile delinquent" who, like Jimmy Porter, refuses the opportunity for self-improvement and social readjustment offered to him by those maintaining institutional control, whom he sees as the enemy. While the narrator could use his talent for long-distance running to win a race, which would better the reputation of the Borstal and get him on the good side of the governor, he defiantly chooses to run in place just short of the finish line, throwing the race and infuriating the powers that be. He ends the story by appealing to working-class loyalty, planning to hand over his story to a "pal"

---

34. Sillitoe, 7.
35. Andrew Burke observes that the utopian promise of mass housing projects in the reconstruction period was fraught with contradictions, evident in the ensuing history of these buildings, which has been marked by neglect, crime, and general disillusionment: "The formal regularity of their modernist design facilitated construction on a mass scale, yet the demands for housing far outstripped production. As a result, the image of the modernist housing scheme, whether in the form of tower blocks or low-rise slabs, is at least initially invested with the allure of a modernity that for many remained out of reach" ("Concrete University," 180).

who has "lived in our terrace for as long as I can remember" and who "will never give me away."[36]

With "Angry" literature at its center, the dominant critical narrative treating realism of the 1950s has prioritized the thematic interest in how social mobility affected white male working-class lives and identities over almost all other concerns, although recent work has increasingly and importantly also focused on postcolonial experiences.[37] Ferrebe has observed similarly that the conventional story of the 1950s has centered uncritically on the Angries and their localized narratives of disillusionment: "It is Jimmy's announcement [in John Osborne's *Look Back in Anger*] that 'there aren't any good, brave causes left' that is most often quoted to encapsulate the decade's reputation for 'minor literature.'"[38] Drawing a parallel between the New Brutalism and the Angry Young Men would add support to the prevailing cultural, social, and political reading of the period. Doing so, however, fails to account for the inclusive social vision, utopian current, and ethical commitment underwriting the New Brutalism—however unrealized the utopia finally remained.

The New Brutalist approach to design and architecture, which promoted a revolutionary kind of mobility within the British built environment while remaining attuned to the desire for human scale, community, and connection, finds an echo in another kind of realist literature from the period that has been comparatively neglected in the shadow of the Angries. This realism, epitomized by Colin MacInnes, uses mobility as a theme and an aesthetic model to make its humanist desire for broad social and political justice explicit. Jed Esty and Colleen Lye offer a way to conceptualize postwar realism beyond work by Sillitoe, Obsorne, and others with their theory of "peripheral realism."[39] In their model, the mobility of labor within a globalizing postwar world underwrites the realist mode of peripheral perspectives, which include the perspectives of any oppressed or nondominant group. Such a socioeconomic perspective is particularly evident in the 1950s fiction of postcolonial migrants who resettle in London from the Caribbean, Africa, India, Ireland,

---

36. Sillitoe, *Loneliness of the Long-Distance Runner*, 54.

37. This trend is undoubtedly influenced by Alan Sinfield's work, as he has powerfully foregrounded analysis of the social, political, and cultural challenges faced by subordinate groups within Britain. The title of Peter Kalliney's book, *Cities of Affluence and Anger*, points to the continued preoccupation with the perspective and experience of the Angry Young Men and their milieu. John Brannigan's *Literature, Culture, and Society in Postwar England, 1945–1965* begins with analysis of the Angry Young Men and working-class writing. The vast number of books and articles with titles referencing 1956, the year John Osborne's *Look Back in Anger* debuted, points to the firm grip that the "Angry" intervention has on postwar cultural history.

38. Ferrebe, *Literature of the 1950s*, 1.

39. See chapter 1 for a more detailed discussion of their theoretical work on realism.

and elsewhere. Shelagh Delaney, although sometimes considered a token "Angry Young Woman," presents a work of peripheral realism with *A Taste of Honey*, although I would argue that her play is less expressive of the hidden labor relations of global capitalism than of the ambivalence of life in the Welfare State for single working-class women. The play begins with a scene that takes no pains to beautify or romanticize industrial Manchester and their "comfortless flat."[40] As Helen sarcastically says to her daughter, Jo, "Anyway, what's wrong with this place? Everything in its falling apart, it's true, and we've no heating—but there's a lovely view of the gasworks, we share a bathroom with the community and this wallpaper's contemporary. What more do you want? Anyway it'll do for us."[41] Ambivalence toward the future marks the conclusion of Delaney's *A Taste of Honey*, as well. Although Jo's mother returns to the city to check in on her heavily pregnant daughter at the end of the play, sending her friend Geoffrey away, the situation remains destabilized. It is unclear whether Jo will return to a life with her mother, moving from one run-down flat to another, persist as a single mother, perhaps with an unconventional family arrangement that accommodates her gay friend Geoffrey, or whether she will proceed to the kind of home envisioned for Arthur and his future family at the end of *Saturday Night and Sunday Morning*.

Colin MacInnes recognized a different kind of realism in Delaney's play. In 1959, he reviewed a production for *Encounter* in which he praises it for being "the first English play I've seen in which a coloured man, and a queer boy, are presented as natural characters, factually, without a nudge or a shudder. It is also the first play I can remember about working class people that entirely escapes being a 'working class play': no patronage, no dogma, just the thing as it is, taken straight."[42] Like Delaney, MacInnes occupied a peripheral position that set him aside from the Angry Young Men as well as the conventionally postcolonial migrants emphasized by Esty and Lye's theory. MacInnes grew up in Australia and returned to England as a young man, and as a result, he wrote from a position of geographical displacement.[43] To emphasize the significance of his displacement, he chose *England, Half English* as the title for his early collected essays. "Born in London," he remarked in 1962, "but not reared there for so many vital years, my feeling for the city has perforce become that of an insider-outsider: everything in London is familiar; yet everything in it

---

40. Delaney, *Taste of Honey*, 7.
41. Delaney, 7.
42. MacInnes, "Taste of Reality," 205.
43. McLeod, *Postcolonial London*, 40.

seems to me as strange."[44] MacInnes also openly identified as a bisexual at a time when homosexuality was still illegal, and so he wrote from a peripheral position in terms of gender, sexuality, and legality.

Alan Sinfield has noted that this position, which can be described as insider-outsider, affected his status among his literary peers. In contrast with Angry novels and plays, which primarily depict characters who identify as masculine, white, and working class, MacInnes depicted a much greater range of gendered, classed, and racial identities in his fiction. Indeed, the narrator in *Absolute Beginners*[45] explicitly distances himself from the "Angries," calling their work "cottage journalism" (81). According to Sinfield, this insider-outsider status put MacInnes into a lineage of social realist writing that aimed to critique society from the margins: "He harked back to the radical social concerns of Wells, Shaw and Orwell, and anticipated the new journalism of the 1960s—fast-moving, welcoming the new, launching into superficially unpromising topics."[46] Sinfield's influence can be felt throughout the extant scholarship on MacInnes; his work is often discussed in relationship to the youth culture movement and New Left sociological studies of the late 1950s or in conjunction with postcolonial approaches to the postwar years—all of which are attuned to the subversive potential of MacInnes's writing. These studies helpfully situate MacInnes within major postwar cultural traditions, but they do not take full account of his unique contributions, which become evident with sustained attention to the aesthetic dimension of his work and his preoccupation with widespread increased mobility. In attending to form, my approach dovetails with Nick Bentley's assessment of MacInnes's intertextual approach to narrative and vernacular experimentation.[47] MacInnes's work, I argue, offers a uniquely mobile and peripheral British vantage point that disturbs the clear opposition between migrant and national, heterosexual family man and gay single man, radical and traditional realist.

---

44. Qtd. in McLeod, 40. Tony Gould found "insider-outsider" to be such a resonant phrase for MacInnes that he chose it as the title for his biography of MacInnes, *Inside Outsider: The Life and Times of Colin MacInnes*.

45. References to MacInnes's *Absolute Beginners* will use in-text citations.

46. Sinfield, *Literature, Politics, and Culture*, 169.

47. Following Sinfield's interest in dominant and subcultural literary expression, Bentley argues that MacInnes's "writing represents a radical experiment with narrative forms and genres that corresponds to his investigation of the submerged worlds of London's 1950s subcultures, a writing that sits uneasily with the dominant critical readings of the period" ("Writing 1950s London," n.p.). Thomas Davis also takes MacInnes's vernacular as his subject, taking a more New Historicist perspective that aligns with Esty and Lye's framework for peripheral realism. For Davis, vernacular in fiction by MacInnes, Sam Selvon, and others "mediate[s] between everydayness and geopolitical disorder" and reveals language as the "site where the constraints and possibilities of political belonging come into being" (*Extinct Scene*, 188).

In this sense, in line with Esty and Lye's characterization of peripheral realism, we can read MacInnes's fiction as attempting "to fill in rather than leapfrog the space between" these oppositions.[48] Moreover, because of the inherent mobility of MacInnes's peripheral position, we can consider his realist method as one that "involves no simple reproduction of the already known and existing but [that] always contains a future open to dynamic change."[49] This quality, I argue below, is formally apparent in the brazenly open-ended and utopian narrative as well as the style and structure of his novel *Absolute Beginners*, which incorporates the effects of other media into the fabric of its realism. MacInnes's fiction suggests that historically documented socioeconomic and geographic mobility is embedded in realist writing of the 1950s, even if it is not always aesthetically overt in the way that it is in more linguistically and syntactically experimental fiction. In claiming mobility as central to the realist mode, new ways open up for thinking about 1950s texts like *Absolute Beginners* that do not fit easily into dominant categories of kitchen sink realism, popular genre fiction, or avant-garde experimentalism.

The following analysis of *Absolute Beginners* demonstrates that MacInnes's reconstruction fiction offers a more broadly socially engaged literary perspective on mobility than that presented by the realism of the Angry Young Men. As peripheral realist writing that turns its gaze outward, the novel is especially attuned to the social effects of mobility and to British efforts or failures to accommodate all of its ostensible citizens. In this way, it echoes and responds to a contemporaneous demand articulated by Doris Lessing and Raymond Williams for a stronger and more ethically responsible sense of community, which they asserted went hand in hand with the realist novel at the height of its powers. Lessing and Williams lamented the narrowness of British life and literature in the late 1950s, with Lessing describing it as petty, frustrating, and parochial.[50] The problem, she argues in relation to the work of the Angry Young Men in particular, is that their protagonists do not see themselves "in relation to any larger vision."[51] Williams, similarly, sees contemporary literature as frustratingly split between the insulated, isolated brand that Lessing observes and the formulaic popular kind, as in the case of the "future fantasies" of science fiction.[52] Neither blames writers exclusively; in fact, they locate the problem more broadly in the unstable and isolating conditions of postwar life. For Lessing, "From Jimmy Porter to Lucky Jim they are saying: 'I am too

---

48. Esty and Lye, "Peripheral Realisms," 287.
49. Esty and Lye, 287.
50. Lessing, "Small Personal Voice," 16.
51. Lessing, 16.
52. Williams, *Long Revolution*, 306.

good for what I am offered.' And so they are."[53] And for Williams: "The realist novel needs, obviously, a genuine community: a community of persons linked not merely by one kind of relationship—work or friendship or family—but many, interlocking kinds. It is obviously difficult, in the twentieth century, to find a community of this sort."[54] In his commitment to realistically representing, from his peripheral perspective, the confluence of social and individual experiences with heightened mobility, MacInnes addresses the call issued by Lessing and Williams. And in foregrounding the problems of community and social connection in his work, he takes up the task of reconstruction fiction.

Like the Smithsons, MacInnes valued the direct expression of life in British culture. Moreover, he explicitly singled out architecture as an antidote to what he described as his "sociological hunger," his desire to know and represent "the real England."[55] In a 1960 essay on the prolific architectural critic and historian Nikolaus Pevsner, whose best-selling, multivolume series *The Buildings of England* remains in print today, MacInnes praises Pevsner's architectural writings in this regard. For MacInnes, the built environment communicated English reality—its history and its visions for the future—in a way that these other media might not always have been able to achieve:

> A paradox, among so many, in our society, seems to me to be the extreme difficulty, among the welter of informational media, of finding exactly what is going on: what England really *is*, and the lives of those therein. Films and TV tell nothing, radio very little, newspapers rare snippets, and plays and novels and social studies much, much less than they could. For any who may be likewise wracked by the pangs of a sociological hunger, Dr. Pevsner offers a very rich fare indeed.[56]

One way of reading MacInnes's London trilogy, then, is in light of this stated dissatisfaction with the contemporary media landscape as it relates to "what England really *is*." Given his appreciation for the role that architecture and architectural discourse plays in countering this dissatisfaction, it makes sense to read his novelistic representation of architecture and geography as invested with special realist purpose. But beyond this thematic link, this appreciation invites a reading of MacInnes's realism as emulating and suggesting architectural realities, formally presenting a newly constructed way of inhabiting modern, postwar Britain. All three of the trilogy novels do this to an extent

---

53. Lessing, "Small Personal Voice," 16.
54. Williams, *Long Revolution*, 312.
55. MacInnes, "Englishness of Dr Pevsner," 125.
56. MacInnes, "Englishness of Dr. Pevsner," 125.

because they provide the perspectives and stories of various kinds of "beginners": newly arrived Nigerian immigrant, freshly minted civil servant, a teenager, a man learning the ropes of the prostitution racket as a first-time ponce, a cop just promoted to the vice squad learning about prostitution from the other side of the legal divide. From their novel positions, these characters bring meaning to their respective environments in fresh ways that have the power to disrupt conventional (most likely middle-class) perceptions of those marginalized, peripheral zones of London's landscape. In what follows, I take *Absolute Beginners* as a main case study because its narration by a teenager offers the most directly suggestive link with the spirit of contemporaneous architectural innovation. Of the three novels, moreover, the second installment is the most formally experimental, emphasizing the expansive potential of the postwar realist mode.

ABSOLUTE BEGINNERS: REAL BRITAIN ON THE MOVE

Absolute Beginners defies easy generic categorization. Contemporaneous critics described it and MacInnes's other London fiction as "documentary novels," but he resisted this label. Instead, he categorized his work as poetic realism: "I would thus describe *City of Spades* or *Absolute Beginners*—no doubt—flatteringly—as poetic evocations of a human situation, with undertones of social criticism of it."[57] Like the rapidly changing, highly mobile city it depicts, *Absolute Beginners* eschews structural and stylistic boundaries wherever possible, demanding that readers be open to the novel's spontaneous, formally adaptable quality. Superficially, it is a coming-of-age novel about an unnamed photographer, the narrator, on the cusp of adulthood in the last year of the 1950s, but it follows few conventions of the traditional *bildungsroman*. Like a Smithsons-inspired snaking network of connected housing units, it strings together a series of largely disconnected episodes for our narrator/protagonist that flow organically and realistically, although not always smoothly, from one to the next.[58] Instead of relying on the conventions of either the marriage-and-family plot that defined most kitchen sink realism of the period or those of the modernist one-day city novel, MacInnes divides the novel into four chapters

---

57. MacInnes, "Sharp Schmutter," 147.

58. MacInnes employs a similarly episodic structure in *City of Spades* (1957) and *Mr. Love and Justice* (1960), but these two novels are more plot-driven as they move back and forth between stories narrated by (*Spades*) or focused on (*Love*) two characters whose lives become increasingly intertwined. The single first-person narrator of *Absolute Beginners* allows for an altogether more meandering text.

simply titled June, July, August, and September. Its pages are bursting at the seams with sociological detail, giving it an ethnographic quality. References to cinema, popular music, and fashion abound. The reader is swept along for the ride and expected to keep pace with trendy vernacular, such as "dig," "cats," and "telly," and with sometimes unwieldy, chatty sentences instead of polished, careful syntax (*Absolute Beginners,* 54, 188, 188). Its attention to real places and commentary on real events—most notably the Notting Hill race riots, which conclude the novel—also make it journalistic. A review in the *New Musical Express* (notably *not* a literary periodical) aptly makes the book sound more like a game than anything else: "Reads like a pinball machine ricocheting towards TILT, with no chance of replay" (*Absolute Beginners,* frontispiece). Novel, ethnography, news source, entertainment: *Absolute Beginners* is a book defined by generic mobility, interrupting and redirecting narrative expectations as it seeks to poetically represent real conditions.

The hybrid, almost improvised structure of the novel allows MacInnes to track both a celebratory as well as exhausted experience of the heightened mobility of late 1950s London life. Pacing is breathless as the narrative moves briskly with colloquial language from scene to scene, rarely dwelling in character interiority, although often featuring the narrator's impassioned views on all matter of topics, from fashion to music to politics. The shift, often jarring, from enjoyment to exhaustion and disorientation, is captured well in a sequence in which the narrator is discussing pop music in a club. Suddenly, without transition, he is lost on the side of a road, his scooter out of gas. "Quite honestly," he remarks, mirroring the reader's likely response, "I don't know quite what happened then, because my next quite clear recollection was batting along a highway on my Vespa, which went on for miles and miles, I don't know where, until the petrol ran out, it stopped, and I was nowhere" (*Absolute Beginners,* 125). Mobility, for this character, enables social connections, self-expression, and opportunities for new cultural experiences, but it also has the potential to take over, to interrupt those aspects of his life and his first-person narration with a disorienting, and potentially dehumanizing, assertion of mobility for the sake of mobility. By the final chapter, in the wake of the Notting Hill race riots, the novel has, in effect, run out of gas. MacInnes has taken the realist form as far as it will go.

By representing fast-paced London life and characters' constant movement through its buildings, streets, and neighborhoods, *Absolute Beginners* represents the promises and the limitations of the new conditions of mobility in Britain at the turn of the 1960s. The omnipresence of mobility is apparent from the very opening scene. From the rooftop of a department store where the narrator is shopping for new records, he observes newly constructed tower blocks as the transparent backdrop to a postindustrial urban landscape in which the boundaries between home, industry, travel, infrastructure, and entertainment are fluid: "I stood beside big new high blocks of glass-built flats, like an X-ray of a stack of buildings with their skins peeled off, and watched the traffic floating down the Thames below them, very slow and sure (chug, chug) and oily, underneath the electric railway bridge (rattle, rattle), and past the power-station like a super-cinema with funnels stuck on it" (*Absolute Beginners*, 39). The mobility of the architecturally transforming city and its new hip music culture permeates the narrator's visual perceptions and expresses itself through the style of his narration. Punctuated by percussive "chugs" and "rattles," the sentence sounds like a line of jazz with a lively rhythm section. In this modernizing urban setting, the narrator takes pleasure in the widespread mobility of the environment and its effects. This relationship with the postwar city is strikingly different from the relationship between Angry characters and their environments, one defined by opposition, constraint, and conflict.

As the opening scene portends, mobility is rarely a problem and almost always a virtue for the narrator. It is the thing that gives him a sense of freedom. This mobile freedom is reiterated in a basic literary sense by the fact that he is a nameless character who can reconstruct his identity and lifestyle at will. Although we do meet his parents and brother—a working-class family that runs a boardinghouse inhabited mainly by immigrants from Cyprus (a highly mobile, if not modern, domestic space in its own right)—his characterization derives mainly from the spaces he chooses to inhabit, frequent, and move through, as well as his social and cultural commentary on city life. Rather than working in a factory or on a building site, he takes advantage of his unfettered teenager status to make money when he can as a freelance photographer who dabbles in advertising and pornography to get by. He and his friends specialize in the mobile and temporary: the circulation of information, people, and trends. They are journalists, hustlers, prostitutes, pimps, gossips, bisexuals, freelancers. They gather and dance at jazz clubs, where the narrator demonstrates to readers his up-to-the-moment knowledge of fashion and subculture styles. He carefully outlines the differences between various subcultures—the mods, trads, Teds, spivs, and so on—down to the details of fabric, cut, and hair partings (*Absolute Beginners*, 60–61). The brisk circulation and proliferation of multiple styles and media that characterizes the narrator's life on every front is represented as a source of stimulation, joy, and liberation.

The connection between freedom and the ephemeral or mobile is most apparent in how the narrator presents his neighborhood and living situation. As a kind of urban version of Pevsner's more rurally oriented *Buildings of*

England series, *Absolute Beginners* invites readers to become acquainted with a "real," gritty London neighborhood of Notting Dale (which he nicknames "Napoli"), a historically working-class area of West London that became home to a significant number of Spanish Civil War refugees in the 1930s and Caribbean emigrants after the 1948 Nationality Act.[59] Wandering through a city neighborhood, the narrator easily could be characterized as a *flâneur*, that quintessential modernist figure. But his guided tour through Napoli is notably realist, and in fact, MacInnes explicitly distances his version of urban rambling from modernist predecessors when he ironically revises one of Virginia Woolf's celebratory lines from *Mrs. Dalloway*. Woolf's narrator muses, "in the triumph and the jingle and the strange high singing of some aeroplane overhead was what she [Clarissa] loved; life; London; this moment of June."[60] In MacInnes's revision, the narrator describes an "absolutely fabulous June day, such as only that old whore London can throw up, though very occasionally" (*Absolute Beginners*, 13). Woolf's lyrical high modernist contemplation of mobilized city life is transformed in *Absolute Beginners* into a roughly hewn, spirited openness to whatever presents itself. As the narrator makes his way through the neighborhood, he is not deeply contemplating the self or the historical or mythical meanings of the city around him, nor is he displaying the workings of his consciousness or memory, as his metropolitan modernist counterparts such as Clarissa Dalloway did.

Instead, in the realist tradition of reconstruction fiction, he is attuned to the visual surface of things. He maps out for the reader key local landmarks that define the neighborhood: the Harrow Road, Grand Union Canal, a mainline rail station, a hospital, gas-works, Kensal Green cemetery, Wormwood Scrubs park, a prison, a sports arena, and "the new telly barracks of the BBC" (*Absolute Beginners*, 44). The space is not romanticized, beautiful, awe inspiring, or nostalgia inducing; nor is it stigmatized as a site of moral or psychological corruption. Rather, it is rendered straightforwardly, often with pleasure, as a surprisingly seductive urban maze with "escape routes" that "cut across

---

59. The voice of the tour guide had become an increasingly familiar postwar sound through radio and television travel programs. Brian Vesey-Fitzgerald's "There and Back" and "Let's Go," for example, became popular BBC Third Programme installments by the late 1940s. In the 1950s, cultural critics like Nikolaus Pevsner, John Summerson, and John Betjeman frequently took audiences to country houses in their writings and broadcasts, and Pevsner published a widely read forty-six-volume county-by-county work of architectural history, *The Buildings of England*, which MacInnes admired in his essay, "The Englishness of Dr. Pevsner." *Absolute Beginners* is a kind of racy urban rejoinder to the preservationist tour guide voices that focused on the English countryside as a middle-class escapist retreat. See chapter 4 for a thorough treatment of this context.

60. Woolf, *Mrs. Dalloway*, 4.

one another at different points, making crazy little islands of slum habitation shut off from the world by concrete precipices, and linked by metal bridges" (*Absolute Beginners*, 44). Like the Smithsons, MacInnes seems to appreciate that London resists the ultra-modernist grid and is instead experienced most organically as a meandering network of anachronistic but vital relics. The houses in the narrator's neighborhood escaped bombing damage during the war but have also been overlooked by slum clearance programs. They are "old Victorian lower-middle tumble-down, built I dare say for grocers and bank clerks and horse-omnibus inspectors who've died and gone and their descendants evacuated to the outer suburbs, but these houses live on like shells, and there's only one thing to do with them, absolutely one, which is to pull them down till not a one's left standing up" (*Absolute Beginners*, 44).

The narrator's direct, unfiltered commentary on London might seem like an obvious avenue for middle-class social critique in the spirit of Orwell's *The Road to Wigan Pier* (1937), but MacInnes takes a different path. The narrator delivers a scathing critique of the proliferation of middle-class "Houses": "Victorian bourgeois palaces that have been made over into flatlets for the new spiv intellectual lot" and renamed with titles such as "Serpentine House," "this 'House' thing being the new way of describing any dump the landlords want to make a fast fiver out of" (*Absolute Beginners*, 86). In contrast with this middle-class brand of renovation, the narrator values the freedom of Napoli. Despite his clear-eyed perception of neglect and poverty, his case for demolition, and his description of the neighborhood as the "residential doss-house of our city," he remarks that "however horrible the area is, you're *free* there!" (*Absolute Beginners*, 45, 46). In the same spirit as the New Brutalist architects, MacInnes's novel celebrates the "rough poetry" that can be dragged from everyday forces at work, and this poetry comes from the freedom to move at will. Freedom, the novel suggests, resides in spaces that facilitate improvised and organic circulation, rather than overly structured or predetermined systems. In this sense, it rejects the thoroughly planned environments proposed in the first decade of postwar reconstruction and instead puts its faith in the citizens who make their way without the benefits of government intervention.

Mobility and improvisation characterize the narrator's personal space, which rejects the picturesque that had so dominated British ideas about design and architecture in the first postwar decade. Instead, he has created a kind of anti-shrine to consumer culture. The one-room flat at the top of his building of converted flats has minimal furniture and decoration, only one chair and several cushions spread out on the floor. No curtains hang in the windows. Thus, although he lives in a dilapidated building, his own flat has a modern sensibility that prioritizes mobility; there is room to move, and sightlines are open within the flat as well as out into the city. He reinforces the mobility by regularly culling his pop cultural belongings: "The only other objects are my record-player, my pocket transistor radio, and stacks of discs and books that I've collected, hundreds of them, which every New Year's Day I have a pogrom of, and sling out everything except a very chosen few" (*Absolute Beginners*, 48–49). This new kind of object world is defined not by preservation and identification, as elaborated in townscape theory, but by circulation, visibility, and easy disposal. For the narrator and the other inhabitants of his building, this object world reflects their social and economic transience. They do not—or, in the case of recent immigrants, cannot—identify with a traditionally English sense of place.

Spontaneous interaction with others characterizes the building as a whole: "The tenants come and go," and there are "regular squatters" (*Absolute Beginners*, 46). The narrator takes the reader through the building with descriptions of several tenants that demonstrate his dual vision of fluid social identities and architectural boundaries. On the floor below him, the Fabulous Hoplite, a fashionable gay man, serves as an unofficial contact for gossip columnists. Meanwhile, the black Mr. Cool inhabits the first floor, and Big Jill, a "Les ponce" (lesbian pimp) lives in a basement room (*Absolute Beginners*, 47–48). In a utopian vein, this diverse cast of characters moves freely in and out of each other's rooms and throughout the building, with little attention in the narration given to socioeconomic struggle or prohibitive differences. Although in a building that needs reconstruction, MacInnes's Napoli flats recall the Smithson's Golden Lane vision for streets in the sky: a celebration of improvised circulation and community. A similar, but less optimistically rendered building, actually a boardinghouse, features in Lynne Reid-Banks's *The L-Shaped Room* (1961), a novel which follows the journey of Jane, a single, pregnant young woman whose parents have thrown her out of their middle-class home. Jane's new housing in Fulham is described as "one of those gone-to-seed houses . . . all dark-brown wallpaper inside and peeling paint outside. . . . There were a couple of prostitutes in the basement; the landlady had been quite open about them. She'd pointed out that there was even an advantage to having them there—namely, that nobody asked questions about anybody."[61] In this case, unlike in MacInnes's novel, the protagonist's improvised living conditions are a sign of downward mobility, which she associates with her feelings of sexual and moral shame. By the end of the novel, she has overcome those feelings and emerged an independent single mother, but to go along with this development, not only has she left behind the sordid southwest London boardinghouse; she has repaired relations with her parents and been offered

---

61. Banks, *The L-Shaped Room*, 1.

an inherited family cottage. By comparison, the gleeful optimism expressed by MacInnes's narrator is remarkable for refusing to adhere to the middle-class supposition that a run-down neighborhood or building equates to moral degeneracy and shame.

Of course, it is possible to read MacInnes's representation of this community and this space not as socially radical but as fetishized, particularly when considering the London trilogy in its entirety. Indeed, Ed Vulliamy has articulated this reading in returning to his own, contrasting memories of life in 1950s Notting Hill as well as in reaching out to those who knew MacInnes. Vulliamy's account centers on MacInnes's sexuality and posits that the London trilogy is more an artifact of MacInnes's sexualized idolization of black men—and therefore a basically racist representation—than it is an open-minded realist exploration.[62] *City of Spades* (1957) most directly supports Vulliamy's characterization of MacInnes's writing, with its dual narration split between the white, upper-class Montgomery Pew and the black Nigerian Johnny Fortune. That novel, the first in the trilogy, presents Pew and his ethnographically inclined friend Theodora as obsessively interested in the lives of African and Caribbean men. Indeed, Theodora claims to fall in love with Johnny, and she gets pregnant as a result of their involvement. Montgomery's concern for Johnny's well-being is written straight, meant to be taken as sincere affection. When the two are getting acquainted, the following exchange takes place: Montgomery admits,

> "I know nothing about you all, Johnny, but I like your people..."
> "We never trust a man who tells us that."
> "Oh, no? No?"
> "We know in five seconds if you like us without you say so. Those who *say* they like us most usually do not."...
> "Well, even if I musn't say I like you, I *do*."[63]

Not long after this exchange, the police arrive, and another immigrant character encourages Johnny to stash any weed he might have in "that white man's pocket," but Johnny rejects the idea, saying, "No, he's my friend, I think."[64]

MacInnes represents Theodora's interest in Johnny, however, with a satirical edge: she works for the BBC, and MacInnes is clearly sending up the efforts of such institutions and their audiences to equate ethnography with a social good, as Theodora's interests are revealed to be smoke screens for infatuation

---

62. Vulliamy, "Absolute MacInnes," n.p.
63. MacInnes, *City of Spades*, 76.
64. MacInnes, 77.

that is decidedly fetishistic. Upon first meeting Theodora, Johnny describes how she "examined me as if I was a zoological exhibit" before explaining in her clinically intellectual way that she plans to host a radio show that features colonial immigrants discussing their experiences as new arrivals.[65] Throughout the narrative, she is represented in an exaggerated way as only being capable of perceiving Johnny in frankly dehumanizing anthropological ways, and Johnny can always see right through her behavior. When her affections for Johnny are not reciprocated beyond the sexual, she concludes in a letter to Montgomery "that love, or even friendship, for those people is *impossible*—I mean as we understand it. . . . It's when you see that distant look that sometimes comes into their opaque brown eyes that you realise it—that moment when they suddenly depart irrevocably within themselves far off towards some hidden, alien, secretive, quite untouchable horizon."[66] That Montgomery, a civil servant who comes from the same class and culture as Theodora, escapes this same satirical fate easily could be read as a blind spot on MacInnes's part or, indeed, as a sign of misogyny that indirectly pervades not only this novel but the trilogy as a whole—another flaw in MacInnes's fictional London that the narrator of *Absolute Beginners* does not perceive even as he interacts with prostitutes and ponces and convinces his girlfriend to pose for pornographic photographs. Women in these novels have voracious sexual appetites and, in the first and third installments, always get pregnant in inconvenient circumstances, thereby physically manifesting the sexual activity that the men would prefer to keep secret for social or legal reasons. If these men are arrested (Johnny in *Spades*, Frankie in *Mr. Love and Justice* [1960]), forced to choose between their careers and relationships (Edward in *Mr. Love and Justice*), or left no choice but to leave Britain altogether (Johnny in *Spades*), then narratively, it is the women who are finally to blame. On the whole, MacInnes's representation of women and black men across the trilogy is a reminder that the utopian freedom experienced by the narrator throughout most of *Absolute Beginners* should be read as hopeful but ultimately limited by constraints that MacInnes represents both directly and indirectly.

In a more direct vein, in the final "September" chapter of the novel, the easygoing freedoms and nonconformities that the narrator associates with mobility are challenged when the Notting Hill race riots erupt. White nationalists and "Ted" thugs assert their power and ability to move unquestioned through areas of West London, forcing immigrant residents into their homes under threat of violence. The narrator describes the scene in his neighbor-

---

65. MacInnes, 125.
66. MacInnes, 330.

hood just before the riots break out with special attention to the lack of life-affirming free movement that he so values: "There in Napoli, you could feel a *hole*: as if some kind of life was draining out of it, leaving a sort of vacuum in the streets and terraces" (*Absolute Beginners*, 172). The violence and the authorities' efforts to keep the news from spreading outside the neighborhood is so disheartening to the narrator that he ultimately claims to lose faith in Britain. His solution is to embrace yet another modern form of mobility that promises freedom. As he heads to Heathrow Airport with plans to flee to Brazil, he claims with his characteristic optimism that "everyone [is] equal in the sky dominion of fast air-travel." (42). Were he to actually get on a plane leaving Britain at the end, the novel would offer a very different meaning; it would suggest that this is a story of a teenager who ultimately fails to take responsibility for his own life as a British citizen; mobility would be a dehumanizing force. Instead, the novel ends with the narrator greeting a newly arrived group of African immigrants descending from a plane. Although it isn't stated explicitly that his faith has been restored, he leaves the queue for his flight in order to welcome them: "Welcome to London! Greetings from England! Meet your first teenager! We're all going up to Napoli to have a ball!" (201). The novel ends with one of the passengers taking his arm and shouting "Greetings!" in return, and then "they all burst out laughing in the storm" (201). With this ending, MacInnes's novel remains open to the possibility that mobility in all its variations can continue to foster freedom and social connection, but it does not provide a false sense of stability. The fallout from the race riots is only just beginning, and it is uncertain what the narrator will do with his life next.[67]

Up until the final chapter, *Absolute Beginners* is mainly a celebratory sociological study of contemporary urban youth and immigrant cultures in which politics has little place. The narrator's older half-brother, Vernon, even complains that the narrator is "a traitor to the working class" with "no social conscience" because he freelances instead of taking a steady job; he does not seem to appreciate that the Welfare State, with its promise of full employment, was created for his own benefit (*Absolute Beginners*, 35). In this respect, the narrator seems to represent what MacInnes observed in general at the time. In a 1960 article for *Encounter* magazine, he wrote, "In contrast with the earlier generation (say, now aged 23–35) that was emancipated by the Welfare state

---

[67]. Ed Vulliamy reads this closing scene as another example of MacInnes's fetishization of black men, as the narrator describes the newly arrived immigrants as "grinning and chattering" and ready for physical affection ("Absolute MacInnes"). This interpretation is certainly defensible, but it doesn't detract from my reading of the ending as essentially ambivalent as a social commentary.

and who, in spite of economic gains, still seem almost ferociously obsessed by class, the kids don't seem to care about it at all."[68] But the fact is that the novel ultimately takes on the most serious social and political conflicts of its moment, abruptly turning from the seemingly superfluous, if entertaining, concerns of its previous chapters. The narrator's social and political awakening at the novel's end is not an embrace of working-class politics, which might align MacInnes more with the Angry Young Men. Instead, it is a commitment to defending multicultural equality by educating the public about social realities. What upsets him most about the riots is that the violence is ghettoized, and that outside "Napoli" everything is going on as normal, shielded from the truth. When he leaves his flat armed, not incidentally, with a flashlight for self-protection, his main goal is to spread the news, to bring the realities of racism and violent injustice to light. Where the narrator is limited in his ability to stop the violence, however, the novel itself, as a realistic representation of the riots, amounts to a powerful call to attention for contemporaneous readers and a bold counteraction against the abusive unhindered mobility of the white nationalists. Most strikingly, then, this novel demonstrates that even the most reputedly apathetic, apolitical citizens of the late 1950s—teenagers—have the potential to awaken and become socially engaged. Unlike other literature of this period that focuses on the lives of young people, MacInnes's novel breaks through the stiflingly silent official response to racial violence and radically bears witness.

This radical realist representation was fleshed out in MacInnes's other writings, in which he claimed that teenagers had the potential to be more than just consumers; they could be a driving force for social change. In several essays in the late 1950s, MacInnes issues warnings to adults to pay attention to teenagers. "The 'two nations' of our society," he writes in 1958 with a deliberate invocation of Benjamin Disraeli,

> may perhaps no longer be those of the "rich" and "poor" (or, to use old-fashioned terms, the "upper" and "working" classes), but those of the teenagers on the one hand and, on the other, all those who have assumed the burdens of adult responsibility. Indeed, the great social revolution of the past fifteen years may not be the one which re-divided wealth among the adults in the Welfare State, but the one that's given teenagers economic power. This piece is about the pop disc industry—almost entirely their own creation; but what about the new clothing industry for making and selling teenage

---

68. MacInnes, "Pop Songs and Teenagers," 56.

garments of both sexes? Or the motor scooter industry they patronize so generously? Or the radiogram and television industries? Or the eating and soft-drinking places that cater so largely for them?[69]

In this essay, MacInnes characterizes teenagers as a "new classless class" with an unconsciously international sensibility."[70] Their wealth, combined with an indifferent attitude toward adults and issues that earlier generations in Britain invested with importance—class, history, the threat of nuclear warfare—lead MacInnes to argue that generational difference, rather than class difference, has the potential to generate historical change.

In his discussion of youth and popular culture in *Absolute Beginners,* John McLeod argues,

> MacInnes creates a narrator who enshrines his optimistic and progressive vision of youthful London, but for the primary purpose of critique. In looking at London through his narrator's eyes, MacInnes attempts not only to explore critically the political shortcomings of new forms of popular culture nurtured by young people at the time, but also to examine at arm's length his idealistic and problematic visions of London which the [1958 Notting Hill Gate] riots had dramatically threatened.[71]

McLeod's argument works against Sinfield's contention that MacInnes "was virtually the only established writer to celebrate youth culture and try to develop its subversive potential."[72] Indeed, MacInnes's essays on popular culture, teenagers, and the novel, as well as *Absolute Beginners,* indicate that youth culture *does* have a revolutionary social potential in his vision, and that this cultural movement should be documented and disseminated in order to break up the stagnant and uninformative adult cultural enterprises—including the novel. Although undoubtedly leftist, the revolutionary potential that MacInnes invests in youth culture is not about a specific political agenda or even an appeal to a universal liberal humanism. As Sinfield points out, "the humane values" of *Absolute Beginners* "are not tied back . . . into the humanism of the classics, but depend upon the absoluteness of the beginners."[73] As I noted above, all three novels in the London trilogy focus on "beginners" of

---

69. MacInnes, 54.
70. MacInnes, 47.
71. McLeod, *Postcolonial London,* 50.
72. Sinfield, *Literature, Politics, and Culture,* 169.
73. Sinfield, 171.

various kinds. All of these beginning character roles have the added effect of creating an opportunity to situate readers as beginners in learning about a part of British life that they most likely previously knew nothing about. In its desire to begin from a clean slate, MacInnes's vision has more in common with the work of the New Brutalist architects than with many of his contemporary novelists. His characters are revolutionary because their stories demand and create a Britain in which everyone is free to move at will across previously prohibitive boundaries.

MacInnes's analysis of teenagers supports his broader vision of an inclusive globalized culture. In a 1957 essay for *Encounter*, "Young England, Half English," he discusses the impact of American culture, especially popular music, on English teenagers: "Potently diffused by the cinema, radio, the gramophone and now TV," American music encouraged English teenagers to identify more with an international youth culture than with any particular set of English cultural attributes.[74] For MacInnes, this shift in identification is a sign of inevitable postwar denationalization: "If a people—like the English—sings about another people—the Americans—then this may be a sign that it is ceasing to be a people in any real sense at all. Perhaps this is happening: perhaps it has to."[75] As *Absolute Beginners*, and also *City of Spades*, suggest, the loosening sense of Englishness experienced by young people created an opportunity for new relations and identifications with the waves of African and Caribbean immigrants arriving in England in the 1950s. Gail Low observes that, in the 1950s, immigrants were prevented from fully assimilating into the dominant English community that continued to value the nuclear family and the private individual: "Discourses of Englishness insisted on the privacy of the national character; its recurrent pattern of symbolism centred on domestic and familial life. Immigrants, in contrast, were characterized precisely by their 'domestic barbarism' and 'incapacity for domestic and familial life.'"[76] As MacInnes's narrators mix with immigrants in the fluid architectural spaces and linguistic registers of his novels, they challenge an inflexible sense of Englishness based on the stability of individual identity, families, and their houses, while also demonstrating the immigrants' capacity to create resilient, even thriving, domestic communities.

---

74. MacInnes, "Young England, Half English," 14.
75. MacInnes, 15.
76. Low, "Streets, Rooms and Residents," 160.

CONCLUSION: MOBILE REALISM AT ITS LIMIT

As a response to the growing number of postwar intellectuals in Britain who claimed to find no valid reason to devote time to reading novels, MacInnes developed a critique and defense of the novel in a long essay published in 1975, titled *No Novel Reader*. He argues therein that the nature and social function of the novel had changed since the nineteenth century. Although he is skeptical about the potential for the novel to singlehandedly create large-scale social transformation, he believes that the form is redeemable and important because it has an informative function. "If the 'great novel' is not . . . characteristic of our fragmented, rapidly changing society," he contends, "what novelists do offer is a far more informed and accurate picture of particular aspects of our lives" than other media.[77] For MacInnes, the "informed and accurate picture" he valued in novels translated specifically to a realism that confronted the social opportunities and injustices of contemporary British life. Accordingly, he indicts those members of the educated white middle class who believe the novel is escapist and has nothing meaningful to contribute to intellectual life: "In shutting themselves off from the novel, its denigrators are also turning against much unknown human experience, and the classes and races to which the novel increasingly belongs."[78] Running parallel to new ways of envisioning the built environment, his argument about the novel is one that values precise, geographically detailed social information and that ultimately promotes inclusiveness.

Both MacInnes and the New Brutalist architects pushed their art forms to the limit of conventional realist and modernist aesthetic categories in order to accommodate and critique the transformations defining Britain as it moved into its second decade of postwar reconstruction. They stand out as hopeful, optimistic interventions that nevertheless take a clear-eyed view of present fluctuating and challenging conditions, expressing mobility without allowing it to be an end in itself. In this sense, they seem to take up the call posed by a recent immigrant in Sam Selvon's story "My Girl and the City": "One must *build* on the things that happen: it is insufficient to say I sat in the underground and the train hurtled through the darkness."[79] MacInnes and the New Brutalists confronted the real "things that happen" and built a socially attentive vision accordingly. The legacy of later disrepair and neglect has often

---

77. MacInnes, *No Novel Reader*, 52.
78. MacInnes, 43–44.
79. Selvon, "My Girl and the City," 176; emphasis added.

overshadowed these instances of late 1950s optimism, but their recovery is essential to creating a more nuanced story of postwar reconstruction fiction and its realist impulses.[80]

---

80. In *The Ministry of Nostalgia*, Owen Hatherley argues that the public modernism epitomized by New Brutalist mass housing projects has recently been "rescued" from the narrative of neglect and decline and redeployed as part of a contemporary "austerity nostalgia." In Hatherley's view, the boom in consumer goods featuring various modernist buildings from the 1930s to the 1960s alongside the repurposing of the actual buildings for an affluent class of homeowners manage "to precisely reverse the original modernist ethos" (29). Writing with a polemical eye toward the sociopolitical challenges facing Britain in 2015, he concludes his study with the claim, "In Britain today we are living through exactly the kind of housing crisis for which council housing was invented in the first place, at exactly the same time as we're alternately fetishising and privatising its remnants" (197).

CHAPTER 4

Country Houses

Nostalgia and the Realist Challenge

O N A SUMMER AFTERNOON, I stood in the long portrait gallery at Knole, a National Trust country house in Kent that has been in the Sackville-West family since 1566. Having made my way through several of the thirteen staterooms laid out in seventeenth-century décor, I paused at the window to look out over the 1,000-acre deer park surrounding the house. The serenity of the view was suddenly disturbed by a figure exiting through one of the wings not open to visitors. He was dressed in a bathrobe and a pair of Wellington boots. My imagination reeled as I tried to map out this character as a genuine aristocrat in the age of *Downton Abbey*. I felt mildly giddy at this apparent glimpse of "real" life that had seeped from the house and blurred the seemingly well-manicured National Trust line between house and museum. Knole as Trust museum would never give me access to Knole as postwar property—a prohibition that only intensified my desire to know what that latter version of the house was really like. Postwar Knole is the version of the house that caused James Lees-Milne, in 1946, to feel "horrified by piles of dust under the chairs from worm borings. The gesso furniture [was] in a terrible state. All the picture labels [wanted] renewing; the silver cleaning; the window mullions mending."[1] It is also the house in which, "the public

---

1. Lees-Milne, *Some Country Houses and Their Owners*, 40.

[amused] themselves by carving their names on the oak door of the gatehouse on days when they [were] not admitted to the state rooms."[2]

Would visitors pay to see heirlooms covered in dust and windows smashed from wartime damage? My secret aristocratic sighting reinforced my scholarly desire to access the historical experience that the National Trust conceals, including—perhaps especially—the damaged postwar house. The experience revealed a voyeuristic fantasy at the heart of the country house museum that simultaneously accepts and rejects the legacy of the British class system. As country houses transform from houses into museums, with their velvet ropes and souvenir guidebooks, visual evidence of the lived-in house of both past and present is withheld selectively to perpetuate desires that structure the dominant cultural understanding of class hierarchy and its historical significance. These once-private homes become hybrid structures in which public narratives assert themselves in order to mask and mystify the private lives that often still exist somewhere behind the scenes.

Novels by Elizabeth Taylor and Elizabeth Bowen interrogate this merger between public and private narratives tied to postwar country houses. Taylor's 1957 novel, *Angel*,[3] reinforces the middle-class investment in the country house genre while questioning the meaning of such an investment. *Angel* refers back to nineteenth-century country house novels such as *Mansfield Park* (1814) and *Jane Eyre* (1847) that are not interested mainly in the aristocratic owners of houses but in the middle- or lower-class characters like Fanny Price and Jane, who dream of upward social mobility as symbolized by the great estates they come to inhabit. This lineage of the modern country house novel emphasizes middle-class fantasies of marriage and romance over and above the point of view of an upper-class owner. Taylor's work of realistic historical fiction reveals the ambivalence of these middle-class fantasies as well as the goal of literary celebrity in the postwar context. Elizabeth Bowen's penultimate novel, *The Little Girls* (1963),[4] which follows the 1959 sale and demolition of her family estate in Ireland, dramatizes the severed link between past and present after World War II, particularly for formerly landed members of the Anglo-Irish Ascendancy. *The Little Girls* reconfigures the relationship between past and present by representing an absent heritage and the thwarted attempt to act in the present with imagined posterity as the driving ethical force.

In their novels informed by realist commitments, Taylor and Bowen reject the distortions of nostalgia even as they take the past as their subject. Taylor does so through the ambivalent portrayal of a foolishly romantic lower-

---

2. Lees-Milne, 41.
3. References to Taylor's *Angel* will use in-text citations.
4. References to Bowen's *The Little Girls* will use in-text citations.

middle-class novelist whose popular success allows her to buy a country house that, in turn, becomes a prison and mausoleum rather than a means of liberation and source of liveliness. Bowen rejects nostalgia by denying the presence of the house as a symbol and by using a fragmented, porous style that makes the false wholeness of nostalgic representations impossible. This style, while more aesthetically experimental than typical realist prose, should still be understood as a manifestation of Bowen's broad commitment to realistic representation. As my analysis will demonstrate, the fragmented structure and contorted syntax create an attentive representation of physical environments and social relations, both past and present, as opposed to a more conventionally modernist approach that deploys fragmentation to render fractured perception, consciousness, or subjectivity. In their portrayals of the past and its implications, these novels offer a way to approach postwar country houses and heritage culture that departs from interpretations that emphasize a romantic yearning for national glory in drab, post-imperial Britain. *Brideshead Revisited* (1945) is, understandably, a default example for such interpretations put forth by literary critics, cultural historians, and architectural historians alike.[5] The scholarly and commercial popularity of narratives like Kazuo Ishiguro's *The Remains of the Day* (1988), Ian McEwan's *Atonement* (2001), and the ITV television series *Downtown Abbey* (2010–15) further indicates the dominant appetite for nostalgia when it comes to country houses in the later twentieth and twenty-first centuries.[6]

Focusing on Taylor and Bowen allows me to show how the critical preoccupation with nostalgia has obscured other culturally significant facets of the postwar country house and its modes of representation. Nostalgia flattens history by projecting a present-tense desire for wholeness onto the past, thereby obscuring the complexities of what really happened. For Susan Stewart, nostalgia is incompatible with real conditions. Nostalgia, she argues, "does not take part in lived experience. Rather, it remains behind and before that experience."[7] Critical approaches to literature that aim to locate and dismantle nostalgia at all costs ironically risk duplicating the very historical flattening

---

5. See, for example: Richard Gill, *Happy Rural Seat: The English Country House and the Literary Imagination*; Simon Joyce, *The Victorians in the Rearview Mirror*; David Littlejohn, *The Fate of the English Country House*; John J. Su, *Ethics and Nostalgia in the Contemporary Novel*; Kevin Walsh, *The Representation of the Past: Museums and Heritage in the Post-modern World*.

6. Owen Hatherley's *The Ministry of Nostalgia* frames cultural examples such as *Downton Abbey* as part of what he terms "Austerity Nostalgia," implying that contemporary political narratives and consumer culture (in 2015) depend on an appealingly nostalgic, yet completely mystified, representation of working-class docility and obedience in the face of tough times.

7. Stewart, *On Longing*, 23.

that they seek to critique. In an effort to understand both the past and its texts in a more nuanced way, I avoid a totalizing emphasis on nostalgia and instead try to establish a relationship between specific qualities of texts and the historical specificities of reconstruction culture that affected the rural landscape, especially the repurposing of country houses as public museums. Through this approach, I argue that Bowen and Taylor intervene in the unfolding lineage of country house novels with narratives that critique an overinvestment in the selective, partial narratives reinforced through heritage culture.[8]

THE MID-CENTURY MUSEUM: NATIONAL NARRATIVES OF EVACUATION AND RECONSTRUCTION

The physical destructiveness of World War II threatened the secular sanctity of the modern public museum. During the blitz, major collections, including those from the British Museum, the National Gallery, the Victoria and Albert Museum, and the National Maritime Museum, were evacuated to the country, often to aristocratic estates. Public museum space was thus markedly empty during the war. As country houses became temporary museums, museums became multipurpose spaces whose sudden emptiness existed uneasily alongside the wartime housing crisis. In the case of the National Maritime Museum, much of the space was occupied by the Admiralty throughout the war, an ironic requisition that closed the gap between actual naval history and its ordered, narrative presentation within the confines of the museum. That gap was also challenged by requests that conceived of the museum as a storage facility for "bombed out" furniture belonging to blitz victims or mobilized soldiers—the inverse of the country house acting as storage facility for bombed out art and artifacts. On April 17, 1943, the director of the National Maritime Museum, Geoffrey Callendar, learned of one such request in an update from Reginald Lowen:

---

8. A number of literary and cultural critics since the late 1990s have investigated the intersection of modern literature and museums and heritage. Most do so by focusing on literary texts that feature museums, collections, visual art, or thematic attention to beauty. See, for example, Barbara J. Black's *On Exhibit: Victorians and Their Museums* (2000), Suzanne Keen's *Romances of the Archive in Contemporary British Fiction* (2001), Catherine Paul's *Poetry in the Museum of Modernism* (2002), Allan Hepburn's *Enchanted Objects* (2010), and Ruth Hoberman's *Museum Trouble: Edwardian Fiction and the Emergence of Modernism* (2011). I add to this body of work by positioning the postwar country house as a private home that transforms into a public museum.

> Mrs. H, at the instigation of FG [a staff member], has asked whether I can store her furniture anywhere in the Museum. She was bombed out, and ever since has had her furniture stored in a room in somebody else's house, but as that somebody is now moving she has to find other quarters. There is only one place here and that would be Neptune's Hall [the main exhibition space in the museum]; but we may have other people asking questions if this is permitted. I believe the furniture is also the property of FG, and he has no home until he comes back from the Service and makes one. I suppose it would have been his mother's as he lived with her.[9]

Rather than announcing and reinforcing the permanence of civilization in the manner of Victorian and Edwardian museums, wartime museums became clearing houses for the temporary. In a different kind of repurposing, the National Gallery became the site of Dame Myra Hess's regular lunch-time piano concert series. Although the series was undoubtedly a significant wartime ritual, it lacked the visual permanence of the art objects that had been moved to storage in the Manod Quarry in Wales. Music exists in time, leaving no trace, no opportunity for the spatial reinforcement of a dominant narrative of national identity or historical significance.[10] This a-spatial use of a structure designed for the visual display and organization of objects underscores the absence of architectural security and permanence during the war. It also suggests that the physical evacuation of wartime museums entailed a symbolic evacuation that made space for new political narratives of an emerging Welfare State.

As Carol Duncan has persuasively shown, the historical roots of the Western public museum as an expression of liberal democracy has meant that, since the nineteenth century, museums have been accepted almost unquestioningly as "important, even necessary, fixtures of a well-furnished state"; they simultaneously announce the new national ideal of liberal democracy and acknowledge the need to provide guidance and structure for the unruly masses.[11] The mechanism of the modern museum thus creates a space for civic

---

9. National Maritime Museum, Museum Archive & Records Centre, NMM14: Box 3, Folder XII, Letter 17th of April 1943 from Reginald Lowen to Sir Geoffrey Callender. At the request of the museum, names have been redacted to "H" and "FG" as a matter of privacy.

10. Such narratives, however, clearly are reinforced by the ritual performance of particular pieces of music. In the case of Dame Myra Hess, those performances were ritualized visually, if not spatially, when they were filmed by documentary filmmaker, Humphrey Jennings.

11. Duncan, "Art Museums and the Ritual of Citizenship," 88. Duncan's reading of the Louvre has been influential for historical theories of the museum. She argues that the Louvre became "the first truly modern art museum," when the French Revolution "designated the Louvre Palace a national museum" (98).

participation and education that normalizes particular narratives while rejecting others. In the immediate postwar period, as Britain faced economic and structural ruin, museums and exhibitions gave voice to reconstructed political narratives by returning with a transformed vision to their Victorian function: responding to the "specter of chaos" through the controlling mechanisms of order, display, and compilation.[12] In 1946, the Council of Industrial Design put on *Britain Can Make It* (BCMI), a design exhibition held at the still empty 90,000 square foot Victoria and Albert Museum. As the first major postwar exhibition, BCMI placed home design at the center of the British plan for economic recovery, with special curatorial emphasis on redirecting technologies of warfare to peace-time production. In its Policy Committee Meeting, the Trade Association announced that BCMI would "represent the best and only the best that modern British industry can produce. . . . [It will be] British industry's first great post-war gesture to the British people and the world."[13] Visitors were introduced to new ways of conceiving interior design elements that were set to redefine the British home: raw materials, heat, light, power, packaging, fashion, appliances.

According to this exhibition narrative, the ideal postwar home was economical, efficient, and tied to the well-being of the national community. Ironically, however, with the central aim of economic recovery, the exhibition was geared explicitly to an export market, and many visitors referred to the exhibition cheekily as "Britain Can't Have It." In the first major postwar moment of national reconstruction via museum exhibition, the material conditions and realities of a new national home and narrative remained conspicuously cordoned off from the people of that nation. By exhibiting this ideal, its curated home and its constituent values in the ritually significant space of the Victoria and Albert Museum, BCMI was an important symbolic gesture for the burgeoning Welfare State—a gesture that linked the civic museum projects of the postwar British nation with those of traditional liberal democracies and a time of global dominance in spite of the real economic austerity facing the nation. In 1951, this exhibition ethos was repeated and intensified by the

---

12. Black, *On Exhibit*, 15. According to Black, "One may perceive the museum as an impulse or spirit that infused the [Victorian] age and many of its projects: the triple-decker novel; collected works; encyclopedias and dictionaries; and phenomena as ordinary as keepsakes, dollhouses, and rock collections or a theory as cataclysmic as Darwin's panoramic evolutionism. Great and small, these system-building projects involved compilation, organization, and display—the three activities fundamental to a museum's work" (4–5). She further argues, following Duncan, that these defining ordering acts were inversely related to the increasing degree of disorder experienced daily within the ever-expanding metropolis of nineteenth-century London.

13. Darling, "Exhibiting Britain," n.p.

Festival of Britain, which explicitly harkened back to the Great Exhibition of 1851 and its "shrine to manufactured things."[14] But whereas the Victorian museum was about cementing and celebrating Britain's imperial power, the postwar exhibition indirectly acknowledged Britain's waning Empire. Instead of presenting global goods, the Festival promoted domestic tourism made accessible to all classes, even if the exhibited objects and explanatory narratives were not actually available across the socioeconomic spectrum. Indeed, as Duncan argues, the architectural affirmation of democratic participation embodied in the public museum exhibition can be understood as a substitute for actual civic engagement: the museum "produces the public as a visible entity by literally providing it a defining frame and giving it something to do. Meanwhile, the political passivity of citizenship is idealized as active art appreciation and spiritual enrichment. Thus the art museum gives citizenship and civic virtue a content without having to redistribute real power."[15] Like anthologies of canonical literary texts, museums reinforce a sense of "greatness" tied to timeless values and universal responses to cultural objects. By consuming those values and objects in the space of the museum—as in the space of the anthology—museumgoers perform an act of surface-level civic participation in singular, public narratives that is divorced from the material political reality of their "real" lives. In other words, museumgoers take part in heritage without contributing historically or actively shaping their own present and future public legacies. Central to Britain's reconstructed postwar exhibition culture was the country house, with its symbolic significance notably open to reconfiguration.

FROM HOUSE TO MUSEUM

Although country houses and the aristocratic class were already under significant pressure for their survival by the 1920s, World War II and its economic aftermath marked a decisive shift in that story of decline. During the war, many country houses were requisitioned for evacuees and army operations. Wartime requisitions often left the houses damaged to the extent that owners could not afford to make full repairs in the aftermath of the war. The financial burdens of reconstruction coupled with Welfare State land reforms and changes in the disbanding of the servant class effectively forced many landlords to sell their houses to the government for demolition and redevel-

---

14. Black, *On Exhibit*, 10.
15. Duncan, "Art Museums and the Ritual of Citizenship," 93–94.

opment. As Peter Mandler describes in *The Fall and Rise of the Stately Home*, the 1940s were a low point for the country house. In particular, the landmark 1947 Town and Country Planning Act decisively reversed any growth of aristocratic estates by nationalizing land development rights. By transforming the way land was valued, the Act ensured that public housing needs, which were substantial after two and a half million homes had been destroyed by wartime bombing, would take precedence over the preservation of private wealth. In addition to such legislation, death duties were raised after the war to levels that were financially prohibitive for many owners. As a result, nearly three hundred country houses were demolished in the decade after the war.

Many houses, however, were transferred to the National Trust. The Trust was a private charity founded in the 1890s to preserve the English landscape: an outgrowth of the Victorian museum boom and general surge in preservationism.[16] By the 1930s, it had become the major institutional body dedicated to preserving country houses and their grounds through the 1936 Country House Scheme. The Scheme, which soared in popularity after the challenges of World War II, allowed the owner to avoid death duties and remain living in the house in exchange for abiding by three conditions: the house, and typically its entire estate and valuable contents, would be transferred to the National Trust; the house would be opened for public access; and the owner would contribute an endowment for maintenance. Transferring to the National Trust was a decision taken reluctantly by many owners, a decision that marked a new phase in a national history no longer materially tied to the active economic power of landed lineage.

James Lees-Milne, secretary to the National Trust Country Houses Committee, cultivated a preservationist aesthetic that helped to transform the country house into a house museum in the postwar period. During and after the war, he visited many "endangered" houses to assess the possibility of donation to the Trust. His diary records the details of his visits to numerous houses where he interacted with notable cultural and political figures, including Vita Sackville-West. Lees-Milne's reflections register the impact of the war on country houses. In a 1944 entry, for instance, he observes how Osterley, a well-known house in Middlesex, just outside of London, had been transformed: "What a decline since 1939! . . . Now total disorder and disarray. Bombs have

---

16. As Patrick Wright notes in *On Living in an Old Country*, postwar conservation is part of a historically continuous commitment to preservationism that extends back to the second half of the nineteenth century, with the founding of the Commons Preservation Society (1865), National Footpaths Preservation Society (1884), and the Society for the Protection of Ancient Buildings (1877), and with the influence of figures like William Morris and John Ruskin (44–45).

fallen in the park, blowing out many windows; the Adam orangery has been burnt out, and the garden beds are totally overgrown."[17] Four years later, on a follow-up visit to Osterley, he laments that donation to the National Trust might not improve the situation: "It is sad to think what the place is bound to become when made over to the public."[18]

For a figure like Lees-Milne, who was himself raised in a country house, preservation entailed more than the recuperative transfer to the National Trust; preservation also entailed the act of recording and contemplating architectural, socioeconomic, and familial ruins. Lees-Milne's diaries capture a way of thinking about country houses that persists to the present day: what a journalist for *The Observer* described in 2011 as "the sadness of these places and their stories, their quiet and dignified tragedy."[19] At Sissinghurst, where Vita Sackville-West lived with her husband, Harold Nicholson, Lees-Milne interweaves a description of the gardens with a deeply sympathetic portrait of Vita as a noble and tragic figure:

> I love her romantic disposition, her southern lethargy concealing unfathomable passions, her slow movements of grave dignity, her fund of human kindness, understanding and desire to disentangle other people's perplexities for them. . . . We talked of love and religion. She told me that she learnt only at twenty-five that her tastes were homosexual. It was sad that homosexual lovers were considered by the world to be slightly comical. The memory of this evening will be ineradicable.[20]

Through this preservationist lens, the postwar story of country houses and national heritage involved humanizing the drama of aristocratic decline. The loss of "living" country houses was equated to the various losses of human life and, as in the case of Sackville-West, the loss of safe private spaces for nonnormative identities that were publicly subject to prejudice and legal punishment. The shifting realities of wartime neglect and personal struggle became intertwined in the preservationist account.

Lees-Milne's reflections on Ham House, near Richmond, capture the layered drama of house, owner, and aristocracy that epitomized the preservationist impulse:

---

17. Lees-Milne, *Some Country Houses and Their Owners*, 50.
18. Lees-Milne, 51.
19. Lee, "The National Trust Doesn't Even Trust Us to Have Our Own Thoughts," n.p.
20. Lees-Milne, *Some Country Houses and Their Owners*, 61.

The grounds are indescribably overgrown and unkempt. I walked round the house, which appeared thoroughly deserted, searching for an entrance. The garden and front doors look as though they had not been used for decades. So I returned to the back door and pulled a bell. Several seconds later a rusty tinkling echoed from distant subterranean regions. While waiting I recalled the grand ball given for Nefertiti Bethell which I attended in this house some ten years ago or more.... The son showed me hurriedly round the house, which is melancholy in the extreme. All the rooms are dirty and dusty. The furniture and pictures have been moved to the country for safety. There is no doubt whatever that, even without the contents, this house is worthy of acceptance because of the superlative interior treatment, the paneling, the exquisite parquetry floors, the extraordinary chimneypieces, the great staircase of pierced balustrades, the velvet hangings, etc. It is a wonderful seventeenth-century house, and from the south windows the garden layout of symmetrical beds, stone gate plinths and ironwork is superb. Once we were away from the father, whom [the son] clearly holds in mortal dread, the son became confidential. He said the family were worth £2 million and did not receive as much as sixpence in each pound; that they had two gardeners instead of twelve, and no indoor servants except a cook (and himself). He told me he was so distracted by looking after the Ham property and the Lincolnshire estate that at times he felt suicidal. I looked straight at him, and knew that the poor man meant it. When I waved goodbye, the faintest flicker of a smile crossed his bucolic face, and a tiny tear was on his cheek.[21]

This actual, if lyrically embellished, scene at Ham House is similar to the fictional one narrated by Charles Ryder in Evelyn Waugh's *Brideshead Revisted*, when Ryder returns to Brideshead after his company has requisitioned the house and grounds. Ryder walks quickly through the "desolated ground-floor rooms, trying doors that were locked, opening doors into rooms piled to the ceiling with furniture," and he finally finds Nanny Hawkins, a prewar relic in whom he hopes, but fails, to find recognition.[22] Like the father and son in Ham House, Nanny Hawkins laments the emptiness of the wartime house but seems utterly unwilling or unable to change; she, too, is mummified. In these scenes at Ham House and Brideshead, Lees-Milne and Waugh depict houseowners and inhabitants who tragically cannot bridge the gap from past to present to future.

---

21. Lees-Milne, 33–35.
22. Waugh, *Brideshead Revisited*, 392.

Lees-Milne's preservationist aesthetic was echoed by many figures of the reconstruction period. Sackville-West, for instance, contributed *English Country Houses* to the "Britain in Pictures" Series in 1941. In a manner characteristic of preservationist rhetoric, she begins the book by claiming that the country house is a symbolically significant entity for English history and national identity: "There is nothing quite like the English country house."[23] She goes on to construct an image of England rooted in aristocratic, eccentric pastoralism. Architectural historians such as John Summerson also participated in the work of preservation through their writing. Summerson became the curator of the Sir John Soane's Museum in 1945 (a post which he retained until 1984) and published *Georgian London* in the same year.[24] He pleaded in the preface, "This research needs doing now, before the age of reconstruction blots out all that vast quantity of minor evidence which, battered and often derelict, cannot be expected to survive long."[25] In the closing pages of *Brideshead Revisited*, Waugh echoes Summerson's resistance to a reconstruction ethos that would demolish evidence of an institutionally hierarchical past in order to create a more equitable future. Charles Ryder nostalgically laments the failure to keep Brideshead alive, and he links that failure to an initial act of reconstruction. When Brideshead Castle is rebuilt as a house, architectural, familial, and spiritual decline begin:

> The builders did not know the uses to which their work would descend; they made a new house with the stones of the old castle; year by year, generation after generation, they enriched and extended it; year by year the great harvest of timber in the park grew to ripeness; until, in sudden frost, came the age of Hooper; the place was desolate and the work all brought to nothing; *Quomodo sedet sola civitas*. Vanity of vanities, all is vanity.[26]

Waugh, Sackville-West, Summerson, Lees-Milne—these writers made careers out of longing. Under their pens, through the discourse and aesthetics of preservation, and supported by organizations like the National Trust, country estates transformed from dying houses into still life house museums.

---

23. Sackville-West, *English Country Houses*, 7.

24. Sir John Soane's museum is one of the most notable precedents for the modern house museum. Through an Act of Parliament in 1833, the notable architect and collector had his house in Lincoln's Inn Fields turned into a permanent public institution.

25. Summerson, *Georgian London*, 9.

26. Waugh, *Brideshead*, 395. In addition to *Brideshead*, a number of Waugh's novels, including *Decline and Fall* and *Handful of Dust* satirically dramatize the encroachment on the aristocracy of the forces of modernization and bourgeois economic mobility as expressed through the redecoration, renovation, and requisition of country houses.

The preservationist vision, however, was not shared by all Britons during reconstruction. According to Peter Mandler, a public relations report on the future of the National Trust in 1944 concluded that, based on strong public opinion, the government should support projects that would convert houses into "centres for drama, art, or similar cultural activities."[27] The public was, not surprisingly, generally against the idea of aristocratic owners living in their homes while the National Trust paid to maintain them. After the hardships faced by all during the war, and considering that many rationing restrictions were not completely lifted until 1954, public opinion about houses in the 1940s reflected a general cultural resistance toward aristocratic privilege and the desire for increased and modernized social services. Owners who did not wish to transfer to the National Trust but also wanted to avoid demolition partnered with private organizations or the government to convert the houses into public spaces such as schools, hospitals, hotels, or, as depicted in Angus Wilson's 1952 novel, *Hemlock and After*, artists' retreats. This public resistance to the National Trust appears, however, to have been generally short lived.

As the economy began to recover from the exigencies of the war in the later 1950s and 1960s, the country house museum took center stage as tourist destination and scholarly subject in a growing culture of affluence and consumerism. Popular BBC Third Programme radio installments, such as Brian Vesey-Fitzgerald's "There and Back" and "Let's Go," helped to create a general cultural discourse that reincorporated the country house into British national life not as an emblem of aristocratic tragedy but as a crucial part of domestic tourism that valued public spectacle.[28] Middle-class families often made an excursion to a country house the centerpiece of a holiday. Houses also became sites of an anthropological academic interest, as public intellectuals like Summerson, John Betjeman, and Nikolaus Pevsner frequently explored the cultural value of the country house in their writing and broadcasts from a point of view that, as Mandler puts it, "saw architecture as 'a witness of phases of human life in the past.'"[29]

This period of revival for the country house in the 1950s and 1960s cemented a fundamental separation that had been put in motion by the war and its aftermath: a separation between houses as material expression of a living, evolving history and the cultural and social values of houses for a largely middle-class, consumer public. The relationship between the physical house

---

27. Mandler, *Fall and Rise*, 324.

28. For Kevin Walsh, the postwar spectacle of heritage was rooted in aristocratic privilege, with a prime example being the increasing public profile and celebrity of the royal family after Elizabeth and Philip married in November of 1947 (*Representation*, 73).

29. Mandler, *Rise and Fall*, 332.

and its social and cultural values was reconstructed under the guise of heritage, which, according to historian Patrick Wright "involves the extraction of history—of the idea of historical significance and potential—from a denigrated everyday life and its restaging or display in certain sanctioned sites, events, images and conceptions. In this process history is redefined as 'the historical,' and it becomes the object of a similarly transformed and generalized public attention."[30] Before World War II and certainly before the twentieth century, the country house and its inhabitants made physically, economically, and politically concrete contributions to British national life; in the postwar era, the country house became most valuable only insofar as it could be put to use in the cultural and scholarly life of those who had never been and would never be part of the aristocratic realm from which the house emerged. National Trust properties are undoubtedly their own form of museum: preserved to re-create different times in the history of the houses.[31] This separation between the house as material expression of historical conditions and the house as vehicle for curated history lesson prompts questions about the political implications of the postwar country house museum.

Carol Duncan argues that since the objects in a public art museum are "recontextualized as art history, the luxury of princes could now be seen as the spiritual heritage of the nation, distilled into an array of national and individual genius."[32] In the country house museum, private wealth becomes public historical narrative just as it does in a public museum, but there is an added spatial component to the visitor experience. The house museum commemorates and celebrates a particular historical narrative not just through its *objets d'art* but through its domestic architecture and relation to the landscape it inhabits. Viewing tapestries and chairs and paintings in their original space reinforces the significance of landed wealth in British history, even if that landed wealth is now no longer generative.[33] Unlike the countless objects that were removed from their original colonial locations in the nineteenth century

---

30. Wright, *On Living in an Old Country*, 65.
31. It is now standard procedure for the National Trust to fill many house libraries with books from a central repository, rather than necessarily displaying the original collections. Manufactured smells of freshly baked bread are frequently piped through the kitchens, as is the scent of freshly washed clothing in laundry rooms (Lee, "The National Trust Doesn't Even Trust Us to Have Our Own Thoughts," n.p.).
32. Duncan, "Art Museums," 95. Duncan uses the Louvre to explain how museums create the false impression of public ownership: "Significantly, [in the Louvre] the new value discovered in the prince's old treasures could be distributed to the many merely by displaying it in a public space.... If the uneducated were unable to use the cultural goods the museum proffered, they could—and still can—be awed by the sheer magnitude of the treasure" (95).
33. This significance is further reinforced beyond the houses themselves within broader consumer culture. Country house-inspired home décor is still held up as a sign of upward

and displayed in the British Museum, country house treasures are shown *in situ*, making not only the objects but the objects' spatial context part of the work of preservation. The house and its parkland become artifacts that, like any museum installation, "take visitors on a kind of mental journey, a stepping out of the present into a universe of timeless values."[34] As the specific contents, architecture, land, and lineage of a country house are transformed into a public site run by government-funded institutions like the National Trust and English Heritage, they become attached to timeless or mythological notions of Englishness that are deeply invested in a preserved class system. Patrick Wright describes the National Trust in particular: "As a registered company the National Trust holds property privately, and yet it does so in what it also works to establish as the national and public interest. . . . The inalienability of the Trust's property can be regarded (and also staged) as a vindication of property relations: a spectacular enlistment of the historically defined categories 'natural beauty' and 'historic interest' which demonstrates how private property simply *is* in the national public interest."[35] This process creates a shared cultural hierarchy of artistic and material value: a vertical hierarchy seemingly made horizontal by virtue of its public status.

One other way of grasping the slippage between the vertical and horizontal that happens through the country house museum is to think, in Susan Stewart's terms, of the gigantic and the miniature. The country house museum unites the gigantic—the large estate, its expansive and defended wealth, and its connection with the natural world—and the miniature—the rooms of the house museum, neatly on display, like a dollhouse. Stewart theorizes a relationship between these scalar extremes in which consumer culture co-opts and reformulates the gigantic as the miniature in order to create and maintain a certain cultural order:

> In contrast to the still and perfect universe of the miniature, the gigantic represents the order and disorder of historical forces. The consumerism of the miniature is the consumerism of the classic; it is only fitting that consumer culture appropriates the gigantic whenever change is desired. We want the antique miniature and gigantic new. And while our daydream may be to animate the miniature, we admire the fall or the death, the stopping, of the giant.[36]

---

social mobility through magazines such as *Town and Country* and retail outlets that occupy prominent locations on Bond Street like Laura Ashley and Ralph Lauren.

34. Duncan, *Civilizing Rituals*, 19.
35. Wright, *On Living in an Old Country*, 47.
36. Stewart, *On Longing*, 86.

By merging the gigantic and the miniature, the country house museum protects landed wealth and the legacy of vertical hierarchy through the tax advantages of donation to institutions like the National Trust. At the same time, the country house museum deflects potentially troublesome counternarratives that would lobby for real socioeconomic equality. As my experience at Knole suggests, however, the country house museum is not an air-tight container for public narrative. Realistic forms of the country house novel in the postwar period, such as those by Taylor and Bowen, demonstrate the frailty of museological containment.

FROM HOUSE MUSEUM TO COUNTRY HOUSE NOVEL: IRONY AND ABSENCE

Just as a museum organizes and displays through an undeniably ideological process of selection, so novels organize, shape, and depict narrative information with ideological consequences. Stewart invokes the museum-like quality of narrative by focusing on its "absolute closure, its clarity of beginnings and endings."[37] The bounded quality of printed texts—even if those texts contain experimental narratives that remain unresolved—marks it off as a space where rituals are established and norms are enforced, a space that is opposed to actively unfolding history in the closure indicated by its definite first and last pages. For Stewart,

> While "lived" history is perceived as open work, work without established beginning or established ending, it is the accomplishment of narrative to provide both origin and eschaton, a set of provisions that are profoundly ideological in the closure they present. Narrative is "about" closure; the boundaries of events form the ideological basis for the interpretation of their significance.[38]

In this sense, we could think of any narrative as akin to a museum, but there is a particular set of implications for novels that deal with the historical significance of houses and heritage.

For such texts as Elizabeth Taylor's *Angel* or Elizabeth Bowen's *The Little Girls*, narrative is an act of boundary setting that has a critical, reflexive relationship to the house museum and questions of heritage within its walls. Nar-

---
37. Stewart, *On Longing*, 22.
38. Stewart, 22.

rative closure, for these texts, is about endings but also about literal, physical enclosure. Both novels approximate the work of a museum through historical fiction and flashback, but in rejecting nostalgia and privileging real conditions, they offer a less ideologically rigid counternarrative in the context of postwar heritage culture. Taylor uses satire to criticize the ahistorical stance of Angel's house museum: a warning that the benefits of popular, middle-class investment in country house culture, with its narratives of socioeconomic mobility, are limited to fantasy. There is always, her novel suggests, a less tidy, historically meaningful "reality" behind the romance of curatorial closure (the two World Wars in the case of *Angel*), and ignoring this reality is untenable if not unethical. In *The Little Girls,* Bowen uses tropes and strategies of absence to reconfigure the relationships among former country house owners, heritage culture, and historical violence. Although the two texts are very different stylistically, Bowen follows Taylor in challenging the pretension of closure in order to represent or imply a more accurate reality that demands attention. But whereas Taylor uses a middlebrow realism as her vehicle, Bowen uses a more formally experimental realism to acknowledge this reality.

Given that the country house novel and postwar country house culture bring together the middle and upper classes, it is useful to note that Taylor and Bowen were from these two distinct cultural and socioecomonic worlds: Taylor, the middle-class daughter of a Reading insurance inspector, and Bowen, the sole inheritor of her family's house and estate, Bowen's Court, and of her family's lineage as part of the Anglo-Irish Ascendency. Despite their different backgrounds, they had a friendly professional relationship and corresponded about writing in the 1940s and 1950s. Taylor clearly admired Bowen's work and looked to her for advice and camaraderie when faced with the challenges of life as a professional writer. Notably, in her letters to Bowen, Taylor makes a point several times of praising Bowen's fiction for its treatment of what is "real." In a 1949 letter following the publication of Bowen's *The Heat of the Day,* Taylor notes how important it is that Bowen has written a book about real people in the real present to capture the wartime experience: "Yes they [the characters] are all real and *physically* real. When they lift a hand, or laugh, it is a real thing that is done. No thin bits, nothing dull. It is wonderful and hopeful that it can be so true and so about *now,* and I think you are the only one to do this and it was brave of you."[39] As the following analysis will show, while Taylor and Bowen shared a commitment to representing the real conditions in their fiction, their perspectives and styles clearly announce two distinct iterations of the postwar country house novel: one indebted to middle-class and

---

39. Taylor, Letter to Elizabeth Bowen. 24 February 1949. Harry Ransom Center 12.1.

middlebrow literary traditions and the other to the decline of landed wealth and a repurposed aesthetics of modernist fragmentation.

Elizabeth Taylor provides a critical middle-class version of the country house narrative in two of her postwar novels. While I will focus primarily on her 1957 novel, *Angel*, her second novel, *Palladian*, published in 1946, is not only a telling work of early reconstruction fiction, as I discussed briefly in chapter 2, but also a generic precedent for *Angel* and compelling counterpoint to Waugh's *Brideshead Revisited*. *Palladian* is a governess novel that takes as its theme the decaying country house and its aristocratic inhabitants, but the narrative of decline refuses the nostalgic yearning for a lost national greatness that Waugh's novel is generally thought to represent. In *Ethics and Nostalgia in the Contemporary Novel*, for instance, John Su reads *Brideshead* as emblematic of a postwar nostalgia concerned with English history and identity as linked to the country house: "The decay of the English country estate in . . . *Brideshead Revisited* . . . evokes a powerful yearning for lost national glory. . . . The diminished condition of the estate is taken to be emblematic of the nation as a whole."[40] In *Palladian*, the desire for continuity through the country estate is blocked at every turn, including that of generic lineage. The novel invokes the gothic and romance traditions in which houses often figure as central characters through intertextual references to Charlotte Brontë's *Jane Eyre* and Daphne Du Maurier's *Rebecca* (1938). But Taylor undercuts nostalgia for these earlier literary fantasies through the decidedly unromantic characters and plot trajectories in her revision of the country house novel. Various inhabitants of the house in *Palladian* undermine its romantic appeal: an alcoholic, an adulterer who has an affair with the working-class landlady of the village pub, a woman who prefers to become a single mother rather than to marry, a live-in servant from the prewar years who clashes with the young, daily charwoman. The modernizing world beyond the boundaries of the estate comes crashing into the house, and, in the end, the house proves its own failure as a shelter for the future generations of Britain: a statue on the grounds falls and kills the only young child of the estate family. *Palladian* is a morbid novel, but one that seems, unlike Waugh's novel, more interested in the emerging forces that encourage the decline than in mourning the values being lost. The novel offers neither a falsely optimistic or opportunistic vision of the future nor a melancholy portrait of old-fashioned values. Its dead-endedness indicates

---

40. Su, *Ethics and Nostalgia in the Contemporary Novel*, 120. In *Victorians in the Rearview*, Simon Joyce similarly reads *Brideshead Revisited* (alongside *Howards End*) through the framework of nostalgia, as "two texts that are redolent with a longing for some of the supposed values of the past, at the same time that they also stage self-reflexive discussions of the benefits and dangers of nostalgia" (41).

Taylor's recognition that the country house novel tradition can no longer serve a romantic role for the middle classes, especially in the austere immediacy of the postwar period, and it foreshadows her search for an alternative iteration of the genre.

Just over ten years later, *Angel* provides this alternative. It is a country house novel that is a work of historical fiction. It reconstructs a time period (1885–1947) while also repurposing the genre to emphasize the new place of country houses within postwar British culture in the late 1950s. Like a country house museum, Taylor's historical narrative of Angel and Paradise House displays the past, but the narrator provides sustained ironic commentary to create critical distance that is missing in the house museum. The novel tells the story of a popular romance novelist, the lower-middle-class Angel Deverell and Paradise House, the estate that she is able to purchase as a result of her literary celebrity. Angel's coming-of-age story takes place at a high point of museum creation at the turn of the twentieth century.[41] This exhibition frenzy accompanies the demise of late Victorian sensation fiction and the birth of literary modernism. By enclosing this period of exhibition frenzy and literary upheaval through an ironic rather than a nostalgic narrative, the novel critiques the revived heritage culture of the 1950s. Through its mode of historical fiction, the novel distinguishes itself from the modern fiction of the earlier twentieth century in the sense that Allan Hepburn has identified: "Whereas modern novels about artworks and collections validate self-expression and ownership, postmodern novels historicize value and critique museum culture."[42] In its representation of Angel and her house, Taylor's novel certainly has these qualities; it establishes a critical vantage point for understanding the role of the country house and heritage culture in the on-going history of middle-class women's writing. Taylor's style, however, is not postmodern. It is consistent, instead, with the characteristics of reconstruction fiction, as *Angel* grapples with social conditions by offering a less nostalgic version of the country house novel that is attentive to the highly curated quality of postwar country houses; at the same time, it delivers a critical take on Edwardian popular culture.

In a time of supposedly greater class equality, *Angel* signals a contradictory, middle-class uneasiness at work in the 1950s and 1960s: the desire to

---

41. Hoberman notes that the late nineteenth century was a high point of museum creation as a result of new legislation: "Between 1890 and 1914 alone, 215 museums were created in Great Britain, their funding facilitated by the passage of two acts: the Museums and Gymnasiums Act of 1891 and the Public Libraries Act of 1892, which made it easier for municipalities to establish museums" (Hoberman, *Museum Trouble*, 13).

42. Hepburn, *Enchanted Objects*, 10–11.

consume a well-curated, nostalgic, saleable version of English aristocratic history—and the class hierarchy that accompanies it—alongside the need to mock and reject social climbing impulses. According to John Su, postwar narratives about the country house signal a conflict between symbols of power, order, and dominance and the historical forces that threaten the stability of those symbols. Although the postwar country house holds, he argues, "longstanding associations with continuity, tradition, and Englishness, . . . its presence belies the cultural turbulence caused by increasing emigration from the colonies; chronic unemployment and economic depression; and the resurgence of regionalism within Scotland, Ireland, and Wales."[43] *Angel* reveals the middle-class desire for continuity, tradition, and Englishness as represented by the country house, but rather than deploy a nostalgic aesthetics, the novel interrogates this middle-class desire by positioning it ironically with an ambivalent treatment of fantasy, romance, history, and the writing profession—all funneled through a desire for the country house life. As Alice Ferrebe has aptly argued about Taylor's writing in general, it "relies upon romance only ultimately to undermine the genre."[44] Instead of wholeness, continuity, and participation in a national narrative, which is *the* promise of a country house, the country house museum that is Paradise House seals Angel's fate of private isolation and affirms her historical redundancy.

Over the course of her life, Angel both fantasizes about life in a country house and actually becomes a country house owner. Her story thus reveals the simultaneous enchantments and dangers of the middle-class attachment to and reconstruction of country house culture. Her narrative begins in adolescence, when she publishes her first novel, *The Lady Irania*, at the age of 16 without having read much of anything beyond the occasional volume of Shakespeare. Despite the doubts and embarrassed fears of her lower-middle-class mother and aunt, Angel quickly becomes infamous—adored by the romance-devouring reading public and joyfully torn apart by highbrow critics.[45] After leaving the cramped rooms above her mother's grocery store in an industrial town, she begins her ascent through various living spaces that ulti-

---

43. Su, *Ethics and Nostalgia in the Contemporary Novel*, 121.
44. Ferrebe, "Elizabeth Taylor's Uses of Romance," 61.
45. As N. H. Reeve has pointed out, Angel's career as a writer of sensationalist novels is a clear reference to the careers of figures such as Marie Corelli and Amanda Ros (*Elizabeth Taylor*, 54). Victoria Stewart, moreover, reads *Angel* alongside E. F. Benson's *Secret Lives* (1932) and Mary Renault's *The Friendly Young Ladies* (1944) in terms of the middlebrow woman writer, with emphasis on the legacy of Corelli. Stewart argues, "Taylor's novel . . . acts as a reminder that while writers of Angel's ilk may not leave a lasting literary legacy, they have a vital importance, in their time, for their readers" ("Woman Writer" 34).

mately leads to her life in a country house, Paradise House, which the owner has abandoned due to prohibitive costs.

As a child, Angel develops a richly detailed but highly incongruous image of Paradise House in her imagination. Although Paradise House is a real place where her Aunt Lottie works as a daily servant, for Angel it emerges as a pastiche of the details she romantically chooses, notably ignoring or erasing the people who reside there. In school, instead of paying attention to "dull lessons," she daydreams about a bedroom for herself in the house: she "tried to imagine it . . . with plush curtains drawn, a fire in the grate, a white satin gown over a chair and herself being laced into her stays by a maid" (*Angel*, 8). As in this image, Angel's recreations of the house are romantic and anachronistic, unfolding in a vague time and place. The days roll on, and her fantasy grows, becoming both more complete and more historically implausible. She closes her eyes

> to create the darkness where Paradise House could take shape, embellished and enlarged day after day—with colonnades and cupolas, archways and flights of steps—beyond anything her aunt had ever suggested. Acquisitively, from photographs and drawings in history-books, she added one detail after another. That will do for Paradise House, was an obsessive formula which became a daily habit. The white peacocks would do; and there were portraits in the Municipal Art Gallery which would do; as would the cedar trees at school. As the house spread, those in it grew more shadowy. Angel herself took over Madam's jewel-box and Madam's bed and husband. (*Angel*, 15)

Paradise House, like the tourist attraction National Trust House that preserves different time periods in different rooms, is divorced from historically situated ownership and occupation. Instead, Paradise House becomes an illusory vehicle for Angel's fiction writing, in which "her sense of period was so vague and her notions of country-life wonderfully sensational. A handsome young man among dogs was going off to shoot his rival in a duel, not pheasants among the autumn foliage; a lady in an Empire gown had been a mistress of Charles the Second" (*Angel*, 123).

The incongruity of Angel's daydreams might seem simply to suggest the natural workings of a child's imagination, but Taylor was also attentive to architectural styles and interior decoration, and with this in mind, Angel emerges as a character who is not only immature but lacking in taste. Architectural critics in the late 1950s often held up stylistic hybridity, which recalled Victorian aesthetics and immediate postwar Townscape theory, as one of the chief markers of poor taste in the modernizing postwar context. John Summerson often made this point in his writings, as he does in this passage that recalls his Victorian childhood boarding school, Riber Castle, in Derbyshire. It is, he laments,

> not only very ugly, but [it] has the rare characteristic of being stylistically unclassifiable.... One can hardly call it "primitive," but primitive, in a way, it is. Not the sort issuing from the innocence of folk-art but with a savagery of its own century bred in the haunted, cluttered mind of a man who has seen the Alps, visited the cathedrals, the castles, the châteaux and absorbed some of the vanity of their builders, with an appetite to convert his wealth into "galleries," "saloons," "canopies," "clerestories," "spiral staircases" and the rest. Had Smedly [the architect] employed a professional he would have got a house unmistakenly, however crudely, stamped with a style—Italian, Norman, Gothic or Baronial. As it was he produced an object of indecipherable bastardy—a true monster.[46]

In Summerson's recollection as well as in Taylor's characterization of Angel's architectural imagination, stylistic and historical collage is an occasion for humor. More deeply, however, it speaks to an underlying anxiety that such confusion will persist, as in the case of Riber Castle, or be popular with the masses, as in the case of Angel's novels that draw on such a sensibility.

Taylor expresses this anxiety by emphasizing Angel's refusal to see things as they are and charting the negative consequences. Initiating a pattern of denial that will continue throughout her life, Angel never visits the house or witnesses her aunt's real labor as a girl. Instead, she becomes convinced and enchanted by her own incongruous image of the house. Despite having no real basis for her ambition, she becomes determined to live there one day and even fabricates stories for her schoolmates to suggest that the house belongs to her family and is destined for her in the future. She tells them, "It is all kept in order and so is the house. There are dust-sheets over the drawing-room and drugget over the carpets, but the housekeeper sees that everything is polished and shining and ready for the day when I can go there myself to live" (Angel, 9–10). Already, Angel thinks of the house not as a site of lived experience, to which her aunt could attest if given the opportunity, but as a space to be aestheticized, curated, and immobilized.

In the early stages of Taylor's novel, the narrator's mocking descriptions of Angel seem harmlessly humorous, but as the novel progresses, a darker undercurrent is gradually revealed. Angel's fantasies have real implications, as they translate to financial success that facilitates her purchase of the real Paradise

---

46. Summerson, "Unromantic Castle," 14.

House. This move does not bring her closer to reality, however; it only intensifies her sense of denial and her obsession with her own private fantasy world. She complains that the house doesn't match up to how she imagined it in her dreams and how she had described it in her first novel: "The ashen look of the stone was a great shock to her. It was all built the wrong way about and was not big enough or decorated enough, and there were no peacocks" (*Angel*, 146). So, she proceeds to alter the reality rather than confront and accept it. When she and her husband, Esmé, return to Paradise House after their honeymoon, "There was scaffolding over the front . . . and patches of new plaster, a smell of paint and putty and a sound of hammering. The balustrade had been mended and the fallen urn put back. Two peacocks had arrived. . . . They moped on the terrace, which they covered with their droppings; they moulted; they sometimes screamed but never fanned out their tail-feathers" (153). Angel's reconstruction of Paradise House brings it closer to fantasy and further from reality, like a house museum. But Taylor's "reconstruction" of Angel's story does the opposite: it undermines the fantasy and reveals its real consequences.

The museological quality of Paradise House symbolizes a menacing sense of historical denial that emerges throughout the novel. Angel does not engage with the world around her; instead, she conceives of her life through the eyes of a posterity that will judge her cultural value. In other words, she thinks of her life as already over, its narrative already sealed off. Given that Angel's life includes two world wars, the political implications of such a premature backward gaze are grave. Taylor's narrative, however, works critically against the pat ideological closure of Angel's house museum to suggest that the complexity and impact of past experience—whether private or public—cannot be entirely shut out. As N. H. Reeve observes, although Angel "does her best to ignore altogether the history, both private and public, that [history] nonetheless shapes her existence" (*Angel*, 42). Angel's personal history always looms: her lower-middle-class roots threaten to break the surface of her faux aristocratic life. She quickly represses, for instance, a "curiously silencing thought": that she once had been offered a job in Paradise House as a lady's maid. She fights against the pressure of this real historical possibility: "She could not—even if she had cared to, and nothing did she desire less—have peopled it with the ghosts of Aunt Lottie's Madam and that other Angelica" (158). The narrator's interjection between the dashes doubles and reinforces the level of mental barricading and emotional boundary-setting that Angel undertakes to prevent historical intrusion.

To keep personal ghosts at bay, Angel also shuts out the national and global history unfolding around her. When Esmé decides to enlist in the Army during World War I, she enters a period of disturbing, furious anti-patriotism, not because of actual political convictions (she is entirely uninformed and apolitical), but because the war effort takes Esmé away and thus disturbs the house museum world in which he merely played a role that she has scripted for him. Her writing career suffers from her inexplicable, extreme pacifism, and so, too, does Paradise House. The funds begin to run out as Angel's fantasy world shrinks and loses appeal for her readers. Reality encroaches upon the house: it "was half shut up and there was nothing to show for Esmé's work on the garden; the lawns were shaggy again and tall grasses grew around the urns and the stone seats on the terrace" (*Angel*, 166). The tragedy of Angel's historical denial culminates in Esmé's return after being honorably discharged when he loses a leg through injury. He returns to Paradise House to find that there is no room, literally, for his wartime experience nor his postwar trauma in the narrative enclosure of the house that Angel stubbornly has maintained. As a result of Angel's refusal to let her "public" personal narrative be influenced by the narratively explosive fact of war, Esmé commits suicide by drowning himself in the lake on Paradise House grounds. The haunting image of his empty wheelchair alongside the water is matched in horror only by Angel's subsequent replacement of it with a large obelisk monument to Esmé, a gesture that recalls Sir Edwin Lutyens's 1919 Cenotaph for those killed in World War I—but, disturbingly, without the public resonance. Esmé could be only an abstract museum object to Angel, a nostalgic memorial to the end of romance rather than a person who had really experienced war.

During World War II, a similar story of historical denial plays out as Angel and Paradise House enter their final days. The physical and symbolic evacuation of wartime museums is reflected in the diminished furnishings: the library has few books, and the telephone "echoe[s] startlingly in the hall, for, . . . the house was very bare of furniture" (*Angel*, 224)—a description that sounds almost exactly James Lees-Milne's description of the wartime Ham House. The few people who visit the house fight their way through weeds. Angel herself dresses in "moth-eaten chinchilla" (237). As she dies, Paradise House lies cold and muffled in snow that "drifts to the lower window-sills" (242). Her final gesture comes through her unofficial will. She orders that the executors "'shall set aside a sum of money to preserve Paradise House as it stands at the time of my'—the word 'death' had been crossed out and 'decease' superimposed—'to be retained as a public memorial and true record of my life'" (251). Even looking ahead to death, Angel insists on the veracity of her fantasy and on the role of the house in faithfully confirming it. Her editorial revision to the will, moreover, only emphasizes the amount of revision necessary to perpetuate such a willfully historically ignorant fantasy.

Angel's conception of a decaying, overgrown, furniture-less Paradise House as a public memorial is deeply and disturbingly ironic: such a house museum is a fittingly empty memorial to mismotivated pacifism and, less directly, to the dangerous appeasement policies supported by many who clung to country house life and hierarchy in the 1930s. Although country houses mostly had lost their connection with actual political power by at least the 1920s, isolated cases in the prewar decade—that of Nancy Astor and the "Cliveden Set," for example[47]—suggest that the insulation of country house life might have serious negative political consequences for the nation. That Angel essentially loses her entire readership constitutes Taylor's critique of writerly and museological projects that are so closed off and dangerously out of touch with the lives of those who make up the real public in 1950s Britain.

With her historical novel, Taylor critically frames a time in which middle-class writers privileged romance and heritage over history. The temporal distance marks off that time period as effectively over yet not without the recognition that the consequences of such romantic yearning would persist in the realm of postwar middle-class country house culture. Through the young art critic, Clive Fennelly, Taylor forecasts the persistence of sentimental appeal for the postwar public. Clive is enamored with the *image* of decayed wealth: "The space, the quiet, the strangeness captivated him; it was so unlike the neat villas, the golden privet hedges, the shaved lawns of the suburbs where he lived. The wildness and the beauty were enhanced for him by Angel herself in her dress of faded, streaky red, her coiled-up hair with not a grey thread in it, her eccentricity which seemed to him so typical of the decaying aristocracy" (*Angel*, 205). Clive is a suburban, middle-class professional who invests in the "performance" of aristocratic life. Only a social-climbing suburbanite, Clive's character implies, could be fooled by Angel's pretensions. He not only buys into the fantasy; he helps to create it: "The prodigious collapse of Paradise House he [Clive] could foretell; the stains already running up the walls, brickwork at the back held together only by matted ivy, floor boards rotting, plaster crumbling" (212). Taylor might be poking fun at herself with this description of Clive's fantasy of ruin; it recalls her own description of the decrepit country house in *Palladian* as well as the deserted house in her 1947 novel, *A Wreath of Roses*. With *Angel*, Taylor also achieves personal historical

---

47. In addition to cultivating pro-Nazi appeasement politics at its 1930s weekend house parties, Cliveden became further notorious in the 1960s during the "Profumo Affair," a sex scandal at the house that led to the resignation of John Profumo and established facts that contributed to the fall of Harold Macmillan's Conservative government in 1963. Cliveden was donated to the National Trust in 1942 and later became an exclusive hotel, which is still managed by the Trust. Nightly rates in the main house run as high as $2,555 per night.

distance from her earlier preoccupation with the collapse of traditional country house life. In narrating Angel's life and the history in which it was necessarily embedded, Taylor dramatizes the cost of conceiving of houses as if they were museums and lives as if they were exhibitions.[48] The novel shows how the operations of heritage transform "the challenge of history" into something "behind us already accomplished and ready for exhibition as 'the past.' Where there was active historicity there is now decoration and display; in the place of memory, amnesia swaggers out in historical fancy dress" (*Old Country* 74). Taylor's self-reflexive version of the country house novel is a disruptively realistic revisionary tool in the midst of country house-centered heritage culture that reintroduces the challenge of history.

ELIZABETH BOWEN'S *THE LITTLE GIRLS*: "THE EVER-EVAPORATING NOW"

Elizabeth Bowen's *The Little Girls* also critiques the postwar heritage industry, but it does so in a more formally experimental way, revealing the emptiness of the posterity-oriented gesture while simultaneously generating the desire for plenitude. Looming large beyond the text as an absent presence is the 1959 sale and demolition of Bowen's Court, the family's estate in Ireland, over which Bowen herself presided as the last and sole inheritor. Within the novel, the critique manifests through the various significant tropes of absence: an empty time capsule, a half-filled cave-museum, a bombed landmark. Formally, the text is characterized by fits and starts and, in general, the untraceable. Plot trajectories trail off into nothing. Characters are thinly sketched, mainly through dialogue, with minimal access to interiority. Structurally, a flashback to 1914 is bracketed by two longer parts set contemporaneously to the publication of the novel in the early 1960s, with little information from a narrator or the characters about the intervening years. Just as the adult characters search for the time capsule they buried as girls, along with its missing contents and their relationships to each other, so the reader searches for meaningful content in the literary time capsule that Bowen creates with the 1914 part of the narrative. By structurally enclosing this flashback with fragmented narration and

---

48. Taylor also explores the country house museum in her short story, "Hare Park," which appears in her 1958 collection, *The Blush*. In "Hare Park," the Duke opens up his country house to the public in order to keep it alive. The "sightseer" cars "looked purposeful and menacing . . . like a funeral procession . . . ; the crowds spread about the terrace, invading the house from all sides, like an army of ants, penetrating in no time the stables and courtyard and lining up for the house itself" (197).

laborious syntax, Bowen provides an alternative, anti-nostalgic way of engaging with and representing the relationship between past and present. Strains of violence, threat, and cruelty run through the novel, suggesting that the past is never entirely sealed up in museums, time capsules, or narratives; it is always open to reanimation and revision, and it always has the potential to reshape the present. Bowen's postwar emphasis on absence and her formally experimental approach registers historical violence and loss not in the spirit of high modernism as a problem of linguistic expression but as the realist desire for narrative wholeness, however fraught that desire may be.

Throughout her career, Elizabeth Bowen was preoccupied with houses and landscape, in particular the Anglo-Irish Big House and its physical and symbolic role in the decline of the Anglo-Irish Ascendancy within the contexts of a newly independent Ireland and Britain's changing position in global power relations.[49] Her fictional and nonfictional engagement with country houses demonstrates both her personal attachment to these places as well as her full awareness of their increasing anachronism as the twentieth century progressed. In 1940, she wrote an essay for *The Bell* entitled "The Big House," in which she describes the Irish country estate as representative of "the good life for which they were first built," although "in a changed world and under changed conditions."[50] In 1942, she published *Bowen's Court*, an extensive history of her family's Big House, and in a 1944 essay entitled, "The Most Unforgettable Character I've Met," she begins by evoking an empty Bowen's Court in an empty landscape:

> A great grey stone house, with rows upon rows of windows, ringed round with silence, approached by grass-grown avenues—has life forever turned aside from this place? So the stranger might ask, approaching my family home in Ireland. It is miles from anywhere you have ever heard of; it is backed by woods with mountains behind them; in front, it stares over empty fields. Generations have lived out their lives and died here. But no—everybody has gone away?[51]

---

49. A number of critics have considered the theme of the Anglo-Irish Big House in Bowen's work. For a recent exemplary discussion of the Big House in *The Last September* and *Bowen's Court*, see Maud Ellmann, *Elizabeth Bowen: The Shadow across the Page*. In *Elizabeth Bowen: The Enforced Return*, Neil Corcoran considers the Anglo-Irish estate in relation to Anglo-Irish history in *A World of Love*. My essay with Phyllis Lassner, "Domestic Gothic, the Global Primitive, and Gender Relations in Elizabeth Bowen's *The Last September* and *The House in Paris*," also discusses the Big House in Bowen's work.

50. Bowen, "The Big House," 30.

51. Bowen, "The Most Unforgettable Character I've Met," 254.

Passages like this one, written during the war after Bowen had made England her adoptive home, recall the preservationist writings of Waugh, Vita Sackville-West, and John Summerson, but Bowen's description is more haunting than melancholy or nostalgic.[52] In the reconstruction decades following the war, moreover, she represents the haunting quality of Big Houses as a historically productive force in its own right, a force that aligns with the generative power of the fictional, imaginative impulse. In the 1964 afterword to a new edition of *Bowen's Court*, reissued in the same year that *The Little Girls* was published, she reflects:

> Loss has not been entire. When I think of Bowen's Court, there it is. And when others who knew it think of it, there it is, also. . . . Knowing, as you now do, that the house is no longer there, you may wonder why I have left my opening chapter, the room-to-room description of Bowen's Court, in the present tense. I can only say that *I* saw no reason to transpose it into the past. There is a sort of perpetuity about livingness, and it is part of the character of Bowen's Court to be, in sometimes its silent way, very much alive.[53]

For Bowen, fiction about the country house novel preserved what was threatened—even if only by focusing on its present absence. The demolition of Bowen's Court not only reinforced but mandated her faith in fiction as a mode of presentation for what is materially absent. Moreover, in her conviction that the writer's and reader's imaginations have the power to meet in order to reconstruct the built environment of the past, she demonstrates a commitment to realist representation as the technique best suited for this task.[54]

---

52. During World War II, Bowen worked for the Ministry of Information providing intelligence on Ireland, which remained neutral. Her relationship with Ireland was therefore multilayered and often ambivalent. For further discussion of this important topic, see Clair Wills's "The Aesthetics of Irish Neutrality during the Second World War" (2004), Allan Hepburn's chapter on *The Heat of the Day* in *Intrigue* (2005), and Saeko Nagashima's "Reading Neutrality and Disloyalty in Elizabeth Bowen's "The Heat of the Day" (2012).

53. Bowen, *Bowen's Court*, 458–59.

54. Inglesby foregrounds her reading of *The Little Girls* with a discussion of the demolition of Bowen's Court and how that experience affected Bowen's personal writing technique and philosophy: "The end of Bowen's Court forced Bowen to examine once again the ways in which we seek to preserve history, personality, and expression in both houses and the small everyday items that most people barely notice. All of the imaginative work she had done concerning the value of places and objects could not completely prepare her to transfer the bricks and mortar of her heritage into the realm of pure language. During this period [the 1950s], she attempted to brace herself for the impact of demolition by flatly denying her material attachment to her home" ("Expressive Objects," 320). In his essay, "A Sort of Lunatic Giant," Eibhear Walshe also uses a biographical framework to set up a brief discussion of *The Little Girls* alongside a more extended analysis of *Eva Trout*. Walshe considers the impact of the sale and demolition of

While *Bowen's Court* and its afterword give readers the information and imagery they need to mentally reconstruct the demolished house, *The Little Girls* takes the opposite tack: it points to what is missing and partial instead of fantastically recreating abundance. Both choices, I argue, signal Bowen's realist sensibilities, the latter as it works against the distortions of lyrically nostalgic aesthetics. In 1951, she recorded a broadcast for the BBC Third Programme called "The Cult of Nostalgia" in which she hoped for the decline of nostalgia and argued that "against it, there is the pressing realism of history."[55] She calls for "a whole generation [to] keep the power of taking its moments 'straight'—not half-overcast by fantasy, not thinned-down by yearning. Why, indeed, should not imagination—without which, granted, happiness is impossible—be able to burn up in the air of today? . . . What has great art done but enclose that eternal 'now'?"[56] Thirteen years later, *The Little Girls* is an effort by Bowen to meet the demands of her own directive in this broadcast. In thematically and structurally enclosing a burnt-up absence, she turns away from an impulse to depict a romanticized or falsely realized past toward the "realism of history," in which people live in an eternal and ever-evaporating "now."

Bowen's faith in the recuperative power of an anti-nostalgic realism as a counterpoint to heritage culture informs every aspect of *The Little Girls*. The novel sketches out a set of relations among Dinah, Clare, and Sheila (known also by their childhood nicknames: Dicey, Mumbo, and Sheikie) as bookended by two time capsules: one that the girls buried at the site of their school in 1914 and one that Dinah is creating in a cave for her local village in the early 1960s. In the present of the novel, Dinah constantly talks about "posterity" and worries about how a future group of explorers or tourists will interpret the objects she has collected for the cave-museum. She is concerned about the lack of a clear narrative that will contribute to public knowledge while preserving the private identities of those who contributed objects. When her friend, Frank, complains that the objects "still all look to me very much the same" (*Little Girls*, 4), Dinah responds with a curatorial gesture that aims to link the objects with individuals: "'Look, though,' she cried with renewed fervour, 'I've been cataloguing, before I forget what's whose'" (5). Her cataloguing efforts are entirely future oriented. As she says to Mrs. Coral, "One should give

---

Bowen's Court as well as Bowen's time living and traveling in Rome on her two final novels. As with Inglesby's study, Walshe's essay makes use of limited historical context in order to argue that these novels are "crucial within Bowen's canon" (151). My own approach is less invested in the question of Bowen's canon or reputation than in how her writing works within broader historical circumstances.

55. Bowen, "Cult of Nostalgia," 101.
56. Bowen, "Cult of Nostalgia," 101.

posterity a break. One must leave posterity some clues! . . . Clues to reconstruct *us* from. Expressive objects. What really expresses people? The things—I'm sure—that they have obsessions about: keep on wearing or using, or fuss when they lose, or can't go to sleep without. You know, a person's only a *person* when they have some really raging peculiarity" (11). Beneath her eager time capsule curation, Dinah lacks confidence in the expressive potential of the things she has collected: "'And the point is, all are completely different! . . . At least,' said Dinah, looking with faint discouragement, or at least misgiving, at the clumps of objects, 'so I've always believed'" (11). Dinah is trying to create a site of historical preservation that, unlike a museum exhibition, privileges individual particularity over a more generalized public narrative. In fact, she protests to Mrs. Coral that the cave is more of a life-size time capsule than a museum, for it will be air-tight, sealed up, inaccessible; as she directly protests, "It's not a museum—or really anything like" (10). As Dinah continues to try and explain the cave and its expressive objects to Mrs. Coral, however, she becomes "exhausted," and her "voice ran down to a pause" (12).[57]

Despite Dinah's efforts to preserve individual history within the cave, the space of the cave is undoubtedly museum-like in its sense of enclosure and timelessness—the liminality that Carol Duncan identifies as crucial to the work of the museum in creating a singular, public narrative through ritual.[58] Bowen's narrator explicitly describes the timelessness of the cave: "It was now within an hour or so of sunset—unpent, brilliant after the rainstorm, long rays over the garden overhead, making wetness flitter, setting afire September dahlias and roses. Down here [in the cave], however, it was some other hour—peculiar, perhaps no hour at all" (*Little Girls,* 5). Not only is the cave a space with no temporal specificity, the description of Frank and Dinah standing in their own light recalls the primitive, symbolically bare moment of Plato's "Allegory of the Cave" only to deny the possibility of generating meaning that is central to the allegory: "Their two tall forms, backs to the entrance, not only overshadowed the table but further darkened the cave—blocking away from it outdoor daylight" (5). The cave is, like any museum, a space in which history is simultaneously narrated and cordoned off from the present. The allusion to Plato's allegory emphasizes the incompleteness of the "reality" presented in the cave. Like a wartime museum or a country house that has been transformed

---

57. A number of critics have considered Bowen's novel in terms of objects (Elizabeth Inglesby), posterity (Andrew Bennett and Nicholas Royle), and the relationship of past and present (Maud Ellmann, Marian Kelly, Anne Wyatt-Brown). While these interpretations offer compelling directions for reading the novel, historical analysis is often limited to biographical information, and none consider the larger context of heritage culture in postwar Britain.

58. Duncan, *Civilizing Rituals,* 20.

into a hospital or arts center, the cave is a repurposed, symbolically unstable space, only a partial record of what has been, as demonstrated by Mrs. Coral's recollection that "chickens were kept down here when I was a girl. . . . Times change" (9). Dinah attempts to enclose the various narratives within the cave through a ritualizing gesture: "Pulling, then tying the cave's curtains together was a ceremony amounting to locking up" (14). The partial enclosure and unlocked quality of curtains, rather than doors, suggests metaphorically that efforts to enclose heritage spaces with finality are fruitless.

All of Dinah's efforts to enclose objects, people, places, and narratives of the past are cut short or reversed in various ways. The third-person narrative voice is one counterpoint to Dinah's failed nostalgic efforts, as Elizabeth Inglesby and Marian Kelly have argued,[59] but Dinah is, herself, aware of the potential pitfalls of her preservation projects from the very beginning of the novel. She remarks self-consciously to Frank, "Did you know I had a predisposition to bury things? . . . I mean, for a purpose. One of the things that's happened to me this evening is, I see what I've been up to down in that cave. . . . That cave idea's been nice, and I'd never call it a fake, but of course it's been really only a repetition.—No, perhaps not so much exactly that as a going back, again, to something begun" (*Little Girls*, 21). After the women agree to dig up the time capsule, Dinah pinpoints her own nostalgia and questions its validity: "But one can miss without knowing what one misses. Miss—can't one?—without even knowing one *is* missing?" (183).[60] Structurally, Bowen counters Dinah's nostalgia-driven burials and enclosures with a larger project of enclosing missing landmarks, objects, narratives, and memories as a sign of the real present, the "eternal now" that cannot be fully contained.[61]

Landmarks and landscape continuously evaporate, as Clare puts it, "into thin air" (*Little Girls*, 76), prompting recognition of the past that has the ability to reshape the women's collective memories as well as their relationships with one another in the present. When Dinah suggests that the women meet at St. Agatha's to dig up the box, Sheila explains that "It's not there. . . . As you

---

59. Kelly uses reader-response theory to argue that, with this novel, "Bowen has finally and definitively attained her goal of giving us a model for rejecting nostalgia" ("Power of the Past" 13).

60. Susan Stewart, building on Freud, describes nostalgia as "sadness without an object" and "the desire for desire" (*On Longing*, 23). Dinah's "missing without knowing one is missing" clearly recalls this Freudian concept.

61. Bowen's novel precedes the moment when general cultural concern about the history of demolition became a dominant public narrative. In 1974, for instance, the Victoria and Albert Museum put on an exhibition, "The Destruction of the Country House," which chronicled a selection of over one thousand houses that had been demolished over the preceding century. See Patrick Wright's *On Living in an Old Country* for an extended study of preservationism in the 1970s and 1980s.

may or may not know, we were shelled at Southstone. . . . They lammed away at us, onward from 1940. . . . [The girls had] been long gone. That old place had not been a school for years. When it was hit it was empty and boarded up." At this point Clare responds with the interjection: "Into thin air" (76). When they arrive at "what had been the site of St. Agatha's grounds and building," it "looked like being impossible to determine" (196). The narrator anticipates the women's discovery of the empty time capsule and echoes Bowen's sentiments in the *Bowen's Court* afterword when it announces: "What is there is there; there comes to be something fictitious about what is not" (196). World War I separates the girls from each other and holds a pronounced place of narrative interruption in the 1914 flashback; World War II is then introduced as a further source of violence and demolition that disturbs the continuity of land, buildings, and historical as well as personal narratives for the postwar era. While World War I is acknowledged as an aesthetic interruption, World War II is figured as a material and existential one. Confronting the destroyed school prompts the characters to imaginatively reanimate the history of violence and loss represented by the building's absence.

In addition to the wars, redevelopment of the rural landscape is a force of historical transformation that the women navigate together. As Dinah says to Clare, "everywhere there's been built over with new houses. . . . And to make pretty little gardens, one quite often uses fragments of gardens which have been there" (*Little Girls*, 191). Outside the cave, the narrator defines the landscape as what "had been an orchard," with "such trees as had not been cleared away . . . seen in the near distance" (14). This haunting, absent orchard is the placeholder between the cave and Dinah's house, Applegate. The house, a 1912-built suburban villa, is another thwarted attempt within the novel to seal up, enclose, and prevent historical intrusion. It has a fabricated version of what Vita Sackville-West had described in 1947 as the "peculiar genius of the English country house," the "knack of fitting in":

> The house bespoke the sound workmanship which had gone into it; nothing had so far blunted the cut angles, gables, or mullions of the plate-glass windows (of which several projected into bays) or modified the new-quarried glare of the whole—which, by contrast, the lush green, wooded and pastoral, rolling Somerset landscape round it enhanced. Applegate promised to be much the same within as it was without, and was. Nothing rattled at night, even in a gale: the windows fitted, the doors shut properly. Neither the staircase nor any floor creaked.[62]

---

62. Sackville-West, *English Country Houses*, 17.

A twentieth-century phenomenon, Applegate is a modern, obstensibly sturdy re-creation of the historically vulnerable structure that formerly occupied its place: a farmhouse that had burnt to the ground one year before the construction of Applegate. Bowen's narrator introduces the farmhouse as a haunting absence through the sun that had "diluted into a misty film" and that "drew out an undertone that was there" (*Little Girls*, 17). Rather than admit and be changed by the haunted past, however, "Applegate stood up to the hour, as it had to others" (17). With this scene, Bowen also historically links the demolition of Bowen's Court and the rise of consumer heritage culture with the destructive burning of many Anglo-Irish big houses during the Irish War of Independence. Indeed, her 1929 novel, *The Last September*, ends with the burning of a Big House, Danielstown, and the suggestion that the family might build a bungalow like Applegate nearby. Like Dinah's house, Sheikie's ultra-modern house seems to deny any connection to historical context. It is unhomely, "overlit," with curtains that "handsomely [sail] apart" when a cord is pulled, "a place to be left to go back to one's own home" (210–11). Dinah's and Sheikie's houses, like the cave-museum, the time capsule, and the country house museum, are the fabricated placeholders for an absent house, its land, and its history. In narrating the empty gesture that these various placeholders make, Bowen contributes a type of preservation work that acknowledges reality rather than nostalgically mourning or romanticizing what is gone.[63]

Missing landmarks in the novel double the missing objects or souvenirs in the empty coffer that the women dig up. In developing a theoretical relation between nostalgia and the souvenir, Susan Stewart writes that "The souvenir speaks to a context of origin through a language of longing, for it is of the necessarily insatiable demands of nostalgia. The souvenir generates a narrative which reaches only 'behind,' spiraling in a continually inward movement rather than outward toward the future."[64] In the un-burial scene, the action appears on the page as follows:

It was there.
   It was empty.
      It had been found. (*Little Girls*, 201)

---

63. Bowen's attention to missing landmarks in this novel resonates with growing contemporaneous popular concern over the destruction of public monuments, such as the Euston Arch. In 1961, the British Transport Commission decided to demolish the Arch, a Roman artifact, in order to modernize Euston Station. The general public and architectural critics, including John Summerson, Nikolaus Pevsner, J. M. Richards, and John Betjeman voiced concern, but to no avail. In 1968, Alison and Peter Smithson wrote a book about the history of the arch: *The Euston Arch and the Growth of the London, Midland & Scottish Railway*.

64. Stewart, *On Longing*, 135.

The literal blank space on the page reinforces that the "It" that the women have found is absence and emptiness. In the case of *The Little Girls*, the *missing* souvenir accomplishes the opposite of what the found and kept souvenir does: it propels the characters "outward toward the future." According to Stewart's narrative logic, the missing objects enhance Bowen's realist critique of nostalgia. The characters are denied access to objects that would take them back, repeatedly, to a nonrepeatable time.

The emptiness of the time capsule, moreover, is put into sharp relief against the house in whose garden it is buried: a glass house called "Blue Grotto." The utter transparency of this biblically named house seems to mock the nostalgic fantasy of hide-and-seek that the coffer represents. If the empty coffer signals a resurrection at the site of the "grotto," it is a resurrection that liberates the concealed objects from the narratives in which the girls attempted to contain them. In fact, not only are the objects liberated; so is the history that those objects represented for Dinah. After the failed un-burial, the women sit uneasily together at Sheila's house, and Dinah becomes increasingly agitated and eager to leave:

> "Your home," pointed out Sheila, "won't run away."
> Dinah examined the speaker, before saying: "that's what it *has* done, Sheikie." She took a shaky gulp at her drink. She added: "Everything has. *Now* it has, you see. Nothing's real any more." (*Little Girls*, 209, emphasis original)

Dinah's nostalgic attachment to the narrative promise of the time capsule, which had held in place the "reality" of her past and her home, is revealed to be fictitious and ephemeral when she confronts the absence of the souvenirs. Propelled into the present and toward the future, Dinah finally submits and rejects her prior desire to recover the souvenirs: "It might be better to have no pictures of places which are gone. Let them go completely" (*Little Girls*, 216). Pictures, Dinah realizes, are yet another partial representation of the real thing. Eibhear Walshe, building on Bennett and Royle, reads the emptiness of the coffer as metonymic for the emptiness of the past in general. "By characterizing the past as dangerously empty," Walshe argues, "Bowen is extending her earlier preoccupations with isolation and unrootedness to a point of uncompromising bleakness, even nightmare."[65] Undoubtedly, the characters in the novel seem isolated and unrooted in the face of the emptiness they encounter, but I would argue that through the structural enclosure of the

---

65. Walshe, "Sort of Lunatic Giant," 156.

flashback that returns the characters and reader to the present, Bowen insists on the acceptance of this "bleak" emptiness as a new condition for a mode of fiction and being that is liberated from nostalgia.[66]

Bowen demonstrates her commitment to the "realism of history" by stylistically and structurally reinforcing a desire for wholeness that remains out of reach. The text reads like realist narrative that is missing selected components, giving it a lumbering, jolting quality. A number of narrative trajectories begin only to disappear or remain unresolved: Dinah's drafted advertisements for the newspaper (*Little Girls*, 28–29), Francis's desire to have a career in the Secret Service (26–27), the possible relationship between Dinah's mother and Clare's father (167).[67] At the level of prose, Bowen's sentence construction is relentlessly passive and her punctuation interruptive. For example: "From above, around, poured on to them [Clare and Dinah] the not wholly untender or hostile noon" (53). On the surface, this style seems typical of the high modernist aesthetic that Bowen cultivated in her earlier novels, but here the style is in the service of a larger realist confrontation with historical loss, with what is no longer physically present. In such rigorously passive sentences, Bowen forces the reader to search for meaning at the level of the sentence; the desire for clear, fully elaborated representation thus drives the reading experience in the same way that the characters are motivated to rediscover times, places, and things that are persistently elusive.

The flashback mirrors this logic structurally. Narratively, the middle section fails to reveal what seems from the first part of the novel to be the crucial piece of information: the secret contribution to the coffer that each woman made. These details aren't revealed until the narrative returns to the 1960s, and the revelation is decidedly anticlimactic (*Little Girls*, 242). Rather than confer meaning on the other two parts of the novel, then, the flashback acts as a digression that, as Susan Stewart suggests, "stands in tension with narrative closure. It is narrative closure opened from the inside out. . . . Instead of offering the reader transcendence, the digression blocks the reader's view,

---

66. Marian Kelly describes the novel not as bleak or nightmarish, but in quite the opposite direction, as triumphant: "When faced with *absence*, Dinah is finally forced to see the past as past, as no longer present" ("Power of the Past," 11). Kelly reads the final line of the novel as confirmation of Dinah's triumphant discovery of the present in place of the past. Upon waking, Dinah uses the grown-up, present-day name of "Clare" instead of the childhood nickname, "Mumbo." She asks, "'Who's there? . . . Mumbo? . . . Not Mumbo. Clare. Clare, where have you been?'" (*Little Girls*, 307).

67. In her essay, "But One Isn't Murdered: Elizabeth Bowen's *The Little Girls*," Sandra Kemp interprets these missing and abortive narratives as evidence of a perverse detective story that "contains internal relations and echoes that point to no meaning beyond the text" (131).

toying with the hierarchy of narrative events."[68] The resounding emptiness, absence, and partiality that characterize the present-day parts of the novel are only intensified by the empty digression of the flashback. Although the literary time capsule appears to enclose a historical moment that was so pivotal for the characters as well as for Britain's collective memory, the emptiness of its content challenges the finality and sufficiency of such narrative enclosure. To attempt in 1964 to lock the interwar period in the museum vault, Bowen's novel suggests, is to confront the impossibility of wholeness and closure; the realities of historical violence and loss defining those years continue to persist.[69]

While Bowen refuses to reveal the contents of the coffer within the flashback segment, she does hint at this persistent historical violence to which the flashback acts as a prelude. Near the end of the flashback, Bowen interrupts the text with a large image of the message on a birthday cake for one of Dinah's schoolmates:

Olive
Many Happy Returns
Of
The day
23rd July
1914 (153)

Just five days before the assassination of Archduke Franz Ferdinand and the beginning of World War I, "many happy returns" is a morbidly ironic if not entirely ominous message. Never again would Europe be able to return to a time that was so historically innocent, and yet so many soldiers were prevented from moving beyond anything but a traumatic repetition. Bowen's flashback "returns to" or "digs up" this prewar period only to reveal the emptiness of its promise to Olive, and to the world, of "many happy returns." The naïve happiness of this historical moment is accompanied by moments of vio-

---

68. Stewart, *On Longing*, 30.

69. For Marian Kelly, the flashback structure forces readers to experience the same isolation-inducing nostalgia that Dinah experiences, and the return to the present calls readers back to the present tense of the text and their own lives. Drawing on Paul Ricoeur, Kelly argues that Bowen's novel makes an analogy between reading and nostalgia: "Reading literally displaces people: like nostalgia, it locates them elsewhere so that their surroundings cease to exist" ("Power of the Past" 13). But the partialness of the flashback and the abrupt return to the present, for Kelly, prevent the reader from indulging freely in nostalgic reading practice and, instead, the reader is forced to "experience the disruption that nostalgia creates" ("Power of the Past" 15).

lence, morbidity, and recklessness that, placed in another year, might seem a normal part of childhood; in 1914, however, it becomes darkly prescient. The girls try to blow up the bicycle shed at Sheila's house (*Little Girls*, 96–97), and when they are playing on the beach, a boy named Trevor climbs up into a "vast iron drain-pipe, flaking with rust. . . . The thing had the look of being a sewer" (159). Dicey later recalls that she imagined that Trevor had never emerged, and she thought of his "wedged-in bones" (288). When the girls decide to bury a time capsule, they include a note that is clearly childlike, yet ominous given its historical context:

> We are dead, and all our fathers and mothers. You who find this, Take Care. These are our valuable treasures, and our fetters. They did not kill us, but could kill You. Here are Bones, too. You need not imagine that they are ours, but Watch Out. No wonder you are so puzzled. Truly Yours, the Buriers of This Box. (147)

In addition to the bones, each girl contributes one mystery item not revealed to the others. We later learn that Clare includes a gun and Sheila puts in a sixth toe that she had removed as a baby (*Little Girls*, 242). There hardly could be a more troublingly ironic gesture as a prelude to the death and disfigurement about to descend on Europe with the start of the war.

Bowen self-reflexively hints at the literary significance of the time capsule with Dinah's mystery object: a volume of Shelley's poetry that she contributes because she "had given him up," thinking "he was WRONG" (242). Along with a scene in which Clare has trouble reciting Wordsworth's "Ode on Intimations of Immortality from Recollections of Early Childhood," a nostalgic poem about not being able to see in the present what once was visible in the past (80), the discarded Shelley volume suggests the insufficiency of Romantic poetry for the task of postwar historical reckoning. "Ozymandias" might suggest that poetry outlives, and therefore preserves, human civilization, but in Bowen's novel, the Romantic affirmation of universal concepts of art and beauty is undone both when Dinah rejects Shelley and when the volume disappears from the coffer. The same goes for the novels that Mrs. Piggot reads in 1914 to escape daily realities: "As for her surroundings, they were nowhere. Feverel Cottage, the sofa, the time of day not merely did not exist for Mrs. Piggot, they did *not* exist. This began to give Clare, as part of them, an annihilated feeling" (94–95, emphasis original). Bowen's decidedly antiromantic, non-escapist, deliberately ponderous and porous novel thus acts as a counterpoint to those read by Mrs. Piggot as well as to the ahistorical ideals of Romanticism.

Near the end of the central flashback segment, Dinah observes a picnic on the beach: she looks back, "up the long stretch, at the far-away picnic—which though in view, in miniature, was in hearing only in gusts and starts" (*Little Girls*, 164). This moment is a metaphor for Bowen's realist approach to representing the past. The task is not to romanticize or to deceptively re-create but to foreground the ever-evaporating "now" as integral to its representation. Ultimately, the experimental realism of *The Little Girls* critiques the impetus of narrative enclosure that defined country house and heritage culture in the 1960s. For Bowen, history is not clearly delimited. As Clare says to Sheila, "Mistakes have histories, but no beginning—*like*, I suppose, history?" (299). Mingling with Clare's thoughts, the narrator takes this attitude toward history further in claiming its righteousness: "Chance, and its agents time and place. Chance is better than choice; it is more lordly. In its carelessness it is more lordly. Chance is God, choice is man" (306). The neo-sacred space of the postwar country house museum is a public celebration of man-made choices, especially the curatorial choices that allow certain narratives to emerge while others remain invisible or unheard. With the conclusive sentiment that "Chance is God, choice is man," Bowen's novel relocates the sacred in that which cannot be chosen, curated, and enclosed. Her novel remains defiantly and realistically open, and in doing so, it preserves a space for that sacred chance to materialize.

UNDER GLASS, BEHIND ROPES

In the grand entrance hall at Knole, one can inspect the holograph manuscript of Virginia Woolf's *Orlando* cased in glass. Ironically, the novel, which is set in a fictionalized Knole, anticipates its own museum-object status in a passage that captures the transformation of Knole from house to artifact collection:

> Rows of chairs with all their velvets faded stood ranged against the wall holding their arms out for Elizabeth, for James, for Shakespeare it might be, for Cecil, who never came. The sight made her [Orlando] gloomy. She unhooked the rope that fenced them off. She sat on the Queen's chair; she opened a manuscript book lying on Lady Betty's table; she stirred her fingers in the aged rose leaves; she brushed her short hair with King James' silver brushes: she bounced up and down upon his bed (but no King would ever sleep there again, for all Louise's new sheets) and pressed her cheek against the worn silver counterpane that lay upon it. But everywhere were little lavender bags to keep the moth out and printed notices, 'Please do

not touch,' which, though she had put them there herself, seemed to rebuke her. The house was no longer hers entirely, she sighed. It belonged to time now; to history; was past the touch and control of the living. Never would beer be spilt here any more, she thought (she was in the bedroom that had been old Nick Greene's), or holes burnt in the carpet. Never two hundred servants come running and brawling down the corridors with warming pans and great branches for the great fireplaces. Never would ale be brewed and candles made and saddles fashioned and stone shaped in the workshops outside the house. Hammers and mallets were silent now. Chairs and beds were empty; tankards of silver and gold were locked in glass cases. The great wings of silence beat up and down the empty house.[70]

Like the "tankards of silver and gold [that] were locked in glass cases," Woolf's manuscript would become part of the house that was its very subject, a house that "belonged to time" and "was past the touch and control of the living." Just as the chairs on which centuries of royalty have reclined remain behind velvet ropes for the twenty-first-century visitor, the manuscript signifies as an object but no longer contributes to the life of the house as a readable text. The larger implication for literary history is that, alongside the history of seventeenth-century, monarchical England, interwar high modernism is, at least partially, sealed into the house museum vault. With the donation of Knole to the National Trust in 1946, almost twenty years after the publication of *Orlando,* and five years after Woolf's death, her experimental, fantastical biography of Vita Sackville-West became part and parcel of a public country house narrative that was anything but avant-garde. Postwar novels such as *Angel* and *The Little Girls* point, respectively, to the danger of overinvesting in house museum culture—accepting romance and nostalgia in place of historical reckoning—and to the impossibility of containing literary history within such ideologically pat museums. As my behind the scenes "sighting" at Knole confirms, no matter how much institutions like the National Trust keep objects under glass and behind the ropes, there is always an uncharted space, and the realist literary imagination is one way of creating and accessing it.

---

70. Woolf, *Orlando,* 157.

CHAPTER 5

Safe Houses

*Seeking Shelter and Connection
Post-Consensus*

REENVISIONING THE PAST was a main preoccupation for writers who challenged the oversimplification of many public narratives emerging within popular heritage culture in the 1950s and 1960s. As the postwar period continued to unfold, the present took priority for realist fiction as the recent past of the postwar consensus was publicly called into question. In a frequently cited 1987 interview for *Woman's Own* magazine, Margaret Thatcher criticized the expectation that the British government had a responsibility to provide for the welfare of individual citizens:

> I think we have gone through a period when too many children and people have been given to understand "I have a problem, it is the Government's job to cope with it!" or "I have a problem, I will go and get a grant to cope with it!" "I am homeless, the Government must house me!" and so they are casting their problems on society and who is society? There is no such thing! There are individual men and women and there are families and no government can do anything except through people and people look to themselves first.[1]

---

1. Thatcher, Interview for *Woman's Own* ("no such thing as society") with Douglas Keay, n.p.

Under Thatcher's Conservative government (1979–90), the foundational vision of a Welfare State that made the collective a priority was exchanged for a one that valued individualism above all else. The leveling ethos of government sponsored social equality—however flawed in its realization—gave way to the emerging Conservative aim of economic growth associated with liberalized markets and private property. Severe cuts in government spending for council housing and public service industries, such as electricity and railways, followed by the privatization of the housing industry and major utilities that had been nationalized in the postwar settlement, transformed the relationship between the state and citizens' security in terms of basic needs.

Alongside a discussion of the history and implications of the privatization of the housing industry, this chapter considers Graham Greene's *The Human Factor* (1978) and Doris Lessing's *The Good Terrorist* (1985),[2] which depict a British society in which shelter and hospitality are no longer guaranteed and isolated individualism is the new, dysfunctional social rule. In these narratives, safe and reliable domestic space is elusive, a condition that recalls the volatility of the blitz and immediate postwar narratives discussed in chapter 2. In *The Slaves of Solitude* (1947) and *At Mrs. Lippincote's* (1945), shared living space had a profound effect on individual identity and narratives of development. Nearly forty years later, homelessness caused by wartime bombing damage finds its echo in homelessness caused by privatization. This echo was, however, not the one emphasized in official government rhetoric. As Owen Hatherley points out,

> "When Thatcherites . . . spoke of "hard choices" and "muddling through," they often evoked the memories of 1941. It served to legitimate [a regime] which constantly argued that, despite appearances to the contrary, resources were scarce and there wasn't enough money to go around; the most persuasive way of explaining why someone (else) was inevitably going to suffer. Ironically, however, this rhetoric of sacrifice was often combined with a demand that the consumers enrich themselves—buy their house, get a new car, make something of themselves, "aspire."[3]

As opposed to this rhetorical deployment of "the Blitz spirit" in the service of an austerity agenda, *The Human Factor* and *The Good Terrorist* use realist technique to confront real material and social conditions by recalling the

---

2. References to Greene's *The Human Factor* and Lessing's *The Good Terrorist* will use in-text citations.

3. Hatherley, *Ministry of Nostalgia*, 16–17.

effects of widespread environmental instability that characterized wartime and the immediate postwar decade.[4]

On the surface, these two texts bear little resemblance to one another. *The Human Factor* is a realist novel about a spy—not a formulaic popular spy novel—peppered with existential and spiritual meditation. It was written late in Greene's career in his trademark straightforward, accessible prose, and it appeared in the final year of the postwar consensus, during which Labour held a small majority and the Conservative party, led by Thatcher since 1975, was about to assume majority rule. Greene's novel thus highlights challenges to the postwar consensus emerging in the 1970s that anticipate the official sea change in governing policy after 1979. *The Good Terrorist*, published six years into Thatcher's term as Prime Minister, represents one woman's misguided dabbling in revolutionary politics, evoked unflinchingly through a more experimental realism that depends on Lessing's masterful use of focalization and representation of narrative time. Despite their thematic and stylistic differences, however, both texts are political novels whose protagonists are reluctantly political. Although Cold War espionage, the racial politics of apartheid South Africa, and IRA terrorism are necessary to the plots of these novels, the main characters are preoccupied by ultimately self-centered domestic concerns that they cannot or would prefer not to reconcile with the political crises shaping the wider world around them. They express a dangerously widening gap between personal experience and civic life—reversing efforts to bridge this gap, which were integral to wartime reconstruction initiatives and to the realist mode of fiction writing.

In the late 1970s and 1980s, with a number of Welfare State initiatives being scaled back, we can again read realistic fiction as a politically charged, world-building tool. Realist strategies, such as Greene's emphasis on the mundane details of the daily life of a spy or Lessing's exhausting real-time narration of life in a squat, help to clarify social realities, mirroring the role of realist fiction in the immediate postwar years. In contrast to the 1940s, however, the late twentieth-century context lacked the utopian or future-oriented impulse of postwar reconstruction initiatives. The community-centered housing estates and confidently vertical tower blocks of the first two postwar decades, in many cases, had fallen into disrepair by the 1970s, signifying for many the reversal or failure of postwar initiatives rather than continued progress.[5] Council

---

4. Hatherley, 16.

5. For Andrew Burke, postwar council housing, especially in tower blocks, has been the major symbol used by contemporary British filmmakers to assess the promises and pitfalls of modernity: "Originally identified with the modernist and modernising enthusiasms of the welfare state, tower blocks now house those who have been left behind or are out of sync with the dominant fantasies of a fully modernised British state" ("Concrete Universality," 178).

housing faced governmental neglect, as did the building industry in general. Construction rates across the United Kingdom slowed dramatically as a result of cuts to government spending on housing after the Conservatives came to power in 1979. While approximately 100,000 council housing units were constructed each year in the 1970s, that number declined to fewer than 30,000 per year by the mid-1980s, and by 1993, council housing construction had halted almost completely.[6] Over the course of the 1980s and early 1990s, Britain experienced the longest sustained fall in nominal house prices since the early 1950s; housing was "no longer seen as a 'safe' asset."[7]

Reconstruction narratives from the 1950s often conveyed faith in the future of the Welfare State, even if muted or complicated, through closing images of repaired or newly built houses and communities. To give an example from earlier in Greene's career, in *The End of the Affair* (1950), the jilted lover and betrayed husband agree to share a house after the death of the woman they both love rather than drifting into despair and isolation. Recall, as well, Colin MacInnes's narrator welcoming newly arrived immigrants to his neighborhood in London. Within the context of the late 1970s and 1980s, *The Human Factor* and *The Good Terrorist* demonstrate nothing of this earlier confidence in rebuilding. Instead, these works articulate the thwarted desire for a "safe house." Basic physical shelters and ideal notions of political or familial homes are threatened or unavailable in post-consensus Britain. In depicting troubled efforts to establish domestic safety and stability that culminate in fraught openness, these narratives critique a society in which individuals are isolated because architectural safety and community-oriented planning are no longer dependable realities.

A "safe house" is a particularly suggestive metaphor for considering the cultural ramifications of and responses to the political, economic, and ideological transformations of the 1970s and 1980s in Britain. It refers to both the private or domestic and the political and economic. As a term, "safe house" has immediate recognition in relation to domestic violence, and it is also close to "safe haven" or refuge, with its implications for refugees and displaced persons. In these cases, "safe house" may have a positive connotation, but the term must immediately be understood as ambiguous because the shelter provided is only temporary. As a political metaphor, the phrase has a functional meaning in Cold War espionage contexts, and in the specific context of postwar Britain, the Welfare State can be understood as a political, economic, and literally architectural safe house through the provisions of citizenship, immigration rights, and welfare programs that include the construction and main-

---

6. Golland, *Systems of Housing Supply and Housing Production in Europe*, 7.

7. Meen, "Ten Propositions in UK Housing Macroeconomics," 425.

tenance of public housing. Economically, moreover, "safe house" is close to the colloquial phrase "safe as houses," which means "certainly, undoubtedly," and has a nineteenth-century meaning in Britain that refers to houses as safe economic investments.[8] The innate ambiguity of the domestic meanings for "safe house" also applies to these political and economic associations in the 1970s and 1980s: the spy, the citizen, and the speculator all operate within systems that are in flux. Any safety is provisional. As the title for this chapter, "Safe Houses" thus refers to this range of meanings and their inherent ambiguities.

Writing about the American context, Mary Louise Pratt uses the phrase productively to describe historical scenarios in which threatened communities obtain basic protection while also finding the space to create identities or nurture ideals. Despite the important differences between American and British contexts, her characterization of safe houses resonates with my focus on the leveling legacy of the Welfare State. For Pratt, safe houses are

> social and intellectual spaces where groups can constitute themselves as horizontal, homogeneous, sovereign communities with high degrees of trust, shared understandings, temporary protection from legacies of oppression.... Where there are legacies of subordination, groups need places for healing and mutual recognition, safe houses in which to construct shared understandings, knowledges, claims on the world that they can then bring into the contact zone.[9]

Against the equality of safe houses, Pratt uses the term "contact zones," which she defines as "social spaces where cultures meet, clash, and grapple with each other, often in contexts of highly asymmetrical relations of power."[10] In Britain in the 1970s and 1980s, metaphoric and literal safe houses of the Welfare State came under threat or disappeared altogether. Social relations were characterized more by the logic of the contact zone than the safe house. Throughout, this chapter makes use of Pratt's term "contact zone" to emphasize the political, economic, and social conditions that were fundamentally unwelcoming to vulnerable populations in Britain in these years.

---

8. According to John Camden Hotten's *The Slang Dictionary: Etymological, Historical and Anecdotal*, compiled in the mid-to-late nineteenth century, "safe houses" is defined as "an expression to satisfy a doubting person; 'Oh! it's as safe as HOUSES,' i.e., perfectly safe, apparently in allusion to the paying character of house property as an investment. It is said the phrase originated when the railway bubbles began to burst, and when people began to turn their attention to the more ancient forms of speculation, which though slow were sure" (n.p.).

9. Pratt, "Arts of the Contact Zone," 6.

10. Pratt, 1. In "Arts of the Contact Zone," Pratt defines the concept of the contact zone in part by distinguishing it from Benedict Anderson's notion of the imagined community (4).

REMOVING THE SAFETY NET: PRIVATIZATION AND INHOSPITALITY AFTER CONSENSUS

Thatcher's election as Prime Minister in 1979 is widely understood as a major turning point in postwar British history.[11] Stuart Laing describes this election as "the final confirmation that the postwar settlement of welfare capitalism (based on full employment) was over."[12] The Welfare State had struggled, even under a Labour government, to fulfill its promises in the context of the global and domestic socioeconomic challenges of the 1970s, but near total reversal was ensured by increased market liberalization and the privatization schemes that came to dominate economic policy under Thatcher's Government in the 1980s. Privatization of public housing programs and major public utilities such as gas, electricity, coal, oil, and telecommunications was the ultimate manifestation of an ideological and political break from social democracy as it had been practiced, relatively unchallenged by both Labour and Conservative governments in Britain, since the 1940s. For political scientist Andrew Gamble, "Selling nationalized industries back into private ownership was visible proof that collectivism could be turned back."[13] Privatization was felt across all aspects of British society, but housing bore the brunt of public spending cuts throughout Thatcher's term.[14] Because public housing was threatened, it became a crucial political issue, as did homelessness.

Homelessness numbers had increased during the 1960s as a result of slum clearance programs. Displaced people were put on long waiting lists to be rehoused. As public concern escalated, numerous charities were founded to address the problem, including Shelter (1966), Crisis (1967), St. Mungo's (1969), and Porchlight (1974). Although data collection was inconsistent until

---

11. As Joseph Brooker notes in *Literature of the 1980s: After the Watershed*, scholarship on any aspect of British life during this period has to account for "the influence of the Conservative governments that administered Britain for the entire decade, and the attempts they made to alter British society and its historical trajectory" (2). This chapter follows Brooker in recognizing the necessity of considering the literature of the period within the context of emerging Thatcherism. But rather than broadly engaging this context, I consider the particularly dramatic changes to housing policy that took effect in the late 1970s and 1980s, which were central to dismantling portions of the Welfare State. Thatcher's reference to housing and homelessness in the *Woman's Own* interview indicates the significance of these issues in debates about the purpose of government in late twentieth-century Britain. Indeed, Brooker's more general overview of the period obliquely acknowledges the importance of housing with several references to architecture and landscape, including "characteristic . . . toytown apartment buildings, converted warehouses, gleaming blocks; . . . the redevelopment of London's Docklands into a Manhattan-on-Thames" (*Literature of the 1980s*, 17).
12. Laing, "Ken Loach: Histories and Contexts," 20.
13. Gamble, "Privatization, Thatcherism, and the British State," 4.
14. Cooper, *Public Housing and Private Property, 1970–1984*, 18.

the 1990s, the National Assistance Board conducted various surveys beginning in 1965, which suggest that the scale of homelessness increased significantly during the 1980s and early 1990s. The number of homeless people likely reached its peak in the early 1990s. According to the 1991 Census, 2,703 people were "sleeping rough" in a given night.[15] As Stephanie Cooper, education officer with the Inner London Education Authority, described the situation in 1985, "In deciding whether or not there would be a future for public housing the future of the welfare state would be called into question."[16] Housing can thus be understood as *the* cultural and political issue of the 1980s just as it was in the 1940s. Because the promise of reconstruction and rehousing was so central to the creation of the postwar Welfare State, in literal and symbolic terms, housing is the issue through which major structural and ideological transformations of British society can be measured.

The Thatcher Government housing policy is most strongly associated with the 1980 Housing Act, which introduced the "right to buy" program. Under this initiative, owner occupation of private property became the economic goal and ideological norm for residents in public housing. The program was popular in the aftermath of 1970s public expenditure cuts, which had led to the physical neglect of much council housing. Norman Ginsburg, Social Policy scholar, explains the popularity of "right to buy" as an outcome of social mobility dependent on consumer culture and the ideal of private property ownership:

> The sociopolitical tide began to turn against council housing in the 1970s, as home ownership came increasingly within the reach of working class families. Mortgaged owner occupied homes became a central element in and the locus for consumer culture. The "fiscal crisis of the state" in the mid 1970s prompted the then Labour government to cut back on investment in maintenance, improvement and development of council housing. This process was greatly enhanced under the Conservative governments from 1979-97. Hence from the tenants' point of view, the advantages of council housing ebbed away, as rents increased above inflation, maintenance and improvement withered, and "right to buy sales" visibly demonstrated governments' lack of commitment to the sector. The spiral of decline over the 1980s and 1990s was, thus, largely engineered by governments, bolstered by an often zealous commitment to widening home ownership. Councils were hamstrung,

---

15. "Homeless and Nowhere to Go . . . 35 years of Homelessness," n.p.
16. Cooper, *Public Housing and Private Property, 1970-1984*, 18.

unable to raise investment funds for maintenance, improvement and new development, and, yet, held politically responsible by tenants.[17]

Council housing projects capturing the optimism of the 1950s were not sustainable without full financial and ideological support from the government. The neglected tower block, in particular, was a highly visible sign of the failure of utopian Welfare State initiatives. One of the early symbolic challenges to the Welfare State was the 1968 gas explosion at the twenty-two-story Ronan Point in Newham, East London. An entire corner of the tower collapsed, leaving three people dead and eleven injured. The tower block, designed by Taylor, Woodrow, and Anglian, was built using an efficient and cost-effective modern construction technique known as Large Panel System building: large concrete panels were prefabricated off-site and then bolted together on-site. The disaster prompted public and governmental concern over the safety of System-built projects. Although architectural design and government policy are not one and the same, events like the Ronan Point accident became easy symbolic touchstones for arguments against public housing, fueling the support for right to buy. As privatization became the rule, the sense of security once conferred on tenants in public housing could, and then would, no longer be guaranteed by the government. Individuals in alliance with corporations and private banks were to take complete responsibility for obtaining and maintaining their own domestic and economic security, and this policy shift can be understood as a strategic move by the Conservative government that projected a vision of nothing short of a new social and economic order.[18]

The Human Factor and *The Good Terrorist* realistically capture and respond to the pressures of the declining Welfare State contact zone with characters who seek safe houses, hospitality, and community belonging. The search for immediate physical shelter reflects the broader need for a system of sociopolitical security, which was once promised by the postwar consensus but no longer is guaranteed to the same extent. Hospitality should be understood not as a simple extension of good will, but as a complex social and philosophical problem defined by contradiction—contradiction that these novels by Greene and Lessing reveal. In Derrida's formulation, unconditional hospitality is an impossible ideal because the inclusive ethos of such hospitality depends on a simultaneous exclusion of the undesirable. The open welcome, in which we "say yes *to who or what turns up*, before any determination," is necessarily yoked to conditional laws or a politics of hospitality that restrict

---

17. Ginsburg, "The Privatization of Council Housing," 118–19.
18. For a full discussion of "Thatcherism" in its political, economic, legal, and ideological manifestations, see *Thatcher's Law*, edited by Andrew Gamble and Celia Wells (1989).

entry.[19] In order for refuge to have meaning, in other words, a danger or threat must still exist that forces limitations upon hospitality. In the late 1970s and 1980s, the dangers and limitations that give hospitality and safe houses value became increasingly prohibitive. Those who could not afford to take part in the "right to buy" program had to take their chances with, in many cases, multiyear waiting lists for public housing. In the meantime, they were forced to find basic shelter, if they could, in over-crowded temporary housing, with relatives, or, as depicted in *The Good Terrorist*, in squats. Rather than invest in the maintenance of public housing with funds from the central government, local councils, facing steep budget cuts, made it difficult for squatters to occupy abandoned housing by cutting electricity and blocking toilets, leaving the structures uninhabitable.

In *The Human Factor*, physical barriers to safety and hospitality are reinforced by a shift away from social inclusiveness, as privatization and morally suspect Cold War politics become the norm in British society. The black South African characters, Sarah and Sam, are permitted to stay in the home of Sarah's white English mother-in-law, but they are hardly welcomed there. The Welfare State was not perfectly hospitable to all of its citizens, as my earlier discussion of Colin MacInnes and the Notting Hill race riots indicates. Determined policies of privatization, however, and Thatcher's later sentiment that there is "no such thing as society," added limiting conditions to the relatively more welcoming framework of the Welfare State that had extended resources to all members of British society, including newly arrived immigrants from former colonies under the Nationality Act (1948). *The Human Factor* anticipates, and *The Good Terrorist* confirms, that the scaled-back socioeconomic safety nets and the disappearance of public housing as reliable physical shelter under the Conservative agenda thus be understood as profoundly and materially inhospitable.

The two works of fiction analyzed in this chapter interrogate the transformed conditions of state-sanctioned hospitality through thematic attention to safety and danger as well as to the hospitable and inhospitable gestures of individuals and communities. Safe houses emerge intermittently, without help from the government or in spite of aggressive tactics to deny access to those

---

19. Derrida and Dufourmantelle, *Of Hospitality,* 77. In Derrida's words: "But even while keeping itself above the laws of hospitality, *the* unconditional law of hospitality needs the laws, it *requires* them. This demand is constitutive. It wouldn't be effectively unconditional, the law, if it didn't *have to become* effective, concrete, determined, if that were not its being as having-to-be. It would risk being abstract, utopian, illusory, and so turning over into its opposite. In order to be what it is, *the* law thus needs the laws, which, however, deny it, or at any rate threaten it, sometimes corrupt or pervert it. And must always be able to do this" (*Of Hospitality,* 79).

spaces of refuge. In the end, both texts reveal safe houses to be unsustainable, inadequate, and incapable of compensating for inhospitable political realities. Structurally and stylistically, through unresolved plots and ironic focalization, these novels remain markedly open. Within a discussion of hospitality, such openness might be read as a gesture that welcomes interpretation. But the irony that this gesture entails—to welcome the reader's agency is to destabilize the characters—only substantiates Derrida's observation that a perfectly open hospitality remains a fantasy. Narrative openness in *The Human Factor* and *The Good Terrorist* creates ambiguity that draws in the reader to grapple with possible meanings suggested by plot and characterization. Character, in this scenario, is malleable when exposed to multiple readings. A less open approach, with neatly resolved plots and clearly signposted difference between character and narrator, would make meaning less ambiguous and thus keep the reader at a distance—a more stable, and possibly more reassuring, sense of character would emerge.

In literary terms, then, these novels suggest that the role of realist fiction in the scaled-back Welfare State is not to provide a safe house of sorts for the reader; it is, instead, to emulate the contact zone and emphasize the elusiveness of safety and hospitality in citizens' daily lives. Without basic provisions of physical shelter and clarified meaning, characters and readers alike become preoccupied with individual safety and superficial comforts over and above collective well-being and sociopolitical efficacy. And yet, the aesthetic accessibility of these texts does constitute an invitation to the reader to perceive and contemplate their fictional worlds. As a response to hostile social and material conditions, these novels refuse to turn inward, resort to abstraction, or oversimplify through the paranoid formulas of dystopia;[20] rather, they seek outward engagement and foster connection through language. In this sense, they exhibit what Lessing herself identified nearly thirty years earlier as the unique promise of committed realist literature to both preserve the integrity of the individual and create a robust social community. She asserted that "the novelist has one advantage denied to any of the other artists. The novel is the only popular art-form left where the artist speaks directly, in clear words, to his audience. Film-makers, playwrights, television writers, have to reach people through a barrier of financiers, actors, producers, directs. The novelist talks, an individual to individuals, in a small personal voice."[21] Thus, even as *The Human Factor* and *The Good Terrorist* reveal the dangers of extreme

---

20. J. G. Ballard's *High-Rise* is an iconic 1970s example of the dystopian response to social problems that picks up on the image of the neglected tower block for its titular symbol.

21. "Small Personal Voice," 21.

individualism, their realism asserts the desire for a more humanistically oriented Britain.

THE HUMAN FACTOR AND THE BORDERLESS IDEAL

Like many of Graham Greene's novels, *The Human Factor* explores the experience and consequences of individual isolation. Characters starved for connection find themselves placed in literal and metaphorical boxes, ultimately alone. Maurice Castle, the MI6 protagonist of *The Human Factor*, fantasizes about a time and place where boxes, walls, and the "safety curtain" are not necessary (*Human Factor*, 206). Early in the novel, Castle steps into a church in Berkhamstead, the village where he grew up and has returned to live as an adult. He hears the parishioners singing a hymn: "There is a green hill far away, without a city wall" (57). This borderless place, perfectly open and hospitable, is an unattainable ideal rather than a realistic goal, as Castle's heavily fortified name intimates. The real world, plagued by divisive categories of nation, ideology, race, and self, continually reasserts itself. Forced to live in that world, Castle has aims that become impossible to reconcile: to protect and enclose himself and those he loves while also striving to break down walls and achieve open connection with other human beings. Recalling Derrida's formulations, Castle's dilemma demonstrates the "insoluble antinomy" of hospitality.[22] While the Soviet safe house, in espionage terms, offers a place of physical and political refuge for Castle at the end of the novel, it also represents the necessary limits of human openness, acceptance, and connection, as the safe house is a temporary point of transition that is also inaccessible to his South African wife and son. In the context of late 1970s Britain, the representation of safety and hospitality in Greene's novel critiques a world in which political and social borders seem increasingly arbitrary while the necessary physical protections are less reliable. The result is moral and spatial isolation and a false sense of autonomy: Castle clings to a belief that only one person alone in a room can be truly safe, but in the espionage context, of course, even this image of secure solitude is troubled by the inevitability that he is being watched and politically manipulated.

Begun in 1967 but not finished until 1978, *The Human Factor* captures the initial decline of the legislative framework and philosophy of the postwar consensus. After Edward Heath's Conservative government came to power in 1970, unemployment grew, and tension between the state and trade unions

---

22. Derrida and Dufourmantelle, *Of Hospitality*, 77.

began to escalate following the Industrial Relations Act of 1971 and the miners' strike in 1972. Conflict with Northern Ireland grew more serious. Terrorism began to spread in England with bombings perpetrated by the IRA, as well as the anarchist group known as the Angry Brigade. Global and domestic recession took its toll, with widespread inflation and skyrocketing oil prices due to the embargo issued by the Organization of Arab Petroleum Exporting Countries as a result of the UK support of Israel alongside other allies in the Yom Kippur War. Domestically, the embargo gave leverage to miners, who sought to protest an anti-inflation cap on pay raises; the government responded to strike action with the institution of the Three-Day Week, a measure introduced to save electricity.[23] When a Labour government was elected in February 1974, it was "the first example of an industrial dispute leading to a change of government in contemporary British history."[24] Despite this symbolically significant election, Labour held a very small parliamentary majority; as a result, any hopes of bolstering the framework of Welfare State socialism drifted away. With Thatcher elected as Conservative party leader in 1975, the late 1970s came to be defined by cuts to public spending, increasing tension as a result of nationalism in Wales and Scotland, and perhaps most dramatically, the Winter of Discontent in 1978–79, in which workers in the public sector refused to accept salary caps as a solution to economic hardship.

Like John le Carré's 1974 novel, *Tinker, Tailor, Soldier, Spy*, *The Human Factor* rejects the formulas and archetypes of spy fiction popularized by Ian Fleming's James Bond franchise and instead realistically chronicles the banal, unglamorous world of Secret Service bureaucracy in the depressed socioeconomic context of the 1970s. In his autobiography, *Ways of Escape* (1980), Greene explains that his aim in writing *The Human Factor* was to humanize the genre of British spy fiction by deromanticizing its adventurous plotlines and redirecting attention to the individual character. He aimed

> to write a novel of espionage free from the conventional violence, which has not, in spite of James Bond, been a feature of the British Secret Service. I wanted to present the Service unromantically as a way of life, men going daily to their office to earn their pensions, the background much like that of any other profession—whether the bank clerk or the business director—an undangerous routine, and within each character the more important private life.[25]

---

23. The Three-Day Week limited commercial electricity use to three consecutive days each week, as specified by the government, from 1 January to 7 March 1974.
24. Laing, "Ken Loach: Histories and Contexts," 19.
25. Greene, *Ways of Escape*, 227.

In other words, *The Human Factor* is first and foremost a work of realism. Like other works of reconstruction fiction, the novel should be read as a realist interruption that intervenes in literary discourses and social conditions. In this case, Greene interrupts the popular espionage genre with a realistic examination of how moral and political conflicts affect the individual and interpersonal relationships. Socially, the novel intervenes by drawing attention to the globally expansive and potentially overwhelming context of the Cold War with a narrative that is comprehensible, yet not oversimplifying, to individual readers.

The Human Factor has been discussed compellingly in relation to the espionage context, in a comparative analysis of Greene's spy novels, and in a discussion of loyalty and morality in Greene's work. For instance, in the introduction to their recent edited volume, *Dangerous Edges of Graham Greene*, Mark Bosco, SJ, and Dermot Gilvary describe *The Human Factor* as a novel that "explores the virtue of disloyalty when it comes to the state secret service apparatus. Greene continues to condemn the wasteland of modern espionage, especially as smaller nations get drawn into shady alliances between the super powers."[26] By discussing Greene's novel alongside Lessing's and in the sociopolitical context of housing during the period, rather than solely in terms of Greene's oeuvre or the spy fiction genre, a reading emerges that emphasizes the broader cultural trend of contemplating hospitality in the years of the waning Welfare State. Understanding Greene's novel in this way foregrounds his interest in the relationship between the private individual and the political realm.

The private life of Maurice Castle, which Greene claimed to want to emphasize over and above the drudgery of daily working life, is closely guarded against a background of malaise, apathy, and frustrated insecurity. The waning of economic and social safety nets is evidenced by the schoolmasters who live on either side of Castle: they earn a salary that provides "no possibility of saving" (*Human Factor*, 18). The entire novel is littered with characters, relationships, houses, and systems for which there is "no possibility of saving," in any sense of the word, whether it be saving a life, money, resources, or ideological certainty. Tellingly, an alternate title for the novel was "Sense of Security."[27] Castle's coworker, Arthur Davis, is wrongly suspected to be the source of an information leak to the Soviets in South Africa, and he is

---

26. Bosco, SJ, and Gilvary, Introduction to *Dangerous Edges*, 11. For other relevant examples, see Robert Snyder's essay, "'He Who Forms a Tie Is Lost': Loyalty, Betrayal, and Deception in *The Human Factor*"; Laura Tracy's essay, "Passport to Greeneland"; and Allan Hepburn's book, *Intrigue*.

27. Snyder, "He Who Forms a Tie," 26.

subsequently killed; in order to protect himself as the true source of the leak, Castle cannot save Davis. When Davis says to Castle, "I'm tired to death of this damned old country, Castle, electricity cuts, strikes, inflation," the foreshadowing suggests that Davis's death is a result of the deception and betrayal that defines both specific espionage activities and the times in which he lives more generally (*Human Factor*, 51). In referencing electricity cuts, strikes, and inflation, Davis clearly alludes to the Three-Day Week and the continuing tension between trade unions and the Labour government after 1974. These are times, moreover, in which not only social and economic systems are failing, but, unbeknownst to Davis, individualism trumps all other affiliation, with dire consequences.

Davis's wrongful death is also a symptom of the lack of moral clarity in Cold War politics, particularly in the South African context. Castle leaks the information ostensibly to resist tacit British support of apartheid, a morally defensible action challenged by the loyalty to the Soviet dictatorship that it entails. MI6 Control, John Hargreaves, also misses the moral motivation and interprets the leak only as a spectacle of power for power's sake. In discussing the motives for the leak, Hargreaves says to Percival, the Service doctor responsible for poisoning Davis: "There are no atomic secrets in Africa: guerrillas, tribal wars, mercenaries, petty dictators, crop failures, building scandals, gold beds, nothing very secret there. That's why I wonder whether the motive may be simply scandal, to prove they [the Soviets] have penetrated the British Secret Service yet again" (*Human Factor*, 31). Scandal, fatigue, and moral hypocrisy, define Britain's international and domestic politics alike. Likewise, the trope of the Soviet mole as plot device has become similarly worn out. In political and narrative terms, disillusionment with the Cold War reigns. Greene channels these characteristics through Castle, who worries, when talking with Cornelius Muller, the racist South African agent, about how many of his agents were incriminated in the scandal: "His own relative safety made him feel shame. In a genuine war an officer can always die with his men and so keep his self-respect" (97). In both South Africa and at home in Britain, official policies increasingly support those who already have power instead of those who are disenfranchised or who are at risk of becoming so. Further, as Castle discovers, any move to extend protections to those who are oppressed under apartheid rule only puts him in the service of yet another super power, and a tyrannical one at that, with its own set of limiting prohibitions. As the Welfare State destabilizes in the context of the Cold War, personal safety and ethical politics are shown to be increasingly incommensurate.

In the context of such insecure times, Maurice Castle's borderless fantasy reflects a disillusion with Cold War politics and the hypocritical ideological affiliations of nation states. Greene explicitly links *The Human Factor* with his frustration over South Africa in *Ways of Escape* (1980): "It was so obvious that, however much opposed the governments of the Western Alliance might pretend to be to apartheid, however much our leaders talked of its immorality, they simply could not let South Africa succumb to black power and Communism."[28] In contrast to this corrupt political scenario, Maurice nostalgically yearns for a time and place in which personal relationships override politics and ideological concerns. It is a fantasy of returning home and capturing the mythically innocent belonging of childhood without the requirements of political affiliation or religious faith. The fantasy itself is his ultimate safe house. When Castle and Sarah are forced to offer hospitality to Cornelius Muller, the man who had once been the enemy of their relationship in South Africa, the tension between personal commitments and political duties comes to the foreground. Later that night, Castle seeks refuge in his fantasy: he allows himself "to strike, like his childhood hero Allan Quatermain, off on that long slow underground stream which bore him on towards the interior of the dark continent where he hoped that he might find a permanent home, in a city where he could be accepted as a citizen, as a citizen without any pledge of faith, not the City of God or Marx, but the city called Peace of Mind" (*Human Factor*, 107).[29] Castle is fixated on an idealized place that escapes the strictures of human and government systems but that nevertheless provides citizenship as a means of participation and an announcement of unconditional inclusion.

To preserve his safe house, his borderless place, Castle ironically constructs, identifies, and reinforces protective walls in all aspects of his life. This strategy allows the two-fold irony of his name to emerge: "Castle" suggests fortified protection even though the ideal he values is borderless, and it references the nationalistic notion that "an Englishman's home is his castle"—a meaning all too pointed for a Soviet mole. He tries to obtain security without

---

28. Greene, *Ways of Escape*, 229.
29. This passage also clearly recalls Conrad's *Heart of Darkness* and, as Snyder claims, the Victorian adventure narrative in general ("He Who Forms a Tie," 29). In *Heart of Darkness* (1902), Charles Marlow narrates his obsession with the "blank" and "dark" spaces on maps, and in particular, "a mighty big river, that you could see on the map, resembling an immense snake uncoiled, with its head in the sea, its body at rest curving afar over a vast country, and its tail lost in the depths of the land. . . . I went on along Fleet Street, but could not shake off the idea. The snake had charmed me" (22–23). Snyder argues that Castle's attachment to the Victorian adventure narrative indicates a rejection of modern-day institutions and belief systems: "The former banker [Castle] whose boyhood hero was Allan Quatermain and whose sole achievement since joining the firm more than thirty years ago consists in having 'reduced the expenses of the [Pretoria] station considerably' is a man defined by his generation's search for some viable model of authenticity, most other candidates having been discredited with the rise of modernism" ("He Who Forms a Tie," 33).

what he perceives to be the cost of arbitrary ideological commitment. When he goes to see Boris, his Soviet controller, he feels "at home" because only Boris knows the full extent of his counterespionage (even more than Castle knows, in fact), but Castle insists that their relationship remain strictly informational: "I've never pretended that I share your faith—I'll never be a Communist" (*Human Factor,* 121). Despite his ostensible resistance to ideology, however, he cannot help but conceive of Boris's role for him as "a bit like a priest must be to a Catholic—a man who received one's confession whatever it might be without emotion" (117). The analogy, and the reality that "there's no one in the world with whom I can talk of everything, except this man Boris whose real name even is unknown to me," gives Castle "a sense of revulsion" (117). He needs the security that Boris provides, but he takes it grudgingly, for ultimately it provides only a continually multiplied absence of existential and ethical certainly.

Castle's troubled loyalty to the Soviets is doubled by his interest in religious sanctuary—as if he suspects that he might be able to exchange his dubious ideological loyalty for a more transcendent and reliable faith. He seeks sanctuary in a church only to leave disappointed, rejected, and as disillusioned with religion as he is with politics. When he goes to look for Boris a second time only to find that the Soviet safe house is no longer there—that even the "official" safe house cannot provide safety—he goes into a church following an urge to confess "*in camera*" (*Human Factor,* 183). Whereas Boris takes Castle's information without requiring a profession of Communist faith, the priest refuses his information on exactly such grounds: Castle is not a Catholic or a Christian of any kind: "'I think what you need is a doctor,' the priest said. He slammed the shutter to, and Castle left the box" (184). Castle spends the novel stepping in and out of "boxes," looking for protection that won't require ideological or religious affiliation. It is ultimately Boris who speaks the truth that Castle refuses to hear—"We live in boxes and it's they who choose the box"—a truth confirmed by the ending of the novel in which Castle is left isolated in the most inhospitable of safe houses: a two-room apartment (or box) in Moscow, with an unreliable telephone line that goes dead (117), emphasizing his ultimately disconnected state.

Snyder also observes the importance of "boxes" in Greene's novel. For him, the trope of boxes indicates Castle's entrapment in the world of espionage: despite his best intentions to avoid ideological affiliation, Castle unwittingly does so as he aligns himself "with the law of expediency governing intelligence networks."[30] In *Intrigue,* furthermore, Allan Hepburn points out that, across

---

30. Snyder, "He Who Forms a Tie," 30.

his oeuvre, "Greene's protagonists frequently enter closets, railroad cars, sheds, out-houses."[31] In addition to causing physical claustrophobia, Hepburn argues that these dark, box-like spaces signify "a recollection of death or near-death experience" that induces "existential panic."[32] Taken together, these readings by Snyder and Hepburn point to the double bind that "the box" represents for Maurice and for Greene: it is appealing as a site for apolitical existential contemplation, even if that contemplation induces panic, but it inevitably implicates him in a larger, if less visible, network of power relations. While Soviet Communism promised homes for all, Castle realizes that there is a price to be paid for the promise of equality: namely, the surrendering of private property and individual autonomy that he clearly values.

Against Boris's proclamation that Castle cannot determine the boundaries of his own life, especially while under Soviet control, Castle struggles to secure the safety of his family without the help of external allegiances. Family is the community to which he tries to pledge allegiance above all others. Where Sarah and Sam are concerned, Castle's thoughts and actions are motivated by the promise of safety throughout the novel. After kissing Sarah, for instance, "he was reassuring himself that what he valued most in life was still safe" (*Human Factor*, 19). And when discussing his time in South Africa with Hargreaves, he remarks, "We're safely married now. But we did have a difficult time out there" (53). They live away from the perceived dangers of London, in quiet Berkhamstead. Ironically, Castle wants to protect his family, but he also needs the barrier of his house and family—his entire domestic space—to protect himself as an individual from the world with its ominously set borders, boxes, and categories. He attends to the physical space and literal sounds of his house in order to create a protective mental border between himself and that world:

> A door was closed softly, footsteps passed along the corridor above; the stairs always creaked on the way down—he thought how to some people this would seem a dull and domestic, even an intolerable routine. To him it represented a security he had been afraid every hour he might lose. He knew exactly what Sarah would say when she came into the sitting-room, and he knew what he would answer. Familiarity was a protection against the darkness of King's Road outside and the lighted lamp of the police station at the corner. (144)

---

31. Hepburn, *Intrigue*, 121.
32. Hepburn, 122.

Castle recreates with his house and family the political ethos of a heavily bordered nation state. Greene leaves no room for doubt about this parallel; Sarah refers to Castle or their family repeatedly as "our own country" (*Human Factor*, 187). When Castle is awaiting help for his escape but expecting the police to discover him first, he clings to the borders of his familial country: "He was unwilling to leave the four walls of the house, even to go into the garden. If the police came he wanted to be arrested in his home, and not in the open air with the neighbours' wives peering through their windows" (203).

Castle ultimately is able to escape England without being caught by the police, but the "country" of his family proves to have insufficient borders against the often concealed violence of international Cold War politics. When Sarah asks Castle, "Are you sure we are safe?," the narrator interjects with the ambivalent truth: "To that question there was no easy answer" (*Human Factor*, 176). Love and relationships cannot provide secure borders in the context of multiple and incompatible political allegiances. As Snyder puts it, "Both [Castle and Sarah] should know from their telephone's being tapped that such an elevation of the private sphere's inviolability over the geopolitics of Cold War espionage is impossible."[33] The brutal history of apartheid South Africa and the failure of England to protest a regime that promotes racial hatred for fear of siding with Communists, haunts the Castle family even after they have escaped to relative safety in Berkhamstead. When Castle reads to Sam from a book of childhood verse, Sam imagines the character in one poem as driven by racial hatred: "'I think all the white people are afraid of him and lock their house in case he comes in with a carving knife and cuts their throats. Slowly,' he added with relish" (*Human Factor*, 174). Castle realizes the limitations of his private familial country: "Sam had never looked more black, Castle thought. He put his arm around him with a gesture of protection, but he couldn't protect him from the violence and vengeance which were beginning to work in the child's heart" (174). Sam's historical memory will not be apolitical, and the consequences are violent. The novel hints at the futility of Castle's efforts to protect his family in the face of historical realities early in the novel. Sarah fears burglars and intruders, so Castle buys a dog to guard the house. Buller, a boxer, turns out to be anything but vicious. As Sarah says to Castle, "You know what he's like with strangers. He fawns on them" (21). Greene depicts the dog barking giddily and drooling down the leg of any and all visitors. Castle resents the dog for failing to symbolize the apolitical, nonideological security that he naïvely imagines family can provide. Indeed, Castle's expectations for Buller and the subsequent disappointment encapsulates the tension between

---

33. Snyder, "He Who Forms a Tie," 29.

the ideological fantasy of the nuclear family as the centerpiece of Western democratic society and the nonideological reality of family life as something that cannot be either protected or contained.

In a novel in which safety is precarious or impossible, domestic hospitality—particularly English hospitality—is a damaged phenomenon. Davis invites Castle into his flat, but instead of a place of comforting refuge, Castle confronts "a stack of dirty dishes in the sink" and a cupboard "stacked with almost empty bottles" (*Human Factor*, 66). Davis offers Castle a drink, but the traditional gesture of hospitality is corrupted, giving the novel a Gothic dimension that portends Davis's impending demise and Castle's eventual exile: "Davis tried to find a whisky bottle containing enough for two glasses. 'Oh well,' he said, 'we'll mix them. They're all blends anyway'" (66). This early difficulty with hospitality foreshadows the fact that Davis's flat is not a safe house, least of all for him. The blended whisky, moreover, metaphorically highlights the fraught attachment to purity and the resistance to ethnic and racial hybridity driving England's postcolonial and Cold War positioning. The presence of symbolic hybridity here, in Davis's un-safe house, only increases the moral gray area for Castle, whose own marriage and child are mixed.

While Davis lacks a safe house through which to find and provide refuge, Castle and Sarah are forced "by order" to turn their home into a hospitable safe house for the wrong kind of guest (*Human Factor*, 61). "They laughed, with a touch of fear," as they imagined "A black hostess for Mr Cornelius Muller. And a black child" (61). The ironic danger of Muller's visit is that it goes well, encouraging a friendship that Castle and Sarah do not want. Although Muller speaks in racist tones about the "many Englishmen who have started with the idea of attacking apartheid and ended trapped by us [BOSS] in a Bantu girl's bed," he changes gears when Sarah is introduced as Castle's wife, "adapting, as naturally as a chameleon, to the colour of soil" (101, 103). He makes "courteous conversation" over dinner, drinks whiskey and port with Castle, and offers a gift to Sarah, which she is obliged to accept as hostess, even though it is from her "old enemy" (103, 104). The evening concludes with a gesture of the most unconditional kind of hospitality, that which comes not from the inherent perfidy of the human world but the unconditional animal one: "Buller licked the bottom of his [Muller's] trousers with undiscriminating affection" (105). The significance of the moment is not lost on Muller, and he takes advantage of the opportunity to announce an obligatory tie between himself and the Castle home: "'Good dog,' Muller said. 'Good dog. There's nothing like a dog's fidelity'" (105). The scene demonstrates the inevitable double bind of the notion of "perfect" hospitality.

Sarah, a black South African, cannot participate with full agency in the dynamics of English hospitality; she is stuck in a liminal contact zone. On the one hand, she is forced to be a hostess to Muller and therefore to accept the hypocritical political allegiance between England and the South African government. On the other, she is begrudgingly accepted as a guest in her mother-in-law's home once Castle has fled to Moscow. Mrs. Castle offers highly conditional hospitality to Sarah and Sam: "This is *my* home, Sarah. It would be convenient to know just how long you plan to stay" (*Human Factor*, 234, emphasis original). "So much a stranger did she [Sarah] feel in this house," that she identifies not as a guest in an English home but as a refugee without rights, desperate for basic physical shelter: "Now she was without Maurice and without a country" (235, 239). On the one hand, Sarah's enforced isolation signifies the breakdown of systems of sociopolitical hospitality beyond the kitchen and the lounge. On the other, her isolation signifies that the breakdown of sociopolitical hospitality extends to the domestic domain, which is pointedly gendered as female. Sarah, as powerless hostess, is forced to accept threatening guests, while Mrs. Castle has the social power to set limits and maintain exclusionary boundaries. The private domain thus transforms from a symbol of Welfare State security into a powerful Cold War weapon to enforce domestic apartheid at the most intimate level.

England, the Soviet Union, and apartheid South Africa are all represented by *The Human Factor* as inhospitable and dangerous. Individuals remain isolated or trapped in undesirable, hypocritical obligations. Castle faces a genuine dilemma that forces him to choose between national and personal commitments. To support Britain's espionage activities against the Soviet Union would translate to support for the apartheid regime in South Africa and endangering Sarah and Sam, making any straightforward condemnation of Communism impossible. Passing on information to the Soviets in South Africa, on the other hand, translates to apartheid resistance that comes with a heavy price. As the scene in Mrs. Castle's house makes clear, it is Sarah who pays this price most directly once Castle has fled to Moscow. Disillusioned by the compromised moral and political frameworks of the Cold War, Castle embodies the bleak image of the individual in the late 1970s who finds solace only when "his door was locked and the Don't Disturb notice was hanging outside" (*Human Factor*, 224).

The Human Factor has been compared by scholars such as Snyder and Laura Tracy with Greene's 1948 novel, *The Heart of the Matter*.[34] I conclude

---

34. Snyder argues that the protagonists of both novels struggle "with a misguided scrupulosity of conscience" ("He Who Forms a Tie," 26), which ultimately reveals the limits of allegedly selfless, disinterested actions. Tracy finds that the two novels point to a more general trend

with another comparison, between *The Human Factor* and *The End of the Affair* (1951), in order to contrast the historical moment of World War II and the inception of the Welfare State with that of the Cold War and challenges to the Welfare State settlement.³⁵ Both novels tell the story of a man and a woman, both couples named Maurice and Sarah, who are kept apart by forces larger than themselves. In *The End of the Affair*, Sarah's religious faith remains a barrier between the two, but after her death, Maurice overcomes his isolation by building a relationship with Sarah's husband, Henry. The two men actually share a house, suggesting that some form of community and political belonging is possible, despite the narrative sacrifice of Sarah. Nearly thirty years later, *The Human Factor* has no antidote for isolation. Maurice ends up alone in Moscow next to a "dusty disconnected telephone," as Boris says, "safe at the centre of the cyclone" (*Human Factor*, 259). Ironically, he is reading *Robinson Crusoe*, the iconic novel of English individualism and self-sufficiency, which is central to Ian Watt's argument for the simultaneous rise of the realist novel and the bourgeois individual. Sarah is left unwelcome and abandoned at Mrs. Castle's house, confronted by a "long unbroken silence" and the realization that "the line to Moscow is dead" (265). The impediments to creating a hospitable, unified community in 1978 are made evident by the fact that Maurice and Sarah end up in separate domestic spaces, as ideologically, politically, geographically, and technologically far apart as possible. Both Moscow and London prove to be oppressive spaces for their guests. Despite the fact that Sarah and Sam have escaped apartheid South Africa, moreover, their final disconnection from Maurice and the unresolved plot affects a kind of narrative apartheid in which the reader resides in the inhospitable space between. The open ending, while emulating hostile conditions, aesthetically invites a readerly desire for social and political reconstruction.

Although the Sarah character is allowed to live in *The Human Factor*, there is still a sacrifice that points to the new vulnerabilities of the late twentieth century: Buller is killed in order to facilitate Castle's smooth, undetected escape from England (*Human Factor*, 218). The sacrifice of Buller is arguably more disturbing in its implications than Sarah's death in *The End of the Affair*. While Sarah's death is figured as religious martyrdom and brings the two men together in a reconstructive vision, Buller's death—the sacrifice of an entirely innocent creature—only guarantees Maurice's individual safety, which comes

---

in Greene's ouevre: the "demand for uncompromising and continuing self-scrutiny" alongside a "utopian . . . ideal of human self-comprehension" ("Passport to Greeneland," 46).

35. Judith Adamson talks briefly about these two novels together when discussing Greene's female characters in her essay, "The Long Wait for Aunt Augusta: Reflections on Graham Greene's Fictional Women."

at the cost of political, moral, and interpersonal connection. Buller's death is not a sign of noble, willing sacrifice or divine intervention; instead, it is symbolic of a world in which sacrifice for the common good is either corrupted as a totalitarian Soviet policy or, in the case of Britain, no longer a sustained value. Where the message of *The End of the Affair* is hopeful rebuilding, the message of *The Human Factor* is bleak deconstruction and persistent apartheid.

THE GOOD TERRORIST: HOSTESS AS HOSTAGE, GUEST AS TERRORIST

The bleakness of isolation and political disconnection that characterizes *The Human Factor* is shown to have violent consequences not for spies and refugees but for average British citizens in Doris Lessing's *The Good Terrorist*. In Lessing's novel, Alice Mellings has given up the security of her upper-middle-class childhood in order to live as a squatter with vaguely communist sensibilities. She commandeers Number 43 Old Mill Road, an abandoned Victorian house that has been slated for demolition and made uninhabitable by the local council. Alice's efforts to "save" the house and to remake it into a home for a group of squatters are ultimately empty gestures. Where the postwar council housing estate symbolizes, at least at some level, government hospitality, the postwar squat is a sign of the state that has abandoned its commitment to provide housing for all. A squat, as such, is cut off from the social dynamics of property ownership, public housing provision, and community planning; it is also cut off physically, without access to sewage systems and power grids.[36] Just as the squat cannot satisfy basic needs or provide full enfranchisement and community belonging for the citizens who seek shelter there, Alice, as the self-appointed head of this isolated household, cannot successfully offer hospitality to the potential guests who truly need shelter. Her obsessive efforts only keep her from taking responsibility for the political actions unfolding around her, which culminate in a fatal car bombing.[37] Critics generally agree on the

---

36. Although squats were isolated from basic services, the Criminal Law Act of 1977 did give limited protection to squatters. It became illegal to force entry upon premises that appeared to be occupied, even if the occupants were not the property owners.

37. It is likely that Lessing's novel was inspired by the story of poet and political radical, Anna Mendelssohn. Mendelssohn, like Alice Mellings (note the closeness of their names), came from a cultured middle-class home, grew increasingly politicized after the 1968 student protests in Paris and events in Europe, agitated for squatters' rights in London, dropped out of university, and was associated with radical anarchist publications and the urban guerillas known as the Angry Brigade. The Angry Brigade's "activities included about two dozen small-

significance of buildings in Lessing's oeuvre as metaphors for British society.[38] Elizabeth Maslen notes, for instance, that buildings are important "as images for social order or disorder,"[39] and Gayle Greene reads the house in *The Good Terrorist* as a "microcosm of English society."[40] More specifically, I argue that, in the context of Thatcher's privatization schemes, *The Good Terrorist* scrutinizes the suggestive link between household and greater sociopolitical community, particularly through the structure of the squat, asking whether such a relationship is effective or even possible. Lessing's novel depicts a historical moment in which the metonymic relation between home and nation, host and government, has become dysfunctional. As in Greene's novel, the new dominant metonymic relation is between home and individual, which proves to be an insufficient model for social welfare.

Theoretically, a hostess only exists when she has guests. In this sense, a hostess is a kind of "hostage" to potential guests.[41] Alice's "hostage" status—her desire for guests and preoccupation with hospitality—dominates the novel at the expense of more overtly political content. The implication is not that the personal or domestic and political must be at odds, however, but that responsible political participation depends at some level on a basically functional system of state hospitality that removes undue burden from individuals in the name of the common good. In other words, the government's failure to guarantee safe housing for all British citizens may force a choice between personal welfare and responsible—or, in Lessing's case, revolutionary—civic

---

scale attacks, primarily bombings of largely unoccupied police stations, businesses, embassies, politicians' residences, and a deserted BBC van at a Miss World beauty pageant in 1970" (Crangle, "Agonies of Ambivalence," 469). After Mendelssohn's fingerprints were found on a magazine around an explosive device in Manchester, she was tried in the 1972 Stoke Newington 8 trial and sentenced to ten years in prison as a result (she served four). For an illuminating discussion of Mendelssohn's life and work, drawing on archival material that provides insight into Mendelssohn's eventual rejection of her past revolutionary commitments, see Sara Crangle's essay "The Agonies of Ambivalence: Anna Mendelssohn, la poétesse Maudite."

38. Lara Feigel observes "the image of a door being slammed ... throughout [Lessing's] novels and autobiographies, both literally and metaphorically," and she reads this architectural trope not as a political or national symbol but in terms of Lessing's autobiography and personal development (*Free Woman*, 11). Susan Watkins, while attentive to Lessing's various political concerns, particularly the links between class, nation, race, and gender, also invests strongly in the force of autobiography in contemplating Lessing's oeuvre as a whole, arguing that "one way to connect the disparate parts in the Lessing corpus is to re-interpret them ... as life writing" (*Doris Lessing*, 29). Watkins brings this autobiographical approach to bear on her reading of *The Good Terrorist* as well, which she describes as a "self-conscious experimentation with the authority of voice" at a moment when Lessing was testing the limits of her own authorial persona (118).

39. Maslen, "Doris Lessing's *The Good Terrorist*," 26.
40. Greene, *Doris Lessing*, 206.
41. Derrida and Dufourmantelle, *Of Hospitality*, 109.

participation. This politically ambivalent position is expressed in Lessing's novel through her choice to focalize the third-person narrative through Alice's narrow, self-centered consciousness and to relate events more or less in real time. These techniques, as will become clear, simultaneously generate a critical reaction to and empathy for the misguided protagonist. The result is a scathingly realistic portrait of contemporary urban life in the mid-1980s, one that emphasizes the dominance of middle-class political naïvety and its unintended horrific consequences.

Unable or unwilling to critically examine her middle-class sensibilities, Alice is capable of relating only to buildings, not people or the systems they create. She forms a "passionate identification with the criticized house," Number 43 Old Mill Road, and when she thinks about its fate of demolition, "her heart [is] full of pain because of the capacious, beautiful and unloved house" (*Good Terrorist*, 26, 5). Even when she is not directly engaged in homemaking duties, which she gladly performs as "housemother," she thinks about the house, mentally cataloguing the rooms, "imagining it clean and ordered" (17, 35). Putting the house in order does not translate in this novel to political integrity. It demonstrates, rather, the limits of middle-class homemaking as a replacement for basic Welfare State provisions.

Alice ostensibly works to create a refuge for the community of squatters at Number 43, but her efforts, like Maurice Castle's, are actually directed toward creating her own fantastical safe house: a reconstruction of her abundant, comfortable, privately owned, middle-class, childhood home. She frequently takes trips to the houses of her divorced mother and father in order to steal things or money, or simply to channel the feeling of the domestic space, before returning to Number 43. In the hall at her mother's house, for instance, she stands, "breathing in the house, *home*; the big, easy-fitting, accommodating house that smelled of friendship" (*Good Terrorist*, 51). In the kitchen of her father's house, her heart aches as she takes in the room, "being large, and with that great wooden table set with bowls of fruit and flower which for Alice were the symbol of happiness" (83). Once back in Number 43, Alice tries to carry with her some of the essential familiarity of those spaces that, for her, represent home and safety. She puts flowers on the kitchen table and prepares soup for the squatters. Privately, she gains "a comforting sense of familiarity" from the house shaking with traffic, since "she seemed to have lived all her life in houses that shook to heavy traffic" (107). Again, like Castle, Alice wants to have it both ways: to reject the protection and community belonging available to her without making herself vulnerable to danger and without ultimately doing what is necessary to really take responsibility for the welfare of others. Alice's fraught attachment to familiarity is distinct from a commitment to humanistic compassion, a crucial distinction for Lessing in defining the value of literary realism. In "A Small Personal Voice," Lessing radically defends the legacy of nineteenth-century realism as a source of inspiration for contemporary writers, explaining that in rereading nineteenth-century novels,

> I was not looking for a firm reaffirmation of old ethical values, many of which I don't accept; I was not in search of the pleasures of familiarity. I was looking for the warmth, the compassion, the humanity, the love of people which illuminates the literature of the nineteenth century and which makes all these old novels a statement of faith in man himself. . . . This is what I mean when I say that literature should be committed.[42]

In representing the limits of Alice's worldview and homemaking efforts, which prioritize familiarity and comfort, Lessing provides the kind of committed realism that she believed had humanistic political value.

Mistaking familiarity for compassion hinders Alice's political engagement. This engagement is also hindered by her intellectual timidity and her conception of national identity as something static and heroic. She does not have the interest nor the discipline to help the squatters by trying to achieve policy reform. She has a bachelor's degree, but her education has no substance. We are told that she "never read anything but newspapers," and that "she used to wonder how it was that a comrade with a good, clear and correct view of life could be prepared to endanger it by reading all that risky equivocal stuff that she might dip into, hastily, retreating as if scalded" (*Good Terrorist*, 66). England, for Alice, is not a political system that can be altered according to the demands of committed progressive politics, as her "comrades" see it. It is, instead, a fixed entity that she wants to preserve and protect, like private property: "It was ours! National characteristics were precious" (237). To think in possessive terms of national characteristics runs counter to the internationalism of class politics that she purportedly supports. When Gordon O'Leary arrives at Number 43 to find out about the "*materiel*," guns delivered to the house for IRA operatives, Alice uses a confused nationalist argument to send him away: "I'm not interested in America or Czechoslovakia or Russia or Lithuania," she tells him (322). "None of us are. We are English revolutionaries and we shall make our own policies and act according to the English tradition. Our own tradition" (322). When another "agent," Peter Cecil, comes to the house in the wake of the car bombing, Alice seeks solace in him as an Englishman: "She thought, *He is English,* was coming to her rescue. . . . He

---

42. Lessing, "Small Personal Voice," 6.

is English, he will understand" (395). England and Englishness, for Alice, are an extension of her middle-class values that prioritize individual comfort and ownership. Her rescue fantasy also links this kind of nationalism with tropes of romance rather than revolution or even pragmatism. It follows, then, that in her version of England the working class is at once idealized and politically redundant:

> Salt of the earth! Alice was dutifully saying to herself, watching this scene of workers fueling themselves for a hard day's work with plates of eggs, chips, sausages, fried bread, baked beans—the lot. *Cholesterol,* agonized Alice, and they all look so unhealthy! They had a pallid greasy look like bacon fat, or undercooked chips. In the pocket of each, or on the tables, being read, was the *Sun* or the *Mirror.* Only lumpens, thought Alice, relieved that there was no obligation to admire them. Building or road workers, perhaps even self-employed; it wasn't these men who would save Britain from itself! (47, emphasis original)

Alice's "politics" entail thinly sketched stereotypes and conventional middle-class rules and attitudes that support her personal fantasy of a safe and comfortable life. She cannot create a household that effectively symbolizes national identity because she does not have an accurate understanding of what that nation and its internal conflicts are really about nor of the real consequences of nationalist feeling in the context of IRA terrorism and in the dismantling of Welfare State provisions.

In place of educated activism and grassroots political engagement, Alice directs her dissatisfaction at unresponsive buildings. When Margaret Thatcher gives a talk at the University of Liverpool, Alice attends to protest. Her violent anger is not articulated in a specific or informed way in terms of Thatcher's policies; it is aimed instead at the university's "great cold lunatic buildings" that

> looked at them through the downpour, and Alice felt murder fill her heart. She knew most of the new universities; had visited them, demonstrated outside them. When she saw one she felt she confronted the visible embodiment of evil, something that wishes to crush and diminish her. The enemy. If I could put a bomb under that lot, she was thinking, if I could . . . (*Good Terrorist,* 253)

Alice does not try to rehabilitate the utopian promise of postwar modernism, or to forge an alliance with the red brick universities that were so influential in cultivating progressive cultural politics in the 1960s and 1970s. She sees only the surfaces of buildings as a backdrop to a political figure who she is supposed to dislike. Instead of fixing systemic problems at their roots, Alice channels her anger toward aesthetics. Her efforts go toward rehabilitating a Victorian house as a squat rather than campaigning to reverse the privatization of council housing.

Alice is fluent in the language of housing and construction. This fluency gives her a sense of self sufficiency, which likens her to Thatcher's model citizen who does not rely on the government to take care of housing for her; she substantiates, instead, Thatcher's claim that "no government can do anything except through people and people look to themselves first."[43] When Alice tries to persuade the local council that the house should be spared demolition—effectively asking the government to get out of the way—she runs through the "vital statistics of the house": "Its size, its solidity, its situation. Said that, apart from a few slates, it was structurally sound. Said it needed very little to make it liveable" (*Good Terrorist*, 23). The teenagers in Graham Greene's "The Destructors" also speak this language, but whereas the teenagers in Greene's story use this knowledge for the modernizing demolition of outdated aesthetic standards, Alice uses it for the preservation of self-reliant, middle-class sensibilities.

She thinks of herself as a house rescuer and of Philip, a builder, as "her saviour, the restorer of the house" (*Good Terrorist*, 40). We are told that she had "rescued" houses in Manchester, Halifax, and Birmingham, "where electricity had flowed obediently through wires, after long abstinence" (63). Electricity was one of the public utilities privatized under Thatcher, and again, embodying Thatcher's ideology of individualism, Alice takes pride in her solo efforts to solve the problem. She casts herself and Philip as messianic heroes who will save the day, and indeed, Lessing's choice of metaphor—the electricity flowing after a period of abstinence—has distinctly sexual overtones that points to Alice's romantic rather than realistic attitude toward housing. At the council office, she watches on hopefully as Mary Williams writes "the words which would—Alice was sure—save the house. For as long as it was needed by Alice and the others. Save it permanently, why not?" (25). Alice has a keen eye for danger and waste that stand in the way of saving the house and transforming it into a comfortable home. When she first surveys Number 43, she notices "electric cables ripped out of the wall . . . dangling, raw-ended. The cooker was pulled out and lying on the floor. The broken windows had admitted rain water which lay in puddles everywhere. There was a dead bird on the floor. It

---

43. Thatcher, "no such thing," n.p.

stank" (6–7). She observes, "This rubbish is a health hazard," and pronounces, "There must be rats" (11). While the other squatters go to political protests, Alice remains at the house, working with Philip to make the house habitable.

Alice's efforts to rescue and repair the neglected house also affirms middle-class values about waste: a safe house and a comfortable home is one in which human waste is hidden and material waste is put to use. One of Alice's proudest moments comes after she and Philip restore the plumbing by digging out the concrete that the council had poured into the toilets. She and Jim dispose of the buckets of "shit" that had been collecting in an upstairs room by burying it in the back garden (*Good Terrorist*, 72). It follows that one of the major setbacks that Alice experiences in the novel occurs when a policeman pokes fun at her efforts to bury the human waste by throwing a bag of shit into the house foyer. This incident is literally dangerous for the squatters, as undisposed human waste can lead to disease, but for Alice the incident is more serious as a metaphorical threat to her homemaking fantasy, where everything is "clean and orderly": shit does not belong in the foyer.[44] At the same time, material waste is another kind of danger that must be avoided in the middle-class home: waste not, want not. The thrifty Alice complains to Jasper and Bert about "Waste. All this *waste*," and orders the men to go "looking in the skips for some furniture" (*Good Terrorist*, 91, 90, emphasis original). When they return with their gleanings, Alice thinks, "'Oh the wicked waste of it all,' she raged, seeing plastic bags full of curtains, which were there because someone had tired of them; a refrigerator, stools, tables, chairs—all of them serviceable, if some needed a few minutes' work to put right" (*Good Terrorist*, 96–97).

Alice's tireless hostessing, repairing, and salvaging efforts add up to an impressive homemaking feat. Her role as a hostess, however, is undermined on two counts: her fellow squatters do not value her efforts, and she does not provide for the truly needy. After Alice and Philip remove the concrete from the toilets, the group gathers around her: "They cheered her, meaning it, but there was mockery too. And there was a warning, which she did not hear, or care about" (*Good Terrorist*, 43). Just as the squat is cut off from the surrounding community, Alice is incapable of forging interpersonal connections and, therefore, from understanding how best to meet other people's needs. Jasper,

---

44. For Gayle Greene, "The futility that informs Lessing's vision in this novel is epitomized by the image of shit. . . . This shit is simply shit, not a resource capable of being transmuted to gold . . . but a revelation . . . of what it's all worth. Moreover, it is 'systemic,' produced both by the physiological system, the body, and by the socioeconomic system, the body politic" (*Doris Lessing*, 218). Sandra Singer also reads the image of "shit" as Lessing's ultimate judgment of Alice: "In the end, rather than a positive valuation of Alice's character as resourceful or resolute, the reader is left with the police officer's comparison of Alice to a bag of shit" ("London and Kabul," 97).

the gay man with whom she shares an icy, sexless relationship, continually negates her domestic impulses: "'We are not here, [. . .] to make ourselves comfortable. We aren't here for that'" (8). For Margaret Rowe, Alice is never a genuine homemaker; rather, she "appropriates the maternal role which she saw her mother, Dorothy, play in the golden days of the Mellings."[45] Alice's relationship with Jasper further enables this fantasy by allowing her to avoid the sexual maturity of adult relationships; instead, with Jasper, she can "play parent and fantasise about playing wife."[46] In lieu of a reciprocated life as hostess and mother, Alice is confined to a solitary fantasy life in which homemaking amounts to political action—a fantasy that the novel reveals to be untenable in reality.

The novel suggests that a hostess is only successful to the extent that she provides refuge for the vulnerable and takes responsibility for their welfare. Under Alice's command, the characters who are genuinely at risk—Jim, Philip, Faye, Monica—are casualties who do not find the hospitality they need.[47] Faye aggressively tells Alice that she doesn't "care about all this domestic bliss, all the house and garden stuff. . . . Any minute now we are going to have hot running water and double glazing, I wouldn't be surprised. For me this is all a lot of shit, do you hear? *Shit!*" (*Good Terrorist*, 112, emphasis original). While Alice is highly sensitive to the implications of the actual "shit" and material waste that intrudes into the house, she seems unable to fully comprehend Faye's use of the word, which classifies Alice's efforts not as necessary but as wasteful. Rejected by Faye and Jasper, Alice turns to the only nonwhite character in the squat, Jim, whom she also idealizes: "She loved Jim, loved his helplessness, his vulnerability, and her own part in alleviating these wounds" (192). But her self-centered perspective backfires: she manages to help Jim get a job at her father's factory but promptly undermines that achievement by stealing money from the company safe—a crime pinned on Jim, for which he is fired. Jim disappears; Faye dies in the car-bombing; Philip dies after he is not given a place in the squat and is forced to live on the streets; Monica is a single mother who remains homeless and locked out from the professed hospitality of Alice's squat. Merely decorative, the flowers on Alice's table are no

---

45. Rowe, *Doris Lessing*, 101.
46. Rowe, 101.
47. As Jean Pickering, among others, has noted, Alice is not the only one who disregards the true needs and wants of the disadvantaged people who seek refuge in the house: "Few of the would-be revolutionaries show much concern for those on whose behalf they wish to overthrow the system. Philip and Jim are the only two working class members of the commune; they want jobs, not revolution" (*Understanding Doris Lessing*, 189).

substitute for the structural safety nets that might have kept these characters alive and socially enfranchised.

Alice cannot offer protection to the people who need it most, and she also fails to provide refuge for the vulnerable birds that she and Pat find while attempting to fix the roof. Recalling Maurice Castle's willingness to sacrifice the dog in *The Human Factor,* Alice stands by as Pat destroys a bird's nest. Alice begins to cry, becoming "hysterical" and "childlike" as Pat takes action: "'A *bird,*' said Pat. 'A *bird,* not a *person.*' She pulled out handfuls of straw and stuff, and flung them out into the air, where they floated down. Then something crashed on to the tiles of the roof: an egg. The tiny embryo of a bird sprawled there. Moving" (*Good Terrorist,* 92, emphasis original). As with the sacrifice of Buller in Greene's novel, the sacrifice of the birds cannot be justified in the name of some greater good. If Alice had fixed the rotting roof beams, which Elizabeth Maslen has aptly called the "fatal flaw" of the house, the destruction of the nest might have been justified as a guarantor of safety for the squatters.[48] But as it is, the act only reinforces the limits and misguided nature of Alice's efforts. For Maslen, the roof beams signify the breakdown of political purpose and the unethical anarchy that comes to dominate the squatters' behavior and aims. "The house is the central image," she argues, "for the ultimate weakness of the group: animal functions are taken care of but wrong-headedness, mirrored by the rotten roof-beams, typifies the group as collective and as individuals."[49] In addition to this metaphoric significance of the rotten roof-beams, there is another implication: physical safety is a prerequisite for a house that is able to nurture healthy relationships and effective sociopolitical communities. Although Alice demonstrates knowledge of construction, plumbing, and electricity, her larger goal is attractive middle-class comfort and self-validation, which she can achieve only at the cost of more human and substantial structural solutions, genuine interpersonal connection, and refuge for the disadvantaged.

For Gayle Greene, Alice's many shortcomings are significant insofar as they demonstrate that she is a failed revolutionary. Greene's critique of Alice may be reasonable if the goal is to condemn her attempt at radical politics, but Lessing's novel asks readers to do more than hold up Alice as a straw man. There is nothing inherently wrong with self-sufficiency or middle-class homemaking; when considered within the context of Thatcher's privatization schemes, moreover, Alice's ineffective fantasy can be understood as a response to the threat of impermanence and isolation, of an inhospitable existence in

---

48. Maslen, "Lessing's *The Good Terrorist,*" 28.
49. Maslen, 28–29.

the contact zone. The narrative suggests that any successful democratically oriented politics, revolutionary or not, depends on a functioning system of hospitality, a system in which basic human needs and welfare have value. Psychologically, Alice believes herself to have been a victim of inhospitality at some formative stage: "It had been with her since she could remember: being excluded, left out" (*Good Terrorist*, 108). She painfully recalls the large parties that her mother used to throw: "All that splendour of hospitality, the big house, the people coming in and out, the meals, the . . ." (347). Alice would have to give up her room to house guests and sleep on the floor of her parents' room. She was, in other words, a condition of her mother's hospitality to others: "When there were parties, when there were people in the house, it seemed Alice became invisible to her mother, and had no place in her own home" (229). As an adult, she is haunted by what Gayle Greene calls "originary dispossession,"[50] and she becomes "possessed . . . by a vision of impermanence; houses, buildings, streets, whole areas of streets, blown away, going, gone, an illusion" (*Good Terrorist*, 133). In Alice's vision, as in the policies of the Thatcher government, the work of postwar reconstruction disappears, leaving its mark on both the psyche and the landscape.[51]

Alice's psychological wound is literalized in an architectural sense when the narrative relocates her mother from a privately owned home into a much more modest flat. When Alice goes to find Dorothy in her new accommodation, Alice enters an unfamiliar neighborhood that confirms the impermanence of her material past: "Not a very nice area; it could just—Alice supposed—be called Hampstead, by someone charitable. Soon she was standing outside a four-storey block of flats, with a small dirty garden in front. Surely her mother was not living here? Yes, her name was on a scrap of paper inserted in a slot opposite 8: Mellings" (*Good Terrorist*, 227). Alice's vision of impermanence and the displacement of her mother are not revolutionary but bleak and threatening to her own middle-class sense of self. In this sense, *The Good Terrorist* recalls the anxiety expressed by writers during World War II, when physical destruction was a constant threat and reality. But in the context of Lessing's novel, without the guaranteed housing provisions of the Welfare State, individuals are forced to attend to their own safety and well-being at

---

50. Greene, *Doris Lessing*, 216.
51. Alice's vision of the destruction of utopian domestic space also recalls an iconic dystopian novel from the period that centers on the modernist tower block, J. G. Ballard's *High Rise* (1975), in which the ideal of tower block living, metonymic for the idealized society, quickly deteriorates. Notably, and intersecting with representations of vulnerable animals in Lessing's and Greene's novels, *High Rise* begins with the disturbing image of a man on a balcony eating a dog.

the cost of engaging meaningfully with society. Indeed, recalling Thatcher's words, it seems that in Lessing's representation of 1980s Britain, "there is no such thing as society" if only because conditions make it increasingly difficult to recognize.[52]

Like Maurice Castle, Alice retreats to her internal safe house when the dangers of the material world are too great: "Alice shut her eyes, retreated inside herself to a place she had discovered long years ago, she did not know when, but she had been a small child. Inside here, she was safe, and the world could crash and roar and scream as much as it liked" (*Good Terrorist*, 130). Similarly, after the terrorist attack, she relates not to her lost "comrade" Faye or to the other squatters who are all dispersing, but to Number 43 and her fantastical version of the safe house:

> She sat on quietly there by herself in the silent house. In the *betrayed* house.... The house might have been a wounded animal whose many hurts she had one by one cleaned and bandaged, and now it was well and whole, and she was stroking it, pleased with it and herself . . . not quite whole, however.... She felt that she could pull the walls of this house, her house, around her like a blanket, where she could snuggle, where she could feel safe. (*Good Terrorist*, 392)

Like Castle's sense of self-loyalty, Alice's ultimate responsibility is to herself and her own safety, a determined individualism that counteracts her efforts to provide hospitable safety to others who are more vulnerable than she is. In this moment, she figures the house as a wounded animal worth saving, again displacing the vulnerabilities of the other squatters and the actual animals, the birds, who are sacrificed to her project. Her disturbing denial of responsibility after the car bombing further indicates not only her alienation from the others but also from herself as a participant in social systems: "Not that Alice believed that she—Alice—had any real reason to feel bad; she hadn't *really* been part of it" (*Good Terrorist*, 393, emphasis original). Representing the more broadly based betrayal of the nation failing to house its population, the squat at Number 43 cannot be a basic safe house or a comfortable home; it is a "trap" that reproduces and reinforces Alice's isolation (288). It can only be a metonym for Alice as one isolated individual representing many like her, not for a functioning national community. The break between houses and polities represented by Alice's narrative and culminating in senseless violence is noth-

---

52. Thatcher, "no such thing," n.p.

ing short of tragic. Lessing's story of isolation, lost homes, destroyed birds' nests, and rotten roof beams is ultimately an allegory warning of the political and moral abandonment of British citizens by their government.

Many critics and reviewers see *The Good Terrorist* as a conservative, reactionary book for Lessing. Gayle Greene foregrounds her analysis of the novel by exclaiming, "What I find horrific about it [*The Good Terrorist*] is the way Lessing seems to turn on her own former beliefs in a mood of savage caricature."[53] Echoing Greene, Margaret Scanlan offers this critique: "Even a surface reading would seem to suggest that the problem is . . . that its political message is far more conservative, both about women and about action, than we might expect from this feminist icon and former member of the Communist Party."[54] And Scanlan aligns herself with "Denis Donoghue's argument that by portraying her terrorists as incompetents, Lessing soothes the middle-class: 'bourgeois liberalism is safe if these are the only opponents it has to face.'"[55] A "surface reading" of the kind that Scanlan suggests could easily support these criticisms. The characters are not only unkind and unlikable; they are, as Donoghue observes, incompetent, irresponsible activists. They traffic in slogans and political jargon without devoting the time to thorough education, analysis, and politically engaged action. There is no doubt that Lessing intends to portray this misfit group in an entirely negative light.

In her 1985 Massey Lectures for the Canadian Broadcasting Corporation, given in the same year that she published *The Good Terrorist*, Lessing spoke pessimistically about the role of young people in politics:

> In the balance against this hopeful fact [of new emerging democracies], we must put a sad one, which is that large numbers of young people, when they reach the age of political activity, adopt a stance or an attitude that is very much part of our times. It is that democracy is only a cheat and a sham, only the mask for exploitation, and that they will have none of it. We have almost reached a point where if one values democracy, one is denounced as a reactionary. I think that this will be one of the attitudes that will be found most fascinating to historians of the future. For one thing, the young people who cultivate this attitude towards democracy are usually those who have never experienced its opposite: people who've lived under tyranny value democracy.[56]

---

53. Greene, *Doris Lessing*, 50.
54. Scanlan, "Language and the Politics of Despair," 183.
55. Scanlan, 192.
56. Lessing, "Laboratories of Social Change," 65.

Alice's mother Dorothy echoes Lessing's Massey Lecture comments in her diatribe against what she sees as the young, spoiled people of Britain. She concludes her conversation with Alice: "And then you are going to build it all up again in your own image! . . . with only one thought in your minds, how to get power for yourselves" (*Good Terrorist*, 354). The obvious parallels between Lessing's views and Dorothy's rant have led critics such as Scanlan to claim that "Dorothy defines the novel's point of view, is its hidden narrator."[57]

Interpreting the novel in light of Lessing's comments and Dorothy's character, however, should not result in a simplistic assumption that it is condemning young women or progressive politics outright. Elizabeth Maslen offers an alternative interpretation, arguing that Lessing's work is concerned generally with individual responsibility for collective morality.[58] Maslen reads *The Good Terrorist* not as an attack on socialism as an ideology, but as an attack on "the ways in which an ideology can be betrayed."[59] I, too, understand *The Good Terrorist* not as an autobiographical signal of Lessing's personal political shortcomings but as a realist text that critiques the broader social conditions that produce characters like Alice. In her more general examination of Lessing's oeuvre and biography, Lara Feigel is enticed by the fact that "freedom as explored in [her] novels . . . is allowed to be contradictory. Communism is never presented as a straightforward answer because she doesn't forget the absurdity of this attempt to subjugate life to a system. . . . This in part explains her frequent changes of opinion. It may have been a desire for liberation that made Lessing join political movements, but it was the same urge that took her away from them."[60] While Feigel's analysis is more personally than analytically oriented, her point here supports a reading of *The Good Terrorist* as determinedly realist. Representing contradiction, whether fictional or autobiographical, rather than papering over it is a characteristic feature of realist writing, especially for writers like Lessing who vocally admired the realist tradition and committed to pursuing it.[61] Lessing captures how Alice's

---

57. Scanlan, "Language and the Politics of Despair," 195. While Lessing would not have had access to Anna Mendelssohn's archive in the 1980s, Sara Crangle's analysis of that material suggests a strong parallel between Dorothy's view, the ideas articulated in Lessing's lecture, and Mendelssohn's complete rejection around the same time of her youthful activities. According to Crangle, "Throughout these materials, Mendelssohn steadfastly rejects her political past, railing against and identifying with the Left and identity politics, feminism included. She professed her innocence, and her loathing of extremism and violence, until her death in 2009" ("Agonies of Ambivalence," 472).

58. Maslen, "Doris Lessing's *The Good Terrorist*," 26.

59. Maslen, 25.

60. Feigel, *Free Woman*, 17–18.

61. Feigel, 17–18.

preoccupation with individual safety comes at the cost of community safety and, ultimately, political responsibility. Moreover, to create a selfish and childish female protagonist does not necessarily prove that Lessing is adopting a reactionary attitude toward women; rather, as her comments from the Massey Lectures indicate, we should consider Alice's "stance and attitude" as "very much part of our times [the Thatcher years]."[62]

The third-person focalization leaves room for ambiguity and irony that calls on the reader to act just as much as it calls out Alice for her misplaced action. Throughout the novel, Lessing encourages us to read the narrative mainly critically but also with a dash of ambivalence, as in the scene where Alice observes the people eating breakfast around her in a greasy café, discussed above. Although the narrator clarifies that the judgmental, naïve reactions to these working-class men ("Salt of the earth!," "*Cholesterol*," "Only lumpens") belong to Alice and not to the narrator, the choice to offer Alice's thoughts through free indirect discourse, before the narrator's clarifications, also appeals to the reader's sense of empathy—or perhaps gullibility. How easy it might be to agree with Alice's stereotypical, thinly conceived ideas and look into matters no further. Lessing's narrative technique at once admonishes Alice and leaves room for readerly identification, the phenomenon that historically has strongly linked the form of the realist novel with the individual subject, as discussed in chapter 2. The reader thus experiences the grim difficulty of experiencing life in the mid-1980s in any way other than through the stranglehold of individualism. Lessing's representational technique is one that prioritizes facing the facts. This approach may not be as transparent or seem as rhetorically or stylistically optimistic as a more propagandistic approach, but, as with immediate postwar reconstruction fiction, it can serve the valuable purpose of clarifying the troubled state of sociopolitical and material conditions.[63]

Against critics who find the bleak vision of the novel to be conservative or reactionary, I argue that it is profoundly effective in its use of focalization and in its treatment of narrative time, which emulates the breathless, overwhelming pace of life without basic safety nets. The reader follows Alice in more or less real time as she scurries about London and throughout the house over the course of only a few days. She is constantly on the move, and she rarely sleeps, not unlike MacInnes's narrator in *Absolute Beginners*, but without the thrill and energetic optimism. The narrator presents her thoughts as strung

---

62. Lessing, "Laboratories of Social Change,"65.
63. In her reading of *The Golden Notebook*, Lara Feigel observes a similar commitment to facing facts in Lessing's writing: "The failures, the *longeurs*, even the moments of stylistic ugliness, ... seemed bravely realistic" (*Free Woman*, 5).

together haphazardly, often strained by emotion and fatigue. Fragmented sentences and a blurred line between the narrator and Alice, moreover, make it as challenging for the reader to find literary stability as it seems to be for Alice to find physical or emotional comfort. It is difficult for a reader not to empathize with Alice's occasional desire for a home-cooked meal at a large kitchen table: the book and the world it represents are exhausting. In Maslen's apt words, the "reader is never allowed to relax on apparently familiar ground."[64] Ultimately, the reader is forced by Lessing's stylistic insistence to pull back from those identifications, to see them again as a move away from community responsibility toward individual isolation. In the aftermath of the attack, Alice allows herself, as she occasionally did,

> to slide back into her childhood where she dwelt pleasurably on some scene or other that she had smoothed and polished and painted over and over again with fresh colour until it was like walking into a story that began, 'Once upon a time there was a little girl called Alice. . . .' But today her mind would not stay in this dream or story, it insisted on coming back into the present, away from her mother who was finally repudiating Alice because of the bombing. (*Good Terrorist*, 395)

Lessing's realism is not an escapist retreat to linear plots and narrative closure. It is a brutal awakening, an insistence on "coming back into the present." Gayle Greene characterizes Lessing's style as particularly demanding in this regard:

> This is realism with a vengeance, but realism with a difference, that disallows the consolation of explanations or origins, of 'sequence' and 'consequence.' . . . *The Good Terrorist* offers none of the usual consolations of narrative; that what has happened in the past accounts for the present, that what we do in the present affects the future, that we can learn through experience, that the next generation will do better than the last.[65]

Although Lessing does not provide a logical set of explanations for the terrorist violence that ends the novel, the dire consequences of turning away from the present and reality are apparent. For Scanlan, Lessing undermines any political value that might come from her investigation of terrorism because she fails to ask any historical questions about the existence of terrorism in Britain in the 1980s. Instead, Scanlan argues, Lessing creates a link "between

---

64. Maslen, "Doris Lessing's *The Good Terrorist*," 26.
65. Greene, *Doris Lessing*, 218.

private madness and terrorist impulses. . . . The novel's pessimism depends heavily on its attribution of terrorism not to social conditions—which might, with whatever difficulty, be articulated or improved—but to unapproachable centers of power and unfathomable madness."[66] Scanlan's assessment is persuasive when the novel is considered primarily as an investigation of terrorism that conflates Lessing's political attitude with Alice's constraining and constrained point of view, but when considered within the broader social context of Thatcher's Britain and with Lessing's use of focalization in mind, the novel does offer a substantial critique of a politics committed to individual safety and self-reliance before collective well-being. Alice's awakening may have come too late, but Lessing's realism makes the adamant case that it is not too late for the engaged reader.[67]

DEAD LINES, DEAD ANIMALS, DEAD BUILDINGS

The Human Factor and *The Good Terrorist* both end with images of disconnection, death, and destruction. In Greene's novel, a dead phone line fails to connect Maurice in Moscow with Sarah in England. The more overtly destructive event of a deadly terrorist attack concludes Lessing's novel. Both incorporate the sacrificial deaths of animals. These scenes of violence toward animals ultimately point to the fact that the human beings cannot make British society safer for the most vulnerable because they are struggling to find security and hospitality for themselves. Similarly, the sacrificial deaths point to the illusory nature of both the ancient ritual of animal sacrifice and the contemporary ideology of Thatcher's individualism. The safe houses for these most vulnerable beings are ultimately unsustainable when the basic safety nets of social assistance are no longer guaranteed. The sacrifice of these animals is rendered even bleaker when it becomes apparent that nothing is to be gained: human civilization will not become more ethical or just or hospitable as a result of the deaths. In fact, the deaths signal the extent to which danger and inhospitality have spread throughout British society, and it is not surprising that these acts of violence foreshadow much larger acts of political violence and betrayal— the terrorist attack in Lessing's novel and Maurice's abandonment of his family—that are similarly void of clear ethical or political benefit.

---

66. Scanlan, "Language and the Politics of Despair," 190, 192.
67. Gayle Greene reads the novel as an indication that "gone is Lessing's belief that the next generation will make a better life than the generation before, and with it, the hope of progress" (*Doris Lessing*, 218).

The doomed searches for "safe houses" in the works of fiction examined here can be read as eulogies for the Welfare State. Indeed, they are narratives that face death, destruction, and isolation without offering a contrived sense of hope for progress or revival; in place of a thriving home and nation, these narratives show the dangers of squats and Moscow safe houses, which both foreground contingency and isolation, providing no connection with the outside social community. Eulogy, however, suggests a melancholy and perhaps a nostalgia inherent in recollection, but like the other works of reconstruction fiction examined in this book, these novels reject melancholic or nostalgic attitudes toward the past. It is, thus, more appropriate to understand these narratives as emergency signals—as air-raid sirens for a new kind of blitz on British citizens. In *The Human Factor*, when Sarah reluctantly meets Dr. Percival in a restaurant to find out information about Maurice's whereabouts, he congratulates her on having the "courage" to meet him at the restaurant. When she asks for clarification, he replies, "Well, this is one of the places the Irish like to bomb. They've thrown a small one already, but unlike the blitz their bombs are quite liable to hit the same place twice" (*Human Factor*, 242). The new blitz on British citizens in the 1970s and 1980s is not only about IRA terrorism but about a more widespread experience of insecurity. The brutal violence of terrorism makes sure that, like real-world British citizens, readers can have no false sense of security, no "city without a wall," through literature. Like the fiction of 1940s reconstruction, these late twentieth-century works of realism bring to light the concerns that should play an urgent part in building a safer world.

CONCLUSION

Reconstruction as Departure and Return

> "Homes are much more than rooms and tables and chairs.
> Homes wait in our hearts till we can make them again"
> —Elizabeth Bowen, "Christmas Toast"[1]

THE TERM "reconstruction" points both to the possibility of something new and to the return of something already past. It is therefore appropriate that the last chapter of this book attended to novels that echoed, with a difference, the anxieties of architectural instability that defined wartime and immediate postwar fiction. It is also appropriate to begin this conclusion by returning to Elizabeth Bowen's wartime writings, in which she herself returned to her anxiety over the transience of tables and chairs only to revise—or reconstruct—her own ideas about the existential implications of housing. As the 1940 epigraph for the introduction made clear, only a few months into the blitz Bowen faced the impermanence of household furnishings with a sense of bleak recognition: "All my life I have said, 'Whatever happens there will always be tables and chairs'—and what a mistake."[2] At that moment, Bowen was preoccupied with the destruction of the world around her. In the 1942 epigraph above, however, Bowen had begun to foster a reconstructive vision. This vision was attuned not only to what had been physically lost; it was also invested, perhaps even more strongly, in a new definition of home that emphasized the power of the imagination in returning and rebuilding. As the various works of postwar literature discussed in this book suggest,

---

1. Bowen, "The Christmas Toast is 'Home!,'" 128–29.
2. Letter to Virginia Woolf, 216.

realistic fictional representation emerged as a necessity in the context of conditions that made real-world rebuilding difficult or even impossible.

Although both epigraphs date to the war, considering them alongside each other points to two simultaneous narratives within reconstruction fiction that this book has charted throughout the postwar years: the often disconcerting narrative of how things are and the cautiously hopeful narrative of how things could be. Even the bleakest representations of the period, *At Mrs. Lippincote's* (1945) at one end and *The Good Terrorist* (1985) at the other, retain a sense of hope in their efforts to clarify the distinctions between reality and untenable fantasies. Likewise, the most explicitly optimistic work of reconstruction fiction, *Absolute Beginners,* acknowledges the darkness at the edge of its bright vision by concluding with the Notting Hill race riots. Even if, as Tony Judt establishes in *Postwar,* the second half of the twentieth century was burdened by the weight and scale of the catastrophic losses of World War II, making those years a kind of "epilogue" to the war, this book has demonstrated that the literature of the period also provided a "prologue" as well as new chapters for a rebuilding world.[3] Postwar reconstruction fiction, through its realistic engagements and representations, expresses not only the will to continue but the determined effort to confront, clarify, and transform social conditions. In Karen Shonfield's analysis of postwar British architecture, she asserts that "utopian aspirations . . . lie behind the very act of building. At the smallest scale building involves transformation, and some investment in the future."[4] The imaginative world building of postwar realism, no matter how bleak, should be understood as similarly invested in the persistence of the social world.

In its ability to conjure up images of return and departure, and in evaluating what is and asserting what could be through realist techniques, the term "reconstruction fiction" has potential that extends beyond the parameters of this book. In the specifically British context, there is more to be said about the flourishing of late twentieth-century historical fiction—"reconstructions" in the vein of Taylor's *Angel* (1957)—that realistically knits together examinations of British culture, social conditions, and the symbol of the wartime or postwar house.[5] Kazuo Ishiguro's *The Remains of the Day* (1988) is one of the more apt examples of this kind of contemporary historical fiction. The novel indirectly returns to two crucial moments of national political reconstruction,

---

3. Judt, *Postwar: A History of Europe Since 1945,* 2.
4. Shonfield, *Walls Have Feelings,* 29.
5. Victoria Stewart's *The Second World War in Contemporary British Fiction* deals with this proliferation of historical fiction that returns to the war for its setting, although her interest is particularly in secrecy.

World War II and the Suez Crisis, from the vantage point of a newly emerging moment of European reconstruction: the fall of the Berlin Wall and the rise of neoliberal capitalism.

Like Bowen's *The Little Girls,* Ishiguro's country house novel is one that calls on the reader to attend to what is missing just as much as they attend to what is present. In the case of *The Remains of the Day,* this strategy enables Ishiguro to issue a political critique and a call to social responsibility in evaluating historical memory. Through the example of the two Jewish maids dismissed by Lord Darlington at the height of his efforts to promote appeasement, the novel points not only to the casualties of the Holocaust and the War in general but also to the damaging consequences of indifference, collaboration, and blind loyalty. Lord Darlington's actions are filtered through the point of view of the butler, Mr. Stevens, who refuses both to challenge Darlington's order and to admit its immorality when the housekeeper, Miss Kenton, presses him to do so. Stevens's unquestioned loyalties and nostalgic unwillingness to see things clearly, to confirm that he witnesses wrongdoing, results narratively in the downfall of his personal relationships and Britain's status on the global stage. He fails to connect emotionally with those who matter most to him: his father and Miss Kenton. In the present of the novel, 1956, Stevens unsuccessfully tries to rekindle—or reconstruct—a life with Miss Kenton just as Darlington Hall has been sold to an American millionaire in order to avoid demolition and as, in the silent historical background, Britain finally cedes imperial authority to the United States in the Middle East as a result of the Suez Crisis. Ishiguro filters these twinned stories of personal tragedy and political retreat through a highly unreliable narrator, the butler of a great house, the quintessential contemporary symbol of prewar Englishness. In doing so, Ishiguro suggests at once that this symbol remains potent and that it can be recuperated in the late 1980s only as a warning to the consequences of denial and the fallout of failing to witness honestly and act ethically. The most crucial actions, emotions, and political commitments in the book are those that happen elsewhere, beyond what Stevens chooses to articulate. By virtue of what it leaves out, the novel insists that Britain needs citizens in the historical present who will meet the world with open eyes and with clarity of purpose, citizens who will heed Bowen's wartime directive to "look out through glass."[6]

In the second decade of the twenty-first century, thirty years after Doris Lessing's portrait of anxious insecurity in the aftermath of the Welfare State, Britain once again finds itself in an age of austerity measures, dramatic public

---

6. Bowen, "Calico Windows," 186. Ian McEwan's *Atonement* is another work of contemporary historical fiction that looks back to the war through the prism of a great house.

spending cuts, and the scaling back of government welfare initiatives. Housing is, again, one of the major issues that circulates in current public discourse as a response to these conditions. Tenants of Newham Council in east London, for example, received notices in 2012 that, due to sky-rocketing property values, the estate could no longer afford to keep rents at an affordable, public housing rate. Newham Council's solution was to sell the estate to a Midlands council in Stoke-on-Trent. Tenants were told to relocate or become classed as "intentionally homeless," which would prohibit them from receiving government assistance.[7] Meanwhile, a catastrophic 2017 fire at Grenfell Tower, a public housing high-rise in North Kensington, has become a symbol of dramatic socioeconomic inequalities and the neglect of social welfare under Theresa May's Conservative Government.

British writers continue to be concerned with the stakes of reconstruction in terms of its effect on peoples' lived social realities, but in this era, reconstruction tends to be associated with private interests and gentrification, while preservation has become the goal of those wishing to protect the world built by the postwar Welfare State. In 2012, novelist Zadie Smith learned that Brent Council had plans to demolish the Willesden Green Library Centre, which included an independent bookshop and a kind of public square, a site that had been a central and much used gathering place for the multicultural, working-class community where Smith grew up. The Council planned to sell the publicly owned space, to be replaced by private luxury flats, a greatly reduced library, retail space, and no bookshop. Smith's own fiction since the publication of *White Teeth* in 2000 has been preoccupied with realistic investigations of place, belonging, and the complex interactions of past and present on interpersonal, multicultural, and cross-class relations in contemporary London. In response to Brent Council's plans to demolish and hand over reconstruction to private interests in Willesden Green, Smith passionately defended the library as well as the legacy of the Welfare State in her *New York Review, Review of Books* essay, "The Northwest London Blues." While she acknowledges that it would be naïve to think that the broad Welfare State of her own childhood, which fully funded her university education, doctors' visits, eyeglasses, and music lessons, could be reintroduced, she cites Tony Judt, who posited in *Ill Fares the Land* that "we need to learn to *think* the state again. . . . We have freed ourselves of the mid-twentieth-century assumption—never universal but certainly widespread—that the state is likely to be the best solution to any given problem. We now need to liberate ourselves from the opposite notion:

---

7. See Michael White's 2012 article for the *Guardian*, "Why Newham Council Is in a Housing Fix," for discussion of this issue.

that the state is—by definition and always—the worst possible option."[8] In the face of proposed demolition and privatization, Smith notes that "the argument in favor of libraries is [not] especially ideological or ethical" and that the stakes of reconstruction aimed at removing access to culture and common public space are high. "A library," she argues,

> is one of those social goods that matter to people of many different political attitudes. All that the friends of Kensal Rise and Willesden Library and similar services throughout the country are saying is: these places are important to us. We get that money is tight, we understand that there is a hierarchy of needs. . . . But they are still a significant part of our social reality, the only thing left on the high street that doesn't want either your soul or your wallet.[9]

In the tradition of earlier reconstruction fiction and the defenses of realism put forth by Elizabeth Bowen, Doris Lessing, and Raymond Williams, Smith posits a link between literature and the common good. In the twenty-first century, she worries that a reconstruction paradigm that leaves behind the idea of the state is also one that leaves behind a fundamental humanism that preserves freedom from ideological or financial submission. With novels like *White Teeth*, *NW* (2012), and *Swing Time* (2016), her commitment to the realist representation of characters navigating London with varying experiences of social, economic, and cultural freedoms—in the vein of Colin MacInnes—illuminates the stakes of such a paradigm and effectively resists it. In this sense, Smith and her work suggest possibilities for a newly conceived, twenty-first-century reconstruction fiction.

Finally, although this book has developed "reconstruction fiction" as a term to account for specific transformations brought on by World War II and the Welfare State, other conflicts that have wrought large-scale destruction or repurposing of living spaces could also be understood as creating a need for realistic reconstruction fiction. At the time of writing this conclusion, the devastating and widespread destruction in Syria as a result of the on-going civil war and terrorism has created the largest crisis of refugees and displaced persons since World War II. The need for perceptive, humanistic reconstruction fiction is as urgent, and more global, than ever.

---

8. Smith, "The Northwest London Blues," n.p., emphasis original
9. Smith, n.p.

BIBLIOGRAPHY

Abercrombie, Patrick, and J. H. Forshaw. *County of London Plan*. London: Macmillan and Co. Limited, 1943.

Adamson, Judith. "The Long Wait for Aunt Augusta: Reflections on Graham Greene's Fictional Women." In *Dangerous Edges of Graham Greene: Journeys with Saints and Sinners*. Ed. Dermot Gilvary and Darren J. N. Middleton. New York: The Continuum International Publishing Group, 2011.

"Alison + Peter Smithson." *Design Museum*. Design Museum, n.d. Web. 17 July 2013.

Aristotle. *Poetics*. In *The Basic Works of Aristotle*. Ed. Richard McKeon. New York: Modern Library, 2001. 1455–87.

Armstrong, Nancy. *Desire and Domestic Fiction: A Political History of the Novel*. Oxford: Oxford University Press, 1987.

———. *How Novels Think: The Limits of Individualism from 1719–1900*. New York: Columbia University Press, 2005.

Association of Building Technicians. *Homes for the People*. London: Paul Elek Publishers, 1946.

Auerbach, Erich. *Mimesis; The Representation of Reality in Western Literature*. 1953. Princeton: Princeton University Press, 2003.

Austerberry, Helen, and Sophie Watson. *Housing and Homelessness: A Feminist Perspective*. London: Routledge, 1986.

Ballard, J. G. *High-Rise*. 1975. Liveright Publishing, 2012.

Banham, Reyner. *The New Brutalism: Ethic or Aesthetic?* New York: Reinhold, 1966.

Beaumont, Matthew. "Introduction: Reclaiming Realism." In *A Concise Companion to Realism*. Ed. Matthew Beaumont. Hoboken: Wiley-Blackwell, 2010. 1–12.

Behrman, S. N. "The Suspended Drawing Room." *The New Yorker* (January 27, 1945): 27–37.

Bennett, Andrew, and Nicholas Royle. *Elizabeth Bowen and the Dissolution of the Novel*. New York: St. Martin's Press, 1995.

Bentley, Nick. "Writing 1950s London: Narrative Strategies in Colin MacInnes's *City of Spades* and *Absolute Beginners*. *Literary London: Interdisciplinary Studies in the Representation of London* (September 2003) 1: 2.

Best, Stephen, and Sharon Marcus. "Surface Reading: An Introduction." *Representations* 108.1 (Fall 2009): 1–21.

Black, Barbara J. *On Exhibit: Victorians and Their Museums*. Charlottesville: University Press of Virginia, 2000.

Bluemel, Kristin. *Intermodernism: Literary Culture in Mid-Twentieth-Century Britain*. Edinburgh: Edinburgh University Press, 2009.

Bosco, Mark, SJ, and Dermot Gilvary. Introduction to *Dangerous Edges of Graham Greene: Journeys with Saints and Sinners*. Ed. Dermot Gilvary and Darren J. N. Middleton. New York: The Continuum International Publishing Group, 2011. 1–17.

Bowen, Elizabeth. "The Big House." In *The Mulberry Tree: Writings of Elizabeth Bowen*. Ed. Hermione Lee. London: Virago Press Limited, 1986. 25–30.

———. *Bowen's Court*. 1942. New York: Ecco Press, 1972.

———. "Calico Windows." 1944. In *People, Places, Things*. Ed. Allan Hepburn. Edinburgh: Edinburgh University Press, 2008. 182–86.

———. "The Christmas Toast Is 'Home!'" In *People, Places, Things*. Ed. Allan Hepburn. Edinburgh: Edinburgh University Press, 2008. 128–31.

———. "The Cult of Nostalgia." In *Listening In*. Ed. Allan Hepburn. Edinburgh: Edinburgh University Press, 2010. 97–102.

———. "English Fiction at Mid-Century." In *People, Places, Things*. Ed. Allan Hepburn. Edinburgh: Edinburgh University Press, 2008. 321–24.

———. Letter to Virginia Woolf. 5 Jan. 1940. In *The Mulberry Tree: Writings of Elizabeth Bowen*. Ed. Hermione Lee. London: Virago Press Limited, 1986. 216–17.

———. *The Little Girls*. 1963. New York: Alfred A. Knopf, 1964.

———. "The Most Unforgettable Character I've Met." In *The Mulberry Tree: Writings of Elizabeth Bowen*. Ed. Hermione Lee. London: Virago Press Limited, 1986. 254–65.

———. "Opening Up the House." In *People, Places, Things*. Ed. Allan Hepburn. Edinburgh: Edinburgh University Press, 2008. 131–33.

Bowlby, Rachel. Foreword to *A Concise Companion to Realism*. Ed. Matthew Beaumont. Hoboken: Wiley-Blackwell, 2010. xiv–xxi.

Brannigan, John. *Literature, Culture, and Society in Postwar England, 1945–1965*. Lampeter: Edwin Mellen Press, 2002.

Brenner, Rachel. *The Ethics of Witnessing: The Holocaust in Polish Writers' Diaries from Warsaw, 1939–1945*. Evanston: Northwestern University Press, 2014.

Brooker, Joseph. *Literature of the 1980s: After the Watershed*. Edinburgh: Edinburgh University Press, 2010.

Brown, Erica, and Mary Grover, eds. *Middlebrow Literary Cultures: The Battle of the Brows, 1920–1960*. Basingstoke: Palgrave Macmillan, 2011.

Bullock, Nicholas. *Building the Post-War World: Modern Architecture and Reconstruction in Britain*. London: Routledge, 2002.

Burke, Andrew. "Concrete Universality: Tower Blocks, Architectural Modernism, and Realism in Contemporary British Cinema." *New Cinemas: Journal of Contemporary Film*. 5.3 (2007): 177–88. Web. 20 Jul. 2012.

Calder, Angus. "UK: Domestic Life, War Effort, and Economy." In *The Oxford Companion to World War II*. Eds. I. C. B. Dear and M. R. D. Foot. Oxford: Oxford University Press, 2005.

Cobley, Evelyn. *Modernism and the Culture of Efficiency: Ideology and Fiction*. Toronto: University of Toronto Press, 2009.

Cohen, Deborah. *Household Gods: The British and Their Possessions*. New Haven: Yale University Press, 2006.

Cole, G. D. H. *Building and Planning*. London: Cassell, 1945.

Conrad, Joseph. *The Heart of Darkness*. 1902. New York: St. Martin's Press, 1996.

Cooper, Stephanie. *Public Housing and Private Property, 1970–1984*. Aldershot: Gower, 1985.

Corcoran, Neil. *Elizabeth Bowen: The Enforced Return*. New York: Oxford University Press, 2004.

Crangle, Sara. "The Agonies of Ambivalence: Anna Mendelssohn, la poétesse Maudite." *Modernism/Modernity* 25.3 (September 2018): 461–89.

Darling, Elizabeth. "Exhibiting Britain: Display and National Identity 1946–1967. "*Designing Britain 1945–1975*." Web.

———. *Re-forming Britain: Narratives of Modernity Before Reconstruction*. London: Routledge, 2007.

Davis, Thomas. *The Extinct Scene: Late Modernism and Everyday Life*. New York: Columbia University Press, 2016.

Deer, Patrick. *Culture in Camouflage: War, Empire, and Modern British Literature*. Oxford: Oxford University Press, 2009.

Dehaene, Michiel. "Surveying and Comprehensive Planning: The 'Co-ordination of Knowledge' in the Wartime Plans of Patrick Abercrombie and Max Lock." In *Man-Made Future: Planning, Education and Design in Mid-Twentieth Century Britain*. Ed. Iain Boyd White. Oxon: Routledge, 2007. 38–58.

Delaney, Shelagh. *A Taste of Honey*. 1959. London: Methuen, 2006.

Derdiger, Paula, and Phyllis Lassner. "Domestic Gothic, the Global Primitive, and Gender Relations in Elizabeth Bowen's *The Last September* and *The House in Paris*." In *Irish Modernism and the Global Primitive*. Ed. Maria McGarrity and Claire Culleton. New York: Palgrave, 2009. 195–214.

Derrida, Jacques, and Anne Dufourmantelle. *Of Hospitality*. Stanford: Stanford University Press, 2000.

Duncan, Carol. "Art Museums and the Ritual of Citizenship." In *Exhibiting Cultures: The Poetics and Politics of Museum Display*. Ed. Ivan Karp and Steven D. Lavine. Washington: Smithsonian Institute Press, 1991. 88–103.

———. *Civilizing Rituals: Inside Public Art Museums*. London: Routledge, 1995.

Ellmann, Maud. *Elizabeth Bowen: The Shadow across the Page*. Edinburgh: Edinburgh University Press, 2003.

Esty, Jed. *A Shrinking Island: Modernism and National Culture in England*. Princeton: Princeton University Press, 2004.

Esty, Jed, and Colleen Lye. "Peripheral Realisms Now." *Modern Language Quarterly* 73.3 (September 2012): 269–88.

Feigel, Lara. *Free Woman: Life, Liberation, and Doris Lessing*. London: Bloomsbury, 2018.

Ferrebe, Alice. *Literature of the 1950s: Good, Brave Causes*. Edinburgh: Edinburgh University Press, 2012.

———. "Elizabeth Taylor's Uses of Romance: Feminist Feeling in 1950s English Fiction." *Literature and History* 19.1 (Apr. 2010): 50–64. Web.

"The Festival of Britain." Museum of London website. 15 Apr. 2002. Web. 3 Jul. 2012.

Forster, E. M. "Mrs. Miniver." 1939. In *Two Cheers for Democracy*. London: Edward Arnold, 1972.

Friedman, Susan Stanford. *Planetary Modernisms: Provocations on Modernity across Time*. New York: Columbia University Press, 2015.

Gamber, Wendy. *The Boardinghouse in Nineteenth-Century America*. Baltimore: Johns Hopkins University Press, 2007.

Gamble, Andrew. "Privatization, Thatcherism, and the British State." In *Thatcher's Law*. Ed. Andrew Gamble and Celia Wells. Cardiff: University of Wales Press, 1989. 1–20.

Gąsiorek, Andrzej. *Post-War Fiction: Realism and After*. London: Edward Arnold, 1995.

Gill, Richard. *Happy Rural Seat: The English Country House and the Literary Imagination*. New Haven: Yale University Press, 1972.

Ginsburg, Norman. "The Privatization of Council Housing." *Critical Social Policy* 25 (2005): 115–35. Web. 20 Jul. 2012.

Golland, Andrew. *Systems of Housing Supply and Housing Production in Europe*. Aldershot: Ashgate, 1998.

Gould, Tony. *Inside Outsider: The Life and Times of Colin MacInnes*. London: Chatto and Windus, 1983.

Green, Henry. *Back*. 1946. Champaign: Dalkey Archive, 2009.

Greene, Gayle. *Doris Lessing: The Poetics of Change*. Ann Arbor: University of Michigan Press, 1994.

Greene, Graham. "The Destructors." In *Twenty-One Stories*. 1954. New York: Viking, 1962. 225–45.

———. *The End of the Affair*. 1951. London: Penguin Books, 1962.

———. *The Human Factor*. London: Penguin, 1978.

———. *Ways of Escape*. 1980. Harmondsworth: Penguin, 1981.

Hamilton, Patrick. *The Slaves of Solitude*. 1947. New York: New York Review of Books, 2007.

Hanley, James. *No Directions*. London: Faber and Faber, 1943.

Hanson, Stuart. *From Silent-Screen to Multi-Screen: A History of Cinema Exhibition in Britain Since 1896*. Manchester: Manchester University Press, 2007.

Hartley, Jenny. *Hearts Undefeated: Women's Writing of the Second World War*. London: Virago, 1994.

Harvey, David. *Spaces of Hope*. Berkeley: University of California Press, 2000.

Hastings, Hugh de Cronin. "Townscape: A Plea for English Visual Philosophy." 1949. In *Architecture Culture, 1943–1968: A Documentary Anthology*. Ed. Joan Ockman. New York: Columbia University Graduate School of Architecture, Planning, and Preservation (Rizzoli), 1993. 114–19.

Hatherley, Owen. *The Ministry of Nostalgia*. London: Verso, 2016.

Hepburn, Allan. *A Grain of Faith: Religion in Mid-Century British Literature*. Oxford: Oxford University Press, 2018.

———. *Enchanted Objects: Visual Art in Contemporary Fiction*. Toronto: University of Toronto Press, 2010.

———. *Intrigue*. New Haven: Yale University Press, 2005.

Hoberman, Ruth. *Museum Trouble: Edwardian Fiction and the Emergence of Modernism*. Charlottesville: University of Virginia Press, 2011.

"Homeless and Nowhere to Go . . . 35 years of Homelessness." *Porchlight* website. 2009. Web. 13 Aug. 2012.

Hornsey, Richard. *The Spiv and the Architect: Unruly Life in Postwar London*. Minneapolis: University of Minnesota Press, 2010.

Hotten, John Camden. *The Slang Dictionary: Etymological, Historical and Anecdotal*. London: Chatto and Windus, 1914. *Project Gutenberg*. Web. 5 July 2016.

Inglesby, Elizabeth. "'Expressive Objects': Elizabeth Bowen's Narrative Materializes." *Modern Fiction Studies* 53.2 (2007): 306–33.

Ishiguro, Kazuo. *The Remains of the Day*. New York: Vintage, 1988.

Jacobs, Alan. *The Year of Our Lord 1943: Christian Humanism in an Age of Crisis*. Oxford: Oxford University Press, 2018.

James, Henry. Preface of *Portrait of a Lady*. 1881. *The Literature Network*, http://www.online-literature.com/henry_james/portrait_lady/0/.

Jameson, Fredric. *The Political Unconscious: Narrative as a Socially Symbolic Act*. Ithaca: Cornell University Press, 1981.

Jones, Nigel. *Through a Glass Darkly: The Life of Patrick Hamilton*. 1991. London: Black Spring Press, 2008.

Joyce, Simon. *The Victorians in the Rearview Mirror*. Columbus: The Ohio State University Press, 2007.

Judt, Tony. *Postwar: A History of Europe Since 1945*. New York: Penguin, 2005.

Kalliney, Peter. *Cities of Affluence and Anger: A Literary Geography of Modern Englishness*. Charlottesville: University of Virginia Press, 2006.

Keen, Suzanne. *Romances of the Archive in Contemporary British Fiction*. Toronto: University of Toronto Press, 2001.

Kelly, Marian. "The Power of The Past: Structural Nostalgia in Elizabeth Bowen's *The House In Paris* and *The Little Girls*." *Style* 36.1 (2002): 1–18. Web.

Kemp, Sandra. "But One Isn't Murdered: Elizabeth Bowen's *The Little Girls*. In *Twentieth-Century Suspense*. Ed. Clive Bloom. New York: St. Martin's, 1990. 130–42.

Labica, Thierry. "War, Conversation, and Context in Patrick Hamilton's *The Slaves of Solitude*." *Connotations* 12:1 (2002/2003), 72–82. Web. 20 Jul. 2012.

Laing, Stuart. "Ken Loach: Histories and Contexts." In *Agents of Challenge and Defiance: The Films of Ken Loach*. Ed. George McKnight. Westport: Greenwood Press, 1997. 11–27.

Lassner, Phyllis. *British Women Writers of World War II: Battlegrounds of Their Own*. Houndmills: Palgrave, 1998.

Le Corbusier. *The City of Tomorrow and Its Planning*. 1929. New York: Dover, 1987.

Lee, Stewart. "The National Trust Doesn't Even Trust Us to Have Our Own Thoughts." *Guardian*. 5 Jun. 2011. https://www.theguardian.com/commentisfree/2011/jun/05/national-trust-stewart-lee.

Lees-Milne, James. *Some Country Houses and Their Owners*. Ed. Michael Bloch. 1975. London: Penguin, 2009.

Lessing, Doris. *The Good Terrorist*. 1985. London: Harper Perennial, 2007.

———. "Laboratories of Social Change." CBC Massey Lectures: *The Prisons We Choose to Live Inside*. Toronto: CBC Enterprises, 1986.

———. "The Small Personal Voice." *A Small Personal Voice*. 1956. Vintage Books, 1975.

Levine, George. *The Realistic Imagination: English Fiction from Frankenstein to Lady Chatterley*. Chicago: University of Chicago Press, 1981.

Light, Alison. *Forever England: Femininity, Literature, and Conservatism between the Wars*. London: Routledge, 1991.

Littlejohn, David. *The Fate of the English Country House*. Oxford: Oxford University Press, 1997.

"London: The Swinging City." *Time*. Time Inc., 15 Apr. 1966. Web. 17 July 2013.

Low, Gail. "Streets, Rooms and Residents: The Urban Uncanny and the Poetics of Space in Harold Pinter, Sam Selvon, Colin MacInnes and George Lamming." In *Landscape and Empire 1770–2000*. Ed. Glenn Hooper. Aldershot: Ashgate, 2005. 159–76.

Lukács, Georg. *Studies in European Realism*. 1948. New York: Grosset & Dunlap, 1964.

Macaulay, Rose. *The World My Wilderness*. London: The Book Club, 1950.

MacInnes, Colin. *Absolute Beginners*. 1959. New York: Dutton, 1985.

———. *City of Spades*. 1957. London: Allison & Busby, 2012.

———. *England, Half English*. 1961. New York: Random House, 1962.

———. "The Englishness of Dr Pevsner." In *England, Half English*. 1961. New York: Random House, 1962. 119–29.

———. *Mr. Love and Justice*. 1960. London: Allison & Busby, 2012.

———. *No Novel Reader*. London: Martin, Brian & O'Keefe, 1975.

———. "Pop Songs and Teenagers." In *England, Half English*. 1961. New York: Random House, 1962. 45–60.

———. "Sharp Schmutter." In *England, Half English*. 1961. New York: Random House, 1962. 146–57.

———. "A Taste of Reality." In *England, Half English*. 1961. New York: Random House, 1962. 205–7.

———. "Young England, Half English." In *England, Half English*. 1961. New York: Random House, 1962. 11–19.

MacKay, Marina. *Modernism and World War II*. Cambridge: Cambridge University Press, 2007.

———. "The Wartime Rise of the Rise of the Novel." *Representations* 119.1 (Summer 2012): 119–43.

MacKay, Marina, and Lindsey Stonebridge, eds. *British Fiction after Modernism: The Novel at Mid-Century*. Houndmills: Palgrave, 2007.

MacNeice, Louis. *Selected Prose of Louis MacNeice*. Oxford: Clarendon Press, 1990.

Mandler, Peter. *The Fall and Rise of the Stately Home*. New Haven: Yale University Press, 1997.

Mao, Douglas, and Rebecca Walkowitz. "The New Modernist Studies." *PMLA* 123.3 (2008): 737–48.

Marcus, Sharon. *Apartment Stories: City and Home in Nineteenth-Century Paris and London*. University of California Press, 1999.

Maslen, Elizabeth. "Doris Lessing's *The Good Terrorist*: Socialist or Anti-Socialist." *Red Letters: A Journal of Cultural Politics* 19 (May 1986): 24–34.

Mass-Observation. "File Report 1622: Some Psychological Factors in Home Building." 1943. *Mass-Observation Online*. University of Sussex. 14 March 2010. Web.

McDonagh, Josephine. "Space, Mobility, and the Novel: 'The spirit of place is a great reality.'" In *A Concise Companion to Realism*. Ed. Matthew Beaumont. Hoboken: Wiley-Blackwell, 2010. 50–67.

McLeod, John. *Postcolonial London: Rewriting the Metropolis*. New York: Routledge, 2004.

Meen, Geoffrey. "Ten Propositions in UK Housing Macroeconomics: An Overview of the 1980s and Early 1990s." *Urban Studies* 33.3 (1996): 425–44. Web. 20 Jul. 2012.

Mellor, Leo. *Reading the Ruins: Modernism, Bombsites and British Culture*. Cambridge: Cambridge University Press, 2011.

Mepham, John. "Varieties of Modernism, Varieties of Incomprehension: Patrick Hamilton and Elizabeth Bowen." In *British Fiction after Modernism: The Novel at Mid-Century*. Eds. Marina MacKay and Lindsey Stonebridge. Houndmills: Palgrave, 2007. 59–76.

Merriman, Peter. "'A New Look at the English Landscape': Landscape Architecture, Movement and the Aesthetics of Motorways in Early Postwar Britain." *Cultural Geographies* 13 (2006): 78–105. Web. 20 Jul. 2012.

Miller, Betty. *On the Side of the Angels*. 1945. New York: Penguin-Virago, 1985.

Miller, D. A. *The Novel and the Police*. Berkeley: University of California Press, 1988.

Moretti, Franco. *Distant Reading*. New York: Verso, 2013.

Morris, Pam. *Realism*. Routledge, 2003.

Mumford, Lewis. *The Culture of Cities*. London: Secker and Warburg, 1938.

Murat, Jean-Christophe. "City of Wars: the Representation of Wartime London in Two Novels of the 1940s: James Hanley's *No Directions* (1943) and Patrick Hamilton's *The Slaves of Solitude* (1947)." *Anglophonia: French Journal of English Studies* 25 (2009): 329–40.

Murdoch, Iris. *The Time of the Angels*. 1966. London: Vintage, 2002.

National Maritime Museum, Museum Archive & Records Centre, NMM14: Box 3, Folder XII, Letter 17th of April 1943 from Reginald Lowen to Sir Geoffrey Callender.

"The New Brutalism." Editorial. *Architectural Design* 25 (January 1955): 1.

Orwell, George. *The Road to Wigan Pier*. 1937. London: Penguin, 2001.

———. "Why I Write." In *A Collection of Essays*. New York: Doubleday, 1954. 313–20.

Osborn, John. *Look Back in Anger*. 1956. New York: Penguin, 1982.

Panter-Downes, Mollie. *London War Notes*. Edited by William Shawn, 1971. London: Persephone Books, 2014.

———. *One Fine Day*. 1947. New York: Penguin-Virago, 1985.

Paul, Catherine. *Poetry in the Museums of Modernism: Yeats, Pound, Moore, Stein*. Ann Arbor: University of Michigan Press, 2002.

Pickering, Jean. *Understanding Doris Lessing*. Columbia: University of South Carolina Press, 1990.

Plain, Gill. *Literature of the 1940s: War, Postwar and 'Peace.'* Cambridge: Cambridge University Press, 2014.

———. *Women's Fiction of the Second World War: Gender, Power, Resistance*. Edinburgh: Edinburgh University Press, 1996.

Pratt, Mary-Louise. "Arts of the Contact Zone." *Profession* 91 (1991): 33–40. Web. 20 Aug. 2012.

Pritchett, V. S. Introduction to *Wuthering Heights* by Emily Brontë. 1847. Boston: Houghton Mifflin, 1956.

Rau, Petra. *Long Shadows: The Second World War in British Fiction and Film*. Evanston: Northwestern University Press, 2016.

Rawlinson, Mark. "*The Slaves of Solitude* and the Second World War." *Critical Engagements* 1.1 (2007): 260–71.

Reeve, N. H. *Elizabeth Taylor*. Tavistock: Northcote House / British Council, 2008.

Reid-Banks, Lynne. *The L-Shaped Room*. 1961. New York: Simon and Schuster, 1962.

Rosner, Victoria. *Modernism and the Architecture of Private Life*. New York: Columbia University Press, 2005.

Rowe, Margaret Moan. *Doris Lessing*. New York: St. Martin's Press, 1994.

Sackville-West, Vita. *English Country Houses*. 1941. London: Collins, 1947.

Scanlan, Margaret. "Language and the Politics of Despair in Doris Lessing's *The Good Terrorist*." *Novel: A Forum on Fiction* 23.2 (Winter 1990): 182–98. Web. 20 Jul. 2012.

Schneider, Karen. *Loving Arms: British Women Writing the Second World War*. Lexington: University Press of Kentucky, 1997.

Scott, J. D. "In the Movement." *Spectator* (1 Oct. 1954): 399–400. Web. 17 July 2013.

Selvon, Sam. *The Lonely Londoners*. 1956. London: Penguin, 2006.

———. "My Girl and the City." In *Ways of Sunlight*. 1957. Burnt Mill: Longman, 1987. 169–76.

Shonfield, Katherine. *Walls Have Feelings: Architecture, Film, and the City*. New York: Routledge, 2000.

Showalter, Elaine. *A Literature of Their Own: British Women Novelists from Brontë to Lessing*. Princeton: Princeton University Press, 1977.

Sillitoe, Alan. *The Loneliness of the Long-Distance Runner*. 1959. New York: Vintage, 1987.

———. *Saturday Night and Sunday Morning*. 1958. New York: Knopf, 1959.

Sinfield, Alan. *Literature, Politics and Culture in Postwar Britain*. Oxford: Basil Blackwell, 1989.

Singer, Sandra. "London and Kabul: Assessing the Politics of Terrorist Violence." In *Doris Lessing: Interrogating the Times*. Ed. Phyllis Sternberg Perrakis, Debrah Rashke, and Sandra Singer. Columbus: The Ohio State University Press, 2010. 92–112.

Smith, Zadie. "The Northwest London Blues." *New York Review of Books*, June 2, 2012, http://www.nybooks.com/daily/2012/06/02/north-west-london-blues/.

———. "Rereading Barthes and Nabokov." In *Changing My Mind: Occasional Essays*. Toronto: Penguin, 2009. 42–57.

Smithson, Alison, and Peter Smithson. "Thoughts in Progress." *Architectural Design* 27 (1957): 113. Web. 17 July 2013.

Snyder, Robert Lance. "'He Who Forms a Tie Is Lost': Loyalty, Betrayal, and Deception in *The Human Factor*." *South Atlantic Review* 73.3 (Summer 2008): 23–43. Web. 20 Jul. 2012.

Spark, Muriel. *The Girls of Slender Means*. 1963. New York: New Directions Books, 1998.

Spencer, Jane. *The Rise of the Woman Novelist: The Rise of the Woman Novelist: From Aphra Behn to Jane Austen*. Hoboken: Blackwell, 1986.

Stewart, Susan. *On Longing: Narratives of the Miniature, the Gigantic, the Souvenir, the Collection*. 1993. Durham: Duke University Press, 2007.

Stewart, Victoria. *The Second World War in Contemporary British Fiction: Secret Histories*. Edinburgh: Edinburgh University Press, 2011.

———. "The Woman Writer in Mid-Twentieth Century Middlebrow Fiction: Conceptualizing Creativity." *Journal of Modern Literature* 35.1 (Fall 2011): 21–36. Web.

Strong, Roy C. *The Destruction of the Country House, 1875–1975*. London: Thames & Hudson, 1974.

Su, John J. *Ethics and Nostalgia in the Contemporary Novel*. Cambridge: Cambridge University Press, 2005.

Summers-Bremner, "Drinking and Drinking and Screaming." In *Long Shadows: The Second World War in British Fiction and Film.* Ed. Petra Rau. Evanston: Northwestern University Press, 2016. 81–101.

Summerson, John. *Georgian London.* 1945. Hammondsworth: Penguin, 1978.

———. "The Unromantic Castle." In *The Unromantic Castle.* London: Thames and Hudson, 1990. 9–16.

Taunton, Matthew. *Fictions of the City: Class, Culture and Mass Housing in London and Paris.* Houndmills: Palgrave Macmillan, 2009.

Taylor, Elizabeth. *Angel.* 1957. London: Virago, 2008.

———. *At Mrs. Lippincote's.* 1945. London: Virago, 2006.

———. "Hare Park." In *The Blush.* 1958. London: Virago, 1986. 193–205.

———. Letter to Elizabeth Bowen. 24 February 1949. Harry Ransom Center 12.1.

———. *Palladian.* New York: Viking, 1947.

Thatcher, Margaret. Interview for *Woman's Own* ("no such thing as society") with Douglas Keay. Margaret Thatcher Foundation. 23 September 1987. Web. 13 Aug. 2012.

Tracy, Laura. "Passport to Greeneland." *College Literature* 12.1 (1985): 45–52. Web. 20 Aug. 2012.

Vale, Brenda. *Prefabs: A History of the UK Temporary Housing Programme.* London: E & FN Spon-Chapman & Hall, 1995.

Vulliamy, Ed. "Absolute MacInnes." *Observer.* 15 April 2007. https://www.theguardian.com/uk/2007/apr/15/britishidentity.fiction.

Walsh, Kevin. *The Representation of the Past: Museums and Heritage in the Post-Modern World.* London: Routledge, 1992.

Walshe, Eibhear. "A Sort of Lunatic Giant." In *Elizabeth Bowen.* Ed. Eibhear Walshe. Dublin: Irish Academic Press, 2009. 150–61.

Watkins, Susan. *Doris Lessing.* Manchester: Manchester University Press, 2010.

Waugh, Evelyn. *A Handful of Dust.* 1934. London: Penguin, 2000.

———. *Brideshead Revisited.* 1945. Harmondsworth: Penguin, 1981.

———. *Put Out More Flags.* 1942. London: Penguin, 2000.

Watt, Ian. *The Rise of the Novel: Studies in Defoe, Richardson and Fielding.* Berkeley and Los Angeles: University of California Press, 1957.

The Wednesday Play. "Cathy Come Home." Ken Loach. BBC, 1966.

White, Michael. "Why Newham Council Is in a Housing Fix." *Guardian.* 24 April 2012. Web.

Williams, Raymond. *The Long Revolution.* 1961. Harmondsworth: Penguin, 1980.

Wills, Clair. "Realism and the Irish Immigrant: Documentary, Fiction, and Postwar Irish Labor," *Modern Language Quarterly* 73.3 (September 2012): 373–94.

Woloch, Alex. *The One vs. the Many: Minor Characters and the Space of the Protagonist in the Novel.* Princeton: Princeton University Press, 2003.

Woolf, Virginia. "Mr. Bennett and Mrs. Brown." In *Modernism: An Anthology of Sources and Documents.* Ed. Vassiliki Kolocotroni, Jane Goldman, and Olga Taxidou. Edinburgh: Edinburgh University Press, 1998. 395–96.

———. "Modern Fiction." In *Modernism: An Anthology of Sources and Documents.* Ed. Vassiliki Kolocotroni, Jane Goldman, and Olga Taxidou. Edinburgh: Edinburgh University Press, 1998. 397.

———. *Mrs. Dalloway*. 1925. New York: Harcourt, 2005.
———. *Orlando*. 1928. Ware: Wordsworth Classics, 1995.
———. *The Years*. 1937. London: Vintage, 1992.
Wright, Patrick. *On Living in an Old Country*. Oxford: Oxford University Press, 2009.

INDEX

Abercrombie, Patrick, 52

Absolute Beginners (MacInnes), 11, 23, 37, 88, 102, 105n58, 108n59, 191, 196; real Britain and, 105–16; realism and, 103, 104, 105, 117

Adam Bede (Eliot), 26

Adorno, Theodor W., 19

aesthetics, 16, 38, 42, 52, 56, 89, 94, 97, 98, 138, 166, 183; modernist, 91, 117; nostalgic, 137; preservationist, 129; realist, 26, 117

Amis, Kingsley, 86

Angel (Taylor), 13, 23, 120, 133, 135, 136–43, 156, 196

Angry Young Men, 19n51, 87, 99, 100n37, 101, 102, 114; realism and, 98, 100, 103

apartheid, 159, 170, 171, 175, 176, 178

Apartment Stories (Marcus), 31

Aristotle, 38

Armstrong, Nancy, 31, 32, 43n1, 57, 58–59, 60

Association of Building Technicians, 54, 55

Astor, Nancy, 142

At Mrs. Lippincote's (Taylor), 5, 9, 22, 29, 45, 56, 57–58, 59, 80, 84, 158, 196; postwar protagonist and, 60–68; realism and, 61, 63, 68; shared space and, 44

Atonement (McEwan), 121, 197n6

Auerbach, Erich, 37, 37n21, 38, 39, 40

Austen, Jane, 31, 33, 33n15

Back (Henry), 56

Ballard, J. G., 9, 166n20, 187n51

Balzac, Honoré de, 27, 28, 30, 31

Beaumont, Matthew, 25, 26, 27

Behrman, S. N., 7

Bell, The, 144

Bennett, Andrew, 147n57, 151

Bentley, Nick, 102

Best, Stephen, 30, 34, 34n16

Betjeman, John, 22, 108n59, 130, 150n63

Beveridge Report, 4, 5, 45

Big House, 144, 144n49, 145, 150

billets, 5, 21, 22, 23, 33, 44, 55, 56, 58, 60, 61, 62, 63, 64, 65, 66

blitz, 1, 5, 14, 15, 83, 122, 158, 194, 195

boardinghouse, 44, 70, 72, 73, 74, 75, 76, 77–78, 79, 80, 88, 107
Bosco, Mark, 169
Bowen, Elizabeth, 1, 6, 9, 11, 12, 21, 23, 34, 36, 40, 55, 120, 122, 133, 134, 143–55, 195, 197, 199; closure and, 134; consumer heritage and, 150; country house novel and, 145; houses/landscape and, 144; interiors and, 55–56; materiality and, 7; nostalgia and, 121, 146; realism and, 3, 146, 152, 155; on technique, 2
Bowen's Court, 134, 143, 144, 145, 150
Bowen's Court (Bowen), 144, 144n49, 145, 146, 149
Bowlby, Rachel, 25, 26
Brenner, Rachel, 39
Brideshead Revisited (Waugh), 121, 128, 129, 135, 135n40
Britain Can Make It (BCMI), 124
British Museum, 122, 132
Brontë, Charlotte, 135
Brontë, Emily, 8, 63
Building and Planning (Cole), 51
Buildings of England, The (Pevsner), 104, 107–8
Bullock, Nicholas, 91

capitalism, 27, 27n5, 29n8, 38; global, 20, 32, 33, 35n19, 36, 37, 101; neoliberal, 197; welfare, 162
Cities of Affluence and Anger: A Literary Geography of Modern Englishness (Kalliney), 20, 89, 100n37
City of Spades (MacInnes), 105, 105n58, 111, 112, 116
civilization, 50n16, 52, 67, 123, 154, 193
Cobley, Evelyn, 50–51
Cohen, Deborah, 46
Cold War, 12, 21, 159, 160, 165, 169, 174, 175; disillusionment with, 170–71; Welfare State and, 176, 177
Cole, G. D. H., 51, 52
communism, 65, 69, 171, 172, 173, 174, 176, 190
community, 52, 53, 73, 111, 116, 164; individual and, 33, 44, 71; national, 188; peripheral, 87; social, 166, 194; solidarity, 84; urban, 93; wartime, 78, 80

Concise Companion to Realism, A (Beaumont), 25
Congrès internationaux d'architecture moderne (CIAM), 91, 92, 93, 94
Conrad, Joseph, 28, 30, 171n29
Conservative government, 142n47, 158, 162n11, 164, 165, 167, 198; housing, 160, 162, 163
Conservative party, 4, 159, 168
Council of Industrial Design, 124
country houses, 130–31; as museums, 122, 131, 133, 143n48; narrative and, 133–43
County of London Plan, 5, 23, 52, 53, 54, 65, 91, 92
cultural life, 43, 46, 130, 131, 132, 140
culture: British, 24, 37, 136, 196; consumer, 23, 109, 163; country house, 134, 142; heritage, 23, 42, 121, 122, 131, 134, 136, 143, 157; interwar, 46–49; literary, 6, 20, 37; national, 6, 20; popular, 86, 110, 115, 116, 136, 157; reconstruction, 44, 49–55, 84, 122

Dangerous Edges of Graham Greene, 169
Darling, Elizabeth, 90–91
Davis, Thomas, 12n30, 17, 102n47
Deer, Patrick, 17
Defoe, Daniel, 31
Dehaene, Michiel, 50
Delaney, Shelagh, 85, 87, 88n9, 101
Derrida, Jacques, 32, 164, 165n19, 166, 167
Desire and Domestic Fiction (Armstrong), 31
"Destructors, The" (Greene), 13–16, 183
development: character, 44, 45, 46, 48, 57, 59, 60, 68, 79, 82; economic, 158; individual, 47, 48, 49, 50n16, 59, 66, 72; intellectual, 48, 75; narrative, 49, 59, 80, 84, 91; plot, 22, 44, 45, 59, 72; social, 49, 57, 58, 84
discourses, 49; aesthetic, 17; architectural, 49, 104; free indirect, 80, 82, 191; housing, 34; literary, 169; national, 20; reconstruction, 5, 21, 49
Disraeli, Benjamin, 114
domesticity, 5, 14, 16, 22, 30, 31, 32, 55, 56, 58, 62, 64, 66, 68, 75n62, 116, 159, 160, 175, 176, 185
Donoghue, Denis, 189
Downton Abbey, 119, 121, 121n6

Du Maurier, Daphne, 135
Duncan, Carol, 123, 123n11, 124n12, 125, 131, 131n32, 147

Eagleton, Terry, 26, 28
economic issues, 37, 48, 124, 161, 168
Eliot, George, 26, 36
Eliot, T. S., 2n4, 18, 36, 51n20
Elizabeth II, 130n28
Emergency Powers (Defence) Act (1939), 44
Encounter, 101, 113, 116
End of the Affair, The (Greene), 160, 177, 178
England, Half English (MacInnes), 101
English Country Houses (Sackville-West), 129
English Heritage, 132
environment, 21, 79; built, 4, 14, 16, 20, 30, 85, 87, 90–93, 100, 104, 145; physical, 59, 87, 121; planned, 59, 109
Esty, Jed, 17, 18, 27, 35, 35n19, 36, 42, 100, 101, 102n47, 103; realism and, 18n48, 37
Ethics and Nostalgia in the Contemporary Novel (Su), 135
evacuation, 7, 122–25

Fall and Rise of the Stately Home, The (Mandler), 126
fascism, 28, 40, 69, 70, 70n53
Feigel, Lara, 179n38, 190, 191n63
feminism, 31; characterization of, 62, 63, 66; scholarship and, 18n46, 27, 30, 32, 58, 64, 84
Ferrebe, Alice, 85, 86, 100, 137
fiction: genre, 9, 25, 30, 103; historical, 23, 134, 196, 196n5, 197n6; middle-class, 61; postwar, 9, 24, 55, 156, 195; realist, 3, 29n8, 157, 166; reconstruction, 5–16; spy, 168–69
Fielding, Henry, 31
flashbacks, 134, 143, 149, 152, 153, 155
Fleming, Ian, 9, 168
focalization, 13, 159, 166, 191, 193
Forshaw, J. H., 52
Forster, E. M., 61
Foucault, Michel, 20, 32
freedom, 34, 51, 107, 199

Freud, Sigmund, 38n23, 63, 148n60

Gamber, Wendy, 72, 73
Gamble, Andrew, 162
Garden City, 90–94, 97–98
Gaskell, Elizabeth, 31
Georgian London (Summerson), 129
Gibberd, Frederick, 91
Gilvary, Dermot, 169
Ginsburg, Norman, 163
Girls of Slender Means, The (Spark), 5
Gissing, George, 28, 30
Golden Lane, 93, 94, 94 fig. 1, 95 fig. 2 and 3
Good Terrorist, The (Lessing), 13, 24, 36, 89, 158, 159, 160, 164, 165, 196; Englishness and, 182; homemaking and, 184, 185; hostess/guest and, 178–93; middle-class sensibilities and, 180, 183; modernism and, 182–83; narrative openness in, 166; politics and, 181, 182, 185, 188–89; realism and, 191–93
Gothic, 13, 30, 59, 60, 67, 82, 135, 139, 175
Green, Henry, 56
Greene, Gayle, 179, 184n44, 186, 187, 189, 192, 193n67; boxes and, 172; demolition and, 16
Greene, Graham, 9, 12, 13–16, 21, 23, 158, 159, 160, 164, 168–78, 179, 183, 186, 193; espionage genre and, 169; individual isolation and, 167; protagonists of, 173, 174
Gropius, Walter, 93
Gunn, Thom, 86

Ham House, 127, 128, 141
Hamilton, Patrick, 12, 13, 22, 23, 33, 56, 57–58; allegory and, 74; boardinghouse novel and, 71–84; domestic space and, 68–69; indirect discourse and, 82; Marxist sympathies of, 70; narrative development and, 59; Priestley and, 69; shared space and, 44; wartime and, 70–71; youth of, 68
Hangover Square (Hamilton), 68, 70n53
Hanley, James, 56
Harvey, David, 29
Hastings, Hugh de Cronin, 90

Hatherley, Owen, 118n80, 121n6, 158
H. D., 22
Heart of the Matter, The (Greene), 176
Heat of the Day, The (Bowen), 134
Heath, Edward, 167
Hemlock and After (Wilson), 130
Hepburn, Allan, 122n8, 136, 145n52, 169n26, 172–73
heritage, 15, 21, 131, 142, 143, 150, 155; cultural, 23, 42, 121, 122, 134, 136, 143, 146, 157; historical significance of, 133; museums and, 122n8, 133
Hess, Dame Myra, 123, 123n10
High-Rise (Ballard), 9, 166n20, 187n51
history, 22n57, 40, 143; cultural, 24, 31, 35n19, 98n31, 121; literary, 10, 18, 25, 27, 31–32, 35, 37, 42, 58, 89, 156; Marxist conceptions of, 30; poststructuralist conceptions of, 33; realism and, 146, 152
home, 15, 16, 46, 124; nation and, 179; single-family, 47, 56; Victorian, 47, 48
homelessness, 3, 54, 87, 158, 162, 163, 185
homemaking, 48, 72–73, 180, 184, 186
Homes for the People, 54, 55
Hornsey, Richard, 20
hospitality, 44, 165, 166, 178, 185, 187; Derrida and, 164; English, 175, 176; insoluble antimony of, 167, 175; politics of, 164; sociopolitical, 176; state, 179
house museums, 125–33; irony/absence and, 133–43
housing: construction of, 92, 93; council, 93, 158, 149–60, 163, 164, 183; crisis, 45, 56, 118n80, 122; cultural/political issues and, 163; implications of, 2, 130, 133, 163, 195; individual and, 46–49; industry, 24; landscape and, 144; market, 87; middle-class, 109; museums and, 125–33; political, 160; postwar, 3–5; shared, 44; transformation of, 9, 163. See also public housing
Housing Act (1980), 163
Howard, Ebenezer, 90, 91
Human Factor, The (Greene), 9, 12, 21, 23, 24, 158, 159, 160, 165, 186, 193, 194; borderless ideal and, 167–78; hospitality and, 176; narrative openness in, 166; realism of, 169

humanism, 37n21, 39, 41, 44, 49, 115, 199
identity, 29, 49, 86, 107, 158, 161; crisis, 66; individual, 56, 58, 65; middle-class, 66; national, 20, 123, 129, 181–82; queer, 20; racial, 102; social, 46, 66, 110; working-class, 66, 100
Ill Fares the Land (Judt), 198
immigrants, postcolonial, 37, 86n2, 87, 88, 90, 100, 105, 110, 112, 113, 116, 117, 160, 165
individual, 29, 43; community and, 33, 44, 71; housing ideals and, 46–49; middle-class, 61; the novel and, 32, 57–59; planning and, 49–55; society and, 84; welfare of, 157
individualism, 22, 24, 46, 49, 51, 73, 77, 158, 167, 170, 191; determined, 188; ideology of, 183; narrative, 80, 82–83, 177; traditional, 49
Industrial Relations Act (1971), 168
Inglesby, Elizabeth, 145n54, 146n54, 147n57, 148
intermodernism, 2n4, 17n45
Intrigue (Hepburn), 172–73
IRA, 168, 181, 182
Ishiguro, Kazuo, 121, 196, 197
isolation, 167, 188, 189, 194

James, Henry, 22
Jameson, Frederic, 28, 29, 30, 32, 34n16, 41
Jane Eyre (Brontë), 13, 60, 120, 135
Jennings, Elizabeth, 86
Jones, Nigel, 68
Joyce, James, 28, 43
Judt, Tony, 196, 198

Kafka, Franz, 72
Kalliney, Peter, 20, 89, 100n37
Kelly, Marian, 147n57, 148, 148n59, 152n66, 153n69
Knole, 119, 133, 155, 156

L-Shaped Room, The (Reid-Banks), 110
Labica, Thierry, 70, 76n63
Labour government, 4, 45, 162, 163, 168, 170

INDEX · 215

Labour party, 159
Laing, Stuart, 162
landmarks, 45, 108, 126, 143, 148, 150, 150n63
landscape, 4, 6, 9, 58, 87, 90, 91, 144, 148, 149, 187; peripheral zone of, 105; postindustrial, 107; postwar, 4; rural, 122, 126, 131, 149
Larkin, Philip, 22
Lasdun, Denys, 88, 92
Lassner, Phyllis, 17, 18n46, 31, 64, 84n66, 144n49
Last September, The (Bowen), 144n49, 150
Le Carré, John, 168
Le Corbusier, 92, 92n23, 93, 93n25
Lees-Milne, James, 15, 119, 126, 127, 128; Ham House and, 141; preservation and, 129
Lefebvre, Henri, 29, 29n8
Lessing, Doris, 8, 13, 24, 34, 36, 158, 159, 164, 166, 169, 178, 194, 199; bourgeois liberalism and, 189; buildings/metaphors and, 179; on contemporary literature, 103–4; home/nation and, 179; politics and, 41, 189, 190; realism and, 40–42, 181, 192–93; on society, 188
Levine, George, 10, 11
Light, Alison, 64
literary criticism, 8, 25, 29, 30; feminist, 31; socialist, 37
literary history, 2, 18, 24, 25, 27, 35, 42, 58, 156; feminist, 31, 32; Marxist, 28, 30
literary theory, 8n22, 25; British socialist, 40–42; feminist, 31; Marxist, 28, 29, 40; the novel, 32–33; peripheral realism, 27, 35–36, 100; realism, 25; surface reading, 34
literature, 33, 34; British, 19, 37; culture and, 35; minor, 100; postwar, 17, 18, 19, 56; realist, 6, 40, 166; wartime, 17
Literature of the 1940s (Plain), 17
Literature of the 1950s: Good, Brave Causes (Ferrebe), 85
Literature of Their Own, A (Showalter), 31
Literature, Politics and Culture in Postwar Britain (Sinfield), 19
Little Girls, The (Bowen), 9, 12, 21, 23, 36, 120, 133, 134, 143–55, 156, 197; realism and, 146, 152, 155

living space, 48, 54, 55, 61, 71, 72; shared wartime, 43, 56, 57, 60, 66, 68, 75, 76; transformed/transforming, 21
London, 20, 21, 23, 56, 70, 71, 73, 74, 80, 82, 83, 86, 87, 88, 91, 101, 105, 198; immigrants in, 100; Notting Hill race riots and, 112; postcolonial immigrants in, 89–90, 100; postwar reconstruction of, 4, 52–54, 92–94; reappropriation of, 89; representation of, 20, 37, 106–9; wartime, 5, 7, 8
London County Council, 52
Loneliness of the Long-Distance Runner, The (Sillitoe), 99
Lonely Londoners, The (Selvon), 89
Long Revolution, The (Williams), 41
Look Back in Anger (Osborne), 99, 100, 100n37
Low, Gail, 116
Lowen, Reginald, 122
Lukács, Georg, 10, 11, 27, 28, 29, 30, 32, 42; realism and, 39, 40, 41
Lutyens, Sir Edwin, 141
Lye, Colleen, 18n48, 27, 35, 35n19, 36, 37, 42, 100, 101, 102n47, 103
Lynn, Jack, 92, 94, 96

Macaulay, Rose, 5
MacInnes, Colin, 11, 12, 21, 23, 34, 37, 85, 90, 101, 105–6, 108, 109, 110, 113, 160, 165, 191, 199; Englishness and, 116; London trilogy of, 103, 104, 105, 111, 112, 115; journalism of, 114–16; realism and, 88, 100, 104, 117; sexual identification of, 102; vision of, 116
MacKay, Marina, 3n7, 8n22, 13, 17
MacNeice, Louis, 50, 52
Madame Bovary (Flaubert) 37
Mandler, Peter, 126, 130
Mann, Thomas, 27, 30, 32
Mansfield Park (Austen), 120
Marcus, Laura, 26n4, 31n10, 34, 34n16, 35
Marcus, Sharon, 30–35, 31n10, 34n16
Marx, Karl, 27n5, 69, 171
Marxism, 19, 20, 20n53, 27, 28, 29, 30, 31, 33, 34, 40–41, 69, 70
Maslen, Elizabeth, 179, 186, 190, 192
Massey Lectures, 189, 190, 191

material conditions, 2, 6, 7, 10, 11, 23, 25, 29, 30, 97, 124, 166, 191
May, Theresa, 198
McDonagh, Josephine, 29n8, 89
McEwan, Ian, 121, 197n6
McLeod, John, 115
Mellor, Leo, 17
Mephisto (Mann), 32
Merriman, Peter, 91
Miller, Betty, 56
Miller, D. A., 32
Mimesis (Auerbach), 37n21, 38, 40
Mr. Love and Justice (MacInnes), 105n58, 112
Mrs. Dalloway (Woolf), 89, 108
mobility, 44, 85–90, 100, 106, 107, 109, 110, 113, 114; aesthetic, 85, 103, 117; built environment and, 90; economic, 42, 93; geographic, 23, 103; heightened, 85–86; narrative, 57, 59, 82; postcolonial migration, 89–90; postwar, 91–92; postwar environment and, 90–94, 97–98; social, 14, 23, 42, 47, 57, 93, 103, 120, 163; socioeconomic, 42, 87, 134; upward, 23, 45, 46, 59, 66, 87, 99
Modern Language Quarterly, 35
modernism, 1, 3, 11, 17, 18, 21, 25, 26, 32, 35, 51, 61, 89, 136, 144; architectural, 90–91; categories of, 16; interwar, 2n4, 11, 156; metropolitan, 90; postwar, 182–83
Modernism and the Culture of Efficiency (Cobley), 51
Modernism and World War II (MacKay), 17
moral conflicts, 169, 189
Moretti, Franco, 32, 33, 33n15, 35n18, 35n19, 36
Morris, Pam, 10, 39, 44
Morris, William, 48, 126n16
Munton, Alan, 70
Murat, Jean-Christophe, 69, 70
Murdoch, Iris, 5
Museum of London, 54
museums, 122, 147; country house, 122, 131, 133, 143n48; Edwardian, 123; heritage and, 122n8, 133; historical roots of, 123; house, 125–33, 133–43; political narratives and, 124–25; public art, 131, 131n32; Victorian, 123, 126; wartime, 122, 123

narratives, 44, 56, 57, 59, 75, 137, 140, 144, 148, 150–51, 153, 158, 160, 192; country house, 135, 136; exhibition, 124; individual, 58; Marxist conceptions of, 29–31, 40; national, 122–25; personal, 149; political, 123, 124; postwar, 137, 158; public, 133, 157; realist, 30–31, 40, 152; techniques, 24, 57, 60, 76, 83, 152; Welfare State, 12
National Gallery, 122, 123
National Maritime Museum, 122
National Trust, 15, 119, 120, 127, 129, 130, 131, 131n31, 132, 133, 138, 142n47, 156; Country House Scheme, 126
Nationality Act (1948), 86, 108, 165
New Brutalism, 23, 85, 88, 109, 116; Angry Young Men and, 99, 100; building materials of, 98; described, 93–98; realist literary innovations and, 98, 100; social/ethical demands and, 97
New Historicism, 30, 31, 32
New Left, 102
New Modernist Studies, 18n45, 26, 26n3
New Musical Express, 106
New Towns, 4, 52, 54, 85, 91, 92
New Wave Cinema, 86, 98n31
New York Review, 198
New Yorker, 3, 7, 45
Nicholson, Harold, 127
Nicklin, Frederick, 94
No Direction (Hanley), 56
nostalgia, 15, 108, 119, 120, 121, 122, 150, 152, 156; austerity, 118n80, 121n6
Notting Hill race riots, 88, 106, 112, 113, 115, 165, 196
NW (Smith), 199

Odyssey, The (Homer), 37, 37n23
On Longing (Stewart), 32–33
On the Side of Angels (Miller), 56
One vs. the Many, The (Woloch), 57
Orlando (Woolf), 155, 156
Orwell, George, 2n4, 7, 11, 47, 48, 49, 69, 72, 102, 109
Osborne, John, 99, 100, 100n37
Osterley, 126, 127

ownership: limited individual, 66; property, 46, 47, 60, 66, 178; public, 131n32

Palladian (Taylor), 67, 135, 142
Panter-Downes, Mollie, 3, 7, 45, 55, 64n44
Park Hill Estates, 94, 96 fig. 5, 97 fig. 6
Pevsner, Nikolaus, 104, 107–8, 108n59, 130, 150n63
Plain, Gill, 7n5, 17, 17n40, 18n46, 18n47, 31, 64
planning, 8, 49, 57; architectural, 50, 50n16; community, 53, 54, 160, 178; comprehensive, 49–50; individual and, 49–55; national, 49; organizational, 21–24; postwar, 42, 55, 56; reconstruction, 5–6, 61; town, 21
Plato, 147–48
plots: apartment, 31; approach to, 2, 9, 12, 39, 44, 45, 59, 68, 135, 143, 166, 168, 170, 177, 192; development of, 22, 72; family, 86n2, 105; marriage/romance, 64, 72, 77, 80, 81, 86n2
Poetics (Aristotle), 38
Political Unconscious: Narrative as a Socially Symbolic Act, The (Jameson), 28
politics, 125, 172, 176, 178, 180, 183, 186, 187, 188–89; Cold War, 170–71, 174; grassroots, 182; identity, 43n1, 190n57; progressive, 181, 190; working-class, 114; young people in, 189
postcolonialism, 16, 18, 19, 20, 32, 35, 89, 90, 100, 101, 102, 175
postmodernism, 10n26, 16, 17, 18, 26, 36, 37n21, 136
Postwar (Judt), 196
postwar context and, 84; war, 80
postwar realism, 3, 5, 27, 30, 32, 36, 90, 105, 196; historical specificity of, 10–13; possibilities for, 37; reevaluation of, 25
power, 137, 161, 173; conservative, 23; economic, 114; sociopolitical, 23
Pratt, Mary Louise, 161
preservation, 14, 15, 21, 23, 108n59, 110, 126n16, 130, 132, 147, 148, 148n61, 198; aesthetics of, 126, 127, 129, 145, 150
Priestley, J. B., 69
privacy, 46, 47, 49, 55, 56, 69, 73, 76, 116
private property, 47, 87, 132, 158, 163, 173, 181

privatization, 24, 87, 158, 162–67, 179, 186, 199
protagonists, 55–60; limits of, 60–68
public housing, 4, 126, 163, 164, 178, 198; privatization of, 162
Put Out More Flags (Waugh), 56

Rachman, Peter, 88
Rational Architecture Movement, 93
Rattigan, Terrence, 22
Rau, Petra, 17, 18n46
Rawlinson, Mark, 69, 70, 71, 83
Re-forming Britain: Narratives of Modernity before Reconstruction (Darling), 90
realism, 17, 18, 44, 45–46, 61, 89, 98–105, 167, 169, 181, 192, 193, 194; championing, 42; domesticity and, 31; experimental, 155, 159; history and, 27, 29, 30, 33, 36, 146, 152; humanism and, 8, 37–42; interruptive, 25, 34; kitchen sink, 105; literary, 3, 22, 27, 30, 181; midcentury, 3, 27, 63; middlebrow, 134; migration and, 89; mobile, 117–18; modernism and, 11, 35; open/incomplete, 36; peripheral, 27, 35, 36, 100, 101; poetic, 105; postwar, 10–13, 32, 90, 100, 196; reconstruction fiction and, 9, 13, 19–20, 34, 60, 108, 194, 199; reinvented, 7, 38, 68; social, 98, 102, 159, 199; theories of, 25–42; war and, 5–16
Realistic Imagination, The (Levine), 10
Rebecca (Du Maurier), 13, 135
reconstruction, 3, 4, 6, 8, 14, 31, 34, 45, 57, 59, 84, 98, 145, 159, 187; community-oriented, 46; documents, 53; engagement with, 21; ethical, 39; narrative of, 122–25; planned, 52; political, 177; postwar, 13, 16, 22, 24, 40, 91–92, 117; realism and, 11, 19–20, 33; representation and, 12; social, 177; wartime, 46, 50, 87
reconstruction fiction, 5–16
Reeve, N. H., 60, 61, 137n45, 140
Reid-Banks, Lynne, 110
relations: economic, 19; interracial/interclass, 12; political, 19; power, 144, 173; social, 6, 19, 121, 161
Remains of the Day, The (Ishiguro), 121, 196, 197
Rent Act (1957), 87
Richardson, Samuel, 31

Richardson, Tony, 88n9
Rise of the Novel, The (Watt), 31
Rise of the Woman Novelist, The (Spencer), 31
Road to Wigan Pier, The (Orwell), 48, 109
Robin Hood Gardens, 94, 96 fig. 4
Robinson Crusoe (Defoe), 177
romance, 9, 30, 56, 61, 120, 134, 135, 136, 137, 141, 142, 156, 182; plot, 59, 66, 77, 80, 81
Rosner, Victoria, 48
Rowe, Margaret, 185
Royle, Nicholas, 147n57, 151
Ruskin, John, 48, 126n16

Sackville-West, Vita, 126, 127, 129, 145, 149, 156
safe houses, 160, 161, 164–66, 171, 172, 175, 180, 188, 194
safety, 3, 23, 165, 167, 175, 187, 191; domestic, 160; individual, 193; physical, 186; provisional, 161
safety nets, 162–67, 186, 191
Saturday Night and Sunday Morning (Sillitoe), 87, 98, 101
Scanlan, Margaret, 189, 190, 192, 193
Schneider, Karen, 18n46, 64, 84n66
Scott, J. D., 86
Scott, Walter, 31
Secret Service, 152, 168, 170
Selvon, Sam, 85, 88, 89, 90, 117
sexuality, 102, 110, 111–12
Shakespeare, William, 137, 155
Shaw, George Bernard, 102
Shelley, Percy, 154
Shonfield, Katherine, 196
Showalter, Elaine, 31, 32
Shrinking Island, A (Esty), 17, 36
Sillitoe, Alan, 87, 98, 99, 100
Sinfield, Alan, 19–20, 19n51, 100n37, 102, 102n47, 115
Slaves of Solitude, The (Hamilton), 13, 22, 44, 45, 56, 57–58, 59, 84, 158; inconsequence and, 68–83; realism and, 84
"Small Personal Voice, A" (Lessing), 8, 41, 181
Smith, Ivor, 88, 92, 94, 96
Smith, Zadie, 22, 198

Smithson, Alison, 88, 92, 93, 94, 104, 109, 150n63; Brutalism and, 96, 98
Smithson, Peter, 88, 92, 93, 94, 104, 109, 110, 150n63; Brutalism and, 96, 98
Snyder, Robert, 171n29, 173, 176, 176n34
Soane, Sir John, 129, 129n24
social conditions, 6, 10, 13, 23, 30, 34, 42, 90, 136, 158, 161, 166, 169, 190, 196
social positions, 35, 45, 46, 57, 62
socialism, 41, 44, 55, 69, 99, 168, 190
socioeconomic context, 21, 37, 44, 49, 87, 88, 100, 103, 100, 103, 110, 125, 133, 134, 162, 165, 168, 198
sociological: approaches, 19, 102, 113; attitudes, 23–24, 104, 106; style, 11–12
sociopolitical context, 5, 6, 23, 24, 53, 118n80, 166, 169, 176, 179, 191
space: critical, 55; domestic, 5, 32, 67, 68, 97, 158, 180, 187n51; gender and, 31; household, 64; novelistic, 55–60; personal, 45, 48; private, 44, 73; public, 17, 75; shared, 44, 66, 72, 73, 76; social, 29n8, 161; socioeconomic, 66
Sparks, Muriel, 5
Spencer, Jane, 31
Spiv and the Architect: Unruly Life in Postwar London, The (Hornsey), 20
squatters, 110, 165, 178, 178n36, 178n37, 180, 184, 186, 188
Stalin, Joseph, 39
Stendahl, 31
Stewart, Susan, 17, 18n46, 32–33, 132, 133, 151, 152; nostalgia and, 121, 148n60; realism and, 33; on souvenir, 150
Stewart, Victoria, 31, 137n45
Stirling, James, 88, 92
Stonebridge, Lyndsey, 3n7, 13, 17
"Streets in the Sky," 90–94, 95 fig. 2, 96 fig. 5, 97–98, 97 fig. 6
Struther, Jan, 61
Studies in European Realism (Lukács), 10, 28, 40
Su, John, 135, 137
subjectivity, 29, 43, 58, 84, 121; extreme stylistic, 28; female, 31; individual, 73
Summers-Bremner, Eluned, 70
Summerson, John, 15, 108n59, 129, 130, 138, 139, 145, 150n63

Swing Time (Smith), 199
syntax, 9, 42, 106, 121, 144

Taste of Honey, A (Delaney), 87, 88, 88n9, 101
Taylor, Elizabeth, 5, 9, 12, 13, 22, 23, 29, 30, 33, 44, B, 57–58, 59, 60–68, 69, 70, 74, 75, 84, 120, 121, 122, 133, 135–43, 196; Bowen and, 134; characterization by, 63, 68, 139; closure and, 134; country house narrative and, 135, 136, 143, 143n48; narrative development and, 59; novelistic vision of, 67; outdated values and, 64; romance and, 137; shared space and, 44
technology, 4, 50, 52, 86; modernist/modernized, 90, 91, 98; production and, 51; warfare, 124
terrorism, 168, 188, 192–93, 199; IRA, 159, 182, 194
Thatcher, Margaret, 23, 24, 85, 157, 159, 182, 188, 191, 193; election of, 4, 162, 168; individualism and, 183; privatization and, 87, 165, 179, 186
Three-Day Week, 168, 168n23, 170
Time of the Angels, The (Murdoch), 5
Tinker, Tailor, Soldier, Spy (Le Carré), 168
To the Lighthouse (Woolf), 38, 63
Tolstoy, Leo, 27, 30
Town and Country Planning, 52, 132n33
Town and Country Planning Act (1947), 91, 126
townscape theory, 90, 91, 138
Tracy, Laura, 176, 176n34
Twenty-Thousand Streets under the Sky (Hamilton), 68

utopianism, 15, 40, 55, 92, 99n35, 100, 103, 110, 112, 159, 164, 182, 187n51, 196

Vesey-Fitzgerald, Brian, 108n59, 130
Victoria and Albert Museum, 45, 122, 124, 148n61
View of the Harbor, A (Taylor), 67
Villette (Brontë), 63
violence, 70, 72, 81, 149, 168, 174, 188, 194; domestic, 160; historical, 134, 144, 153; political, 174, 192, 193; racial, 112, 113, 114
vision, 7, 12; aesthetic, 52; civic, 8; postwar, 55; social, 35; sociopolitical, 53; utopian, 92

Vulliamy, Ed, 111, 113n67

Wain, John, 86
Walshe, Eibhear, 145–46n54, 151
wartime life, 7, 45, 56, 58
Watt, Ian, 8n22, 31, 43n1, 57, 58, 177
Waugh, Evelyn, 56, 75n62, 128, 129, 129n26, 135, 145
Ways of Escape (Greene), 168, 171
welfare, 160, 180; social, 179, 198
Welfare State, 3, 4, 6, 12, 14, 17, 19, 24, 37, 41, 52, 59, 61, 66, 84, 113–14, 163, 166, 168, 169, 170; BCMI and, 124; challenges to, 158, 159, 161, 162, 198; Cold War and, 176, 177; construction of, 21, 23; framework of, 165; future of, 160; homemaking and, 180; housing in, 88, 164; land reforms of, 125; life in, 101; reconstruction fiction and, 16; socialist policies of, 44, 99; struggles of, 162, 162n11; vision of, 158
Wells, H. G., 102
White Teeth (Smith), 198, 199
Williams, Raymond, 28, 103, 199; realism and, 40, 41, 42, 84, 104
Wilson, Angus, 130
Woloch, Alex, 32, 57, 64, 84
Woolf, Virginia, 1, 18, 47, 48, 62, 75, 89, 108, 155; on Edwardian realism, 3; on human character, 1; manuscript of, 156; modernism and, 32, 36, 43; realism and, 38
Wordsworth, William, 154
working class, 4, 23, 47, 48, 49, 66, 87, 92, 93, 98, 99–100, 101, 102, 107, 108, 113, 114, 182, 191, 198
World My Wilderness, The (Macaulay), 5
World War II, 2, 18, 26, 28, 31, 35, 37, 40, 44, 50, 58, 72; aftermath of, 6; challenges of, 122, 126; context of, 43, 60; identity and, 86; impact of, 43, 84; literary scholarship and, 17–18; losses of, 196
Wreath of Roses, A (Taylor), 67, 142
Wren, Christopher, 14, 15
Wright, Patrick, 126n16, 131, 132
Wuthering Heights (Brontë), 8, 8n22

Years, The (Woolf), 47, 62

Zola, Emile, 28

www.ingramcontent.com/pod-product-compliance
Lightning Source LLC
Chambersburg PA
CBHW020653230426
43665CB00008B/416